NOVELS

OF

SIR EDWARD BULWER LYTTON

Library Edition

THE CAXTON NOVELS

VOL. III.

"MY NOVEL"

OR

VARIETIES IN ENGLISH LIFE

BY PISISTRATUS CAXTON

BY

SIR EDWARD BULWER LYTTON, BART.

NEQUE ENIM NOTARE SINGULOS MENS EST MIHI.
VERAM IPSAM VITAM ET MORES HOMINUM OSTENDERE.
Phædrus

LIBRARY EDITION—IN FOUR VOLUMES

VOL. I.

PHILADELPHIA
J. B. LIPPINCOTT & CO.
1865.

MY NOVEL.

BOOK FIRST.

INITIAL CHAPTER.

SHOWING HOW MY NOVEL CAME TO BE WRITTEN.

SCENE, *The Hall in Uncle Roland's Tower* — TIME, *Night* — SEASON, *Winter.*

MR. Caxton is seated before a great geographical globe, which he is turning round leisurely, and "for his own recreation," as, according to Sir Thomas Browne, a philosopher should turn round the orb of which that globe professes to be the representation and effigies. My mother having just adorned a very small frock with a very smart braid, is holding it out at arm's-length, the more to admire the effect. Blanche, though leaning both hands on my mother's shoulder, is not regarding the frock, but glances towards PISISTRATUS, who, seated near the fire, leaning back in the chair, and his head bent over his breast, seems in a very bad humor. Uncle Roland, who has become a great novel-reader, is deep in the mysteries of some fascinating third volume. Mr. Squills has brought *The Times* in his pocket for his own special profit and delectation, and is now bending his brows over "the state of the money market," in great doubt whether railway shares can possibly fall lower; for Mr. Squills, happy man! has large savings, and does not know what to do with his money, or, to use his own phrase, "how to buy in at the cheapest, in order to sell out at the dearest."

Mr. Caxton (musingly).—It must have been a monstrous long journey. It would be somewhere hereabouts, I take it, that they would split off.

My Mother (mechanically, and in order to show Austin that she paid him the compliment of attending to his remarks).—Who split off, my dear?

"Bless me, Kitty," said my father, in great admiration, "you ask just the question which it is most difficult to answer. An ingenious speculator on races contends that the Danes, whose descendants make the chief part of our northern population (and indeed, if his hypothesis could be correct, we must suppose all the ancient worshippers of Odin), are of the same origin as the Etrurians. And why, Kitty—I just ask you, why?"

My mother shook her head thoughtfully, and turned the frock to the other side of the light.

"Because, forsooth," cried my father, exploding—"because the Etrurians called their gods 'the Æsar,' and the Scandinavians called theirs the Æsir, or Aser! And where do you think this adventurous scholar puts their cradle?"

"Cradle!" said my mother, dreamily—"it must be in the nursery."

Mr. Caxton.—Exactly—in the nursery of the human race—just here [and my father pointed to the globe,] bounded, you see, by the river Halys, and in that region which, taking its name from Ees, or As (a word designating light or fire,) has been immemorially called *Asia*. Now, Kitty, from Ees or As our ethnological speculator would derive not only Asia, the land, but Æsar, or Aser, its primitive inhabitants. Hence he supposes the origin of the Etrurians and the Scandinavians. But if we give him so much, we must give him more, and deduce from the same origin the Es of the Celt and the Ized of the Persian, and—what will be of more use to him, I dare say, poor man, than all the rest put together—the Æs of the Romans, that is, the God of Copper-Money—a very powerful household god he is to this day!

My mother looked musingly at her frock, as if she were taking my father's proposition into seriòus consideration.

"So perhaps," resumed my father, "and not unconformably with sacred records, from one great parent horde came all those various tribes, carrying with them the name of their beloved Asia; and, whether they wandered north, south, or west, exalting their own emphatic designation of 'Children of the Land of Light' into the title of gods. And to think" (added Mr. Caxton pathetically, gazing upon that speck in the globe on which his forefinger rested), — "to think how little they changed for the better when they got to the Don, or entangled their rafts amidst the icebergs of the Baltic — so comfortably off as they were here, if they could but have stayed quiet."

"And why the deuce could not they?" asked Mr. Squills.

"Pressure of population, and not enough to live upon, I suppose," said my father.

PISISTRATUS (sulkily).— More probably they did away with the Corn Laws, sir.

"*Papæ!*" quoth my father; "that throws a new light on the subject."

PISISTRATUS (full of his grievances, and not caring three straws about the origin of the Scandinavians).— I know that if we are to lose £500 every year on a farm which we hold rent-free, and which the best judges allow to be a perfect model for the whole country, we had better make haste and turn Æsir, or Aser, or whatever you call them, and fix a settlement on the property of other nations — otherwise, I suspect, our probable settlement will be on the parish.

MR. SQUILLS (who, it must be remembered, is an enthusiastic Free-trader).— You have only got to put more capital on the land.

PISISTRATUS.— Well, Mr. Squills, as you think so well of that investment, put *your* capital on it. I promise that you shall have every shilling of profit.

MR. SQUILLS (hastily retreating behind *The Times*).

— I don't think the Great Western can fall any lower; though it *is* hazardous — I can but venture a few hundreds ——

PISISTRATUS. — On our land, Squills? Thank you.

MR. SQUILLS. — No, no — anything but that — on the Great Western.

Pisistratus relaxes into gloom. Blanche steals up coaxingly, and gets snubbed for her pains.

A pause.

MR. CAXTON. — There are two golden rules of life; one relates to the mind, and the other to the pockets. The first is — If our thoughts get into a low, nervous, aguish condition, we should make them change the air; the second is comprised in the proverb, "It is good to have two strings to one's bow." Therefore, Pisistratus, I tell you what you must do — Write a Book!

PISISTRATUS.—Write a Book!—Against the abolition of the Corn Laws? Faith, sir, the mischief's done. It takes a much better pen than mine to write down an Act of Parliament.

MR. CAXTON. — I only said "Write a book." All the rest is the addition of your own headlong imagination.

PISISTRATUS (with the recollection of The Great Book rising before him). — Indeed, sir, I should think that that would just finish us!

MR. CAXTON (not seeming to heed the interruption). — A book that will sell. A book that will prop up the fall of prices! A book that will distract your mind from its dismal apprehensions, and restore your affection to your species, and your hopes in the ultimate triumph of sound principles — by the sight of a favorable balance at the end of the yearly accounts. It is astonishing what a differerence that little circumstance makes in our views of things in general. I remember when the bank in which Squills had incautiously left £1,000 broke, one remarkably healthy year, that he became a great alarmist, and said that the country was on the verge of ruin; whereas you see now, when, thanks to a long succession of sickly seasons, he has a surplus capital to risk in the Great Western, he is firmly persuaded that England was never in so prosperous a condition.

Mr. Squills (rather sullenly). — Pooh, pooh.

Mr. Caxton.—Write a book, my son — write a book. Need I tell you that Money or Moneta, according to Hyginus, was the mother of the Muses? Write a book.

Blanche and my Mother (in full chorus). — O yes, Sisty — a book — a book! you must write a book.

"I am sure," quoth my Uncle Roland, slamming down the volume he had just concluded, "he could write a devilish deal better book than this; and how I come to read such trash, night after night, is more than I could possibly explain to the satisfaction of an intelligent jury, if I were put into a witness-box, and examined in the mildest manner by my own counsel."

Mr. Caxton. — You see that Roland tells us exactly what sort of a book it shall be.

Pisistratus. — Trash, sir?

Mr. Caxton. — No — that is, not necessarily trash —

but a book of that class which, whether trash or not, people can't help reading. Novels have become a necessity of the age: you must write a novel.

PISISTRATUS (flattered, but dubious).—A novel! But every subject on which novels can be written is preoccupied. There are novels of low life, novels of high life, military novels, naval novels, novels philosophical, novels religious, novels historical, novels descriptive of India, the Colonies, Ancient Rome, and the Egyptian Pyramids. From what bird, wild eagle, or barn-door fowl, can I

"Pluck one unwearied plume from Fancy's wing?"

MR. CAXTON (after a little thought).—You remember the story which Trevanion (I beg his pardon, Lord Ulswater) told us the other night. That gives you something of the romance of real life for your plot—puts you chiefly among scenes with which you are familiar, and furnishes you with characters which have been very sparingly dealt with since the time of Fielding. You can give us the Country Squire, as you remember him in your youth; it is a specimen of a race worth preserving —the old idiosyncrasies of which are rapidly dying off, as the railways bring Norfolk and Yorkshire within easy reach of the manners of London. You can give us the old-fashioned Parson, as in all essentials he may yet be found; but before, you had to drag him out of the great Tractarian bog; and, for the rest I really think that while, as I am told, many popular writers are doing their best, especially in France, and perhaps a little in England, to set class against class, and pick up every stone in the kennel to shy at a gentleman with a good coat on his back, something useful might be done by a few good-humored sketches of those innocent criminals a little better off than their neighbors, whom, however we dislike them, I take it for granted we shall have to endure, in one shape or another, as long as civilisation exists; and they seem, on the whole, as good in their present shape as we are likely to get, shake the dice-box of society how we will.

Pisistratus.—Very well said, sir; but this rural country-gentleman life is not so new as you think. There's Washington Irving——

Mr. Caxton.—Charming; but rather tne manners of the last century than this. You may as well cite Addison and Sir Roger de Coverley.

Pisistratus.—*Tremaine* and *De Vere*.

Mr. Caxton.—Nothing can be more graceful, nor more unlike what I mean. The Pales and Terminus I wish you to put up in the fields are familiar images, that you may cut out of an oak-tree—not beautiful marble statues, on porphyry pedestals, twenty feet high.

Pisistratus—Miss Austin; Mrs. Gore in her masterpiece of *Mrs. Armytage;* Mrs. Marsh, too; and then (for Scotch manners) Miss Ferrier!

Mr. Caxton (growing cross).—Oh, if you cannot treat on bucolics, but what you must hear some Virgil or other cry "Stop thief," you deserve to be tossed by one of your own "short-horns." [Still more contemptuously]—I am sure I don't know why we spend so much money on sending our sons to school to learn Latin, when that Anachronism of yours, Mrs. Caxton, can't even construe a line and a half of Phædrus. Phædrus, Mrs. Caxton—a book which is in Latin what Goody Two-Shoes is in the vernacular!

MRS. CAXTON (alarmed and indignant).—Fie! Austin! I am sure you can construe Phædrus, dear.

Pisistratus prudently preserves silence.

MR. CAXTON.—I'll try him—

> "Sua cuique quum sit animi cogitatio
> Colorque propius."

What does that mean?

PISISTRATUS (smiling).—That every man has some coloring matter within him, to give his own tinge to——

"His own novel," interrupted my father. "*Contentus peragis!*"

During the latter part of this dialogue, Blanche had sewn together three quires of the best Bath paper, and she now placed them on a little table before me, with her own ink-stand and steel pen.

My mother put her finger to her lip, and said, "Hush!" my father returned to the cradle of the Æsar; Captain Roland leant his cheek on his hand, and gazed abstractedly on the fire; Mr. Squills fell into a placid doze; and, after three sighs that would have melted a heart of stone, I rushed into—MY NOVEL.

CHAPTER II.

"THERE has never been occasion to use them since I've been in the parish," said Parson Dale.

"What does that prove?" quoth the Squire, sharply, and looking the Parson full in the face.

"Prove!" repeated Mr. Dale, with a smile of benign, yet too conscious superiority — "What does experience prove?"

"That your forefathers were great blockheads, and that their descendant is not a whit the wiser."

"Squire," replied the Parson, "although that is a melancholy conclusion, yet if you mean it to apply universally, and not to the family of the Dales in particular, it is not one which my candor as a reasoner, and my humility as a mortal, will permit me to challenge."

"I defy you," said Mr. Hazeldean, triumphantly. "But to stick to the subject (which it is monstrous hard to do when one talks with a parson), I only just ask you to look yonder, and tell me, on your conscience — I don't even say as a parson, but as a parishioner — whether you ever saw a more disreputable spectacle?"

While he spoke, the Squire, leaning heavily on the Parson's left shoulder, extended his cane in a line parallel with the right eye of that disputatious ecclesiastic, so that he might guide the organ of sight to the object he had thus unflatteringly described.

"I confess," said the Parson, "that, regarded by the eye of the senses, it is a thing that in its best day had small pretensions to beauty, and is not elevated into the picturesque even by neglect and decay. But, my friend, regarded by the eye of the inner man — of the rural philosopher and parochial legislator — I say it is by neglect and decay that it is rendered a very pleasing feature in what I may call 'the moral topography of a parish.'"

The Squire looked at the Parson as if he could have beaten him; and, indeed, regarding the object in dispute not only with the eye of the outer man, but the eye of law and order — the eye of a country gentleman and a justice of the peace, the spectacle *was* scandalously disreputable. It was moss-grown; it was worm-eaten; it was broken right in the middle; through its four socketless eyes, neighbored by the nettle, peered the thistle: — the thistle! a forest of thistles! — and, to complete the degradation of the whole, those thistles had attracted the donkey of an itinerant tinker; and the irreverent animal was in the very act of taking his luncheon out of the eyes and jaws of — THE PARISH STOCKS.

The Squire looked as if he could have beaten the Parson; but, as he was not without some slight command of temper, and a substitute was luckily at hand, he gulphed down his resentment, and made a rush — at the donkey!

Now the donkey was hampered by a rope to its fore-feet, to the which was attached a billet of wood, called technically "a clog," so that it had no fair chance of escape from the assault its sacrilegious luncheon had justly provoked. But, the ass turning round with unusual nimbleness at the first stroke of the cane, the Squire caught his foot in the rope, and went head over heels among the thistles. The donkey gravely bent down, and thrice smelt or sniffed its prostrate foe; then, having convinced itself that it had nothing farther to apprehend for the present, and very willing to make the best of the reprieve, according to the poetical admonition, "Gather your rosebuds while you may," it cropped a thistle in full bloom close to the ear of the Squire; — so close, indeed, that the Parson thought the ear was gone; and with the more probability, inasmuch as the Squire, feeling the warm breath of the creature, bellowed out with all the force of lungs accustomed to give a View-hallo!

"Bless me, is it gone?" said the Parson, thrusting his person between the ass and the Squire.

"Zounds and the devil!" cried the Squire, rubbing himself as he rose to his feet.

"Hush," said the Parson, gently. "What a horrible oath!"

"Horrible oath! If you had my nankeens on," said the Squire, still rubbing himself, "and had fallen into a thicket of thistles, with a donkey's teeth within an inch of your ear!" ——

"It is not gone, then?" interrupted the Parson.

"No—that is, I think not," said the Squire, dubiously and he clapped his hand to the organ in question. "No! it is not gone!"

"Thank Heauen!" said the good clergyman, kindly.

"Hum," growled the Squire, who was now once more engaged in rubbing himself. "Thank heaven indeed, when I am as full of thorns as a porcupine! I should like to know what use thistles are in the world."

"For donkeys to eat, if you will let them, Squire," answered the Parson.

"Ugh, you beast!" cried Mr. Hazledean, all his wrath re-awakened, whether by reference to the donkey species, or his inability to reply to the Parson, or perhaps by some sudden prick too sharp for humanity — especially humanity in nankeens — to endure without kicking; "Ugh, you beast!" he exclaimed, shaking his cane at the donkey, which, at the interposition of the Parson, had respectfully recoiled a few paces, and now stood switching its thin tail, and trying vainly to lift one of its fore-legs — for the flies teased it.

"Poor thing!" said the Parson, pityingly. "See, it has a raw place on the shoulder, and the flies have found out the sore."

"I am devilish glad to hear it," said the Squire, vindictively.

"Fie, fie!"

"It is very well to say 'Fie, fie.' It was not you who fell among the thistles. What's the man about now, I wonder?"

The parson had walked towards a chestnut-tree that stood on the village green; he broke off a bough — returned to the donkey — whisked away the flies, and then tenderly placed the broad leaves over the sore, as a protection from the swarms. The donkey turned round its head, and looked at him with mild wonder.

"I would bet a shilling," said the Parson, softly, "that this is the first act of kindness thou hast met with this many a day. And slight enough it is, Heaven knows."

With that the Parson put his hand into his pocket, and drew out an apple. It was a fine, large, rose-cheeked apple — one of the last winter's store, from the celebrated tree in the parsonage garden; and he was taking it as a present to a little boy in the village, who had notably distinguished himself in the Sunday-school. "Nay, in common justice, Lenny Fairfield should have the preference," muttered the Parson. The ass pricked up one of its ears, and advanced its head timidly. "But Lenny Fairfield would be as much pleased with twopence; and what could twopence do to thee?" The ass's nose now touched the apple. "Take it, in the name of Charity," quoth the Parson; "Justice is accustomed to be served last:" and the ass took the apple. "How had you the heart?" said the Parson, pointing to the Squire's cane.

The ass stopped munching, and looked askant at the Squire.

"Pooh! eat on; he'll not beat thee now."

"No," said the Squire, apologetically. "But, after all, he is not an Ass of the Parish; he is a vagrant, and he ought to be pounded. But the pound is in as bad a state as the stocks, thanks to your new-fashioned doctrines."

"New-fashioned!" cried the Parson, almost indignantly, for he had a great disdain of new fashions — "They are as old as Christianity; nay, as old as Paradise, which, you will observe, is derived from a Greek or rather a Persian word, and means something more than 'garden,' corresponding," pursued the Parson, rather pedantically, "with the Latin *vivarium*, viz., grove or park full of innocent dumb creatures. Depend on it, donkeys were allowed to eat thistles there."

"Very possibly," said the Squire, drily. "But Hazeldean, though a very pretty village, is not Paradise. The stocks shall be mended to-morrow — ay, and the pound too, — and the next donkey found trespassing shall go into it, as sure as my name's Hazeldean."

"Then," said the Parson, gravely, "I can only hope that the next parish may not follow your example; or that you and I may never be caught straying."

CHAPTER III.

PARSON DALE and Squire Hazeldean parted company · the latter to inspect his sheep, the former to visit some of his parishioners, including Lenny Fairfield, whom the donkey had defrauded of his apple.

Lenny Fairfield was sure to be in the way, for his mother rented a few acres of grass-land from the Squire, and it was now hay-time. And Leonard, commonly called Lenny, was an only son, and his mother a widow. The cottage stood apart, and somewhat remote, in one of the many nooks of the long, green, village lane. And a thoroughly English cottage it was — three centuries old at least; with walls of rubble let into oak frames, and duly whitewashed every summer, a thatched roof, small panes of glass, an old doorway raised from the ground by two steps. There was about this little dwelling all the homely rustic elegance which peasant life admits of; a honeysuckle was trained over the door; a few flower-pots were placed on the window-sills; the small plot of ground in front of the house was kept with great neatness, and even taste; some large rough stones on either side the little path having been formed into a sort of rock-work, with creepers that were now in flower; and the potato-ground was screened from the eye by sweet-peas and lupine. Simple elegance, all this, it is true; but how well it speaks for peasant and landlord, when you see that the peasant is fond of his home, and has some spare time and heart to bestow upon mere embellishment. Such a peasant is sure to be a bad customer to the ale-house, and a safe neighbor to the Squire's preserves. All honor and praise to him, except a small tax upon both, which is due to the landlord!

Such sights were as pleasant to the Parson as the most beautiful landscapes of Italy can be to the *dilettante*. He paused a moment at the wicket to look around him, and distended his nostrils voluptuously to inhale the smell of the sweet-peas, mixed with that of the new-mown hay in the fields behind, which a slight breeze bore to him. He then moved on, carefully scraped his shoes, clean and well-polished as they were — for Mr. Dale was rather a beau in his own clerical way, — on the scraper without the door, and lifted the latch.

Your virtuoso looks with artistical delight on the figure of some nymph painted on an Etruscan vase, engaged in pouring out the juice of the grape from her classic urn. And the Parson felt as harmless if not as elegant a pleasure in contemplating Widow Fairfield brimming high a glittering can, which she designed for the refreshment of the thirsty haymakers.

Mrs. Fairfield was a middle-aged, tidy woman, with that alert precision of movement which seems to come from an active, orderly mind; and as she now turned her head briskly at the sound of the Parson's footstep, she showed a countenance prepossessing, though not handsome—a countenance from which a pleasant, hearty smile, breaking forth at that moment, effaced some lines that in repose spoke "of sorrows, but of sorrows past;" and her cheek, paler than is common to the complexions even of the fair sex, when born and bred amidst a rural population, might have favored the guess that the earlier part of her life had been spent in the languid air and "within-doors" occupations of a town.

"Never mind me," said the Parson, as Mrs. Fairfield

dropped her quick curtsey, and smoothed her apron; "if you are going into the hay-field, I will go with you; I have something to say to Lenny—an excellent boy."

WIDOW.—Well, sir, and you are kind to say it; but so he is.

PARSON.—He reads uncommonly well, he writes tolerably; he is the best lad in the whole school at his Catechism and in the Bible lessons; and I assure you, when I see his face at church, looking up so attentively, I fancy that I shall read my sermon all the better for such a listener!

WIDOW (wiping her eyes with the corner of her apron).—'Deed, sir, when my poor Mark died, I never thought I could have lived on as I have done. But that boy is so kind and good, that when I look at him sitting there in dear Mark's chair, and remember how Mark loved him, aud all he used to say to me about him, I feel somehow or other as if my goodman smiled on me, and would rather I was not with him yet, till the lad had grown up, and did not want me any more.

PARSON (looking away, and after a pause).—You never hear anything of the old folks at Lansmere?

"'Deed, sir, sin' poor Mark died, they han't noticed me nor the boy; but," added the Widow, with all a peasant's pride, "it isn't that I wants their money; only it's hard to feel strange-like to one's own father and mother!"

PARSON.—You must excuse them. Your father, Mr. Avenel, was never quite the same man after that sad event which—but you are weeping, my friend; pardon me.

Your mother is a little proud; but so are you, though in another way.

Widow. — I proud! Lord love ye, sir, I have not a bit o' pride in me! and that's the reason they always looked down on me.

Parson. — Your parents must be well off; and I shall apply to them in a year or two on behalf of Lenny, for they promised me to provide for him when he grew up, as they ought.

Widow (with flashing eyes). — I am sure, sir, I hope you will do no such thing; for I would not have Lenny beholden to them as has never given him a kind word sin' he was born!

The Parson smiled gravely, and shook his head at poor Mrs. Fairfield's hasty confutation of her own self-acquittal from the charge of pride; but he saw that it was not the time or moment for effectual peace-making in the most irritable of all rancors, viz.: that nourished against one's nearest relations. He therefore dropped the subject, and said:—"Well, time enough to think of Lenny's future prospects; meanwhile, we are forgetting the hay-makers. Come."

The widow opened the back door, which led across a little apple orchard into the fields.

Parson. — You have a pleasant place here; and I see that my friend Lenny should be in no want of apples. I had brought him one, but I have given it away on the road.

Widow. — Oh, sir, it is not the deed — it is the will;

as I felt when the Squire, God bless him! took two pounds off the rent the year he — that is, Mark — died.

PARSON.— If Lenny continues to be such a help to you, it will not be long before the Squire may put the two pounds on again.

"Yes, sir," said the Widow, simply; "I hope he will."

"Silly woman!" muttered the Parson. "That's not exactly what the schoolmistress would have said. You don't read nor write, Mrs. Fairfield; yet you express yourself with great propriety."

"You know Mark was a schollard, sir, like my poor, poor sister; and though I was a sad stupid girl afore I married, I tried to take after him when we came together."

CHAPTER IV.

THEY were now in the hay-field; and a boy of about sixteen, but, like most country lads, to appearance much younger than he was, looked up from his rake, with lively blue eyes beaming forth under a profusion of brown curly hair.

Leonard Fairfield was indeed a very handsome boy — not so stout nor so ruddy as one would choose for the ideal of rustic beauty; nor yet so delicate in limb and keen in expression as are those children of cities, in whom the mind is cultivated at the expense of the body; but still he had the health of the country in his cheeks, and was not without the grace of the city in his compact figure and easy movements. There was in his physiognomy something interesting from its peculiar character of innocence and simplicity. You could see that he had been brought up by a woman, and much apart from familiar contact with other children; and such intelligence as was yet developed in him was not ripened by the jokes and cuffs of his coevals, but fostered by decorous lecturings from his elders, and good-little-boy maxims in good-little-boy books.

PARSON.— Come hither, Lenny. You know the benefit of school, I see: it can teach you nothing better than to be a support to your mother.

LENNY (looking down sheepishly, and with a heightened glow over his face).— Please, sir, that may come one of these days.

PARSON.— That's right, Lenny. Let me see! why, you must be nearly a man. How old are you?

Lenny looks up inquiringly at his mother.

PARSON.— You ought to know, Lenny; speak for yourself. Hold your tongue, Mrs. Fairfield.

LENNY (twirling his hat, and in great perplexity).— Well, and there is Flop, neighbor Dutton's old sheep-dog. He be very old now.

PARSON.— I am not asking Flop's age, but your own.

LENNY.— 'Deed, sir, I have heard say as how Flop and I were pups together. That is, I — I ——

For the Parson is laughing, and so is Mrs. Fairfield; and the hay-makers, who have stood still to listen, are laughing too. And poor Lenny has quite lost his head, and looks as if he would like to cry.

PARSON (patting the curly locks, encouragingly). Never mind; it is not so badly answered, after all. And how old is Flop?

LENNY. — Why, he must be fifteen year and more.

PARSON. — How old, then, are you?

LENNY (looking up, with a beam of intelligence). — Fifteen year and more.

Widow sighs and nods her head.

"That's what we call putting two and two together," said the Parson. "Or, in other words," and here he raised his eyes majestically towards the hay-makers—"in other words — thanks to his love for his book - - simple as he stands here, Lenny Fairfield has shown himself capable of INDUCTIVE RATIOCINATION."

At those words, delivered *ore rotundo*, the hay-makers ceased laughing; for even in lay matters they held the Parson to be an oracle, and words so long must have a great deal in them.

Lenny drew up his head proudly.

"You are very fond of Flop, I suppose?"

"'Deed he is," said the Widow, "and of all poor dumb creatures."

"Very good. Suppose, my lad, that you had a fine apple, and that you met a friend who wanted it more than you, what would you do with it?"

"Please you, sir, I would give him half of it."

The Parson's face fell. — "Not the whole, Lenny?"

Lenny considered. — "If he was a friend, sir, he would not like me to give him all?"

"Upon my word, Master Leonard, you speak so well that I must e'en tell the truth. I brought you an apple, as a prize for good conduct in school; but I met by the way a poor donkey, and some one beat him for eating a thistle, so I thought I would make it up by giving him the apple. Ought I only to have given him the half?"

Lenny's innocent face became all smile; his interest was aroused. — "And did the donkey like the apple?"

"Very much," said the Parson, fumbling in his pocket, but thinking of Leonard Fairfield's years and understanding; and moreover, observing, in the pride of his heart, that there were many spectators to his deed, he thought the meditated twopence not sufficient, and he generously produced a silver sixpence.

"There, my man, that will pay for the half-apple which you would have kept for yourself." The parson again patted the curly locks, and, after a hearty word or two with the other hay-makers, and a friendly "Good-day" to Mrs. Fairfield, struck into the path that led towards his own glebe.

He had just crossed the stile, when he heard hasty but timorous feet behind him. He turned, and saw his friend Lenny.

LENNY (half-crying, and holding out the sixpence). — Indeed, sir, I would rather not. I would have given all to the Neddy.

PARSON. — Why, then, my man, you have a still greater right to the sixpence.

Lenny. — No, sir; 'cause you only gave it to make up for the half-apple. And if I had given the whole, as I ought to have done, why I should have had no right to the sixpence. Please, sir, don't be offended; do take it back, will you?

The Parson hesitated. And the boy thrust the sixpence into his hand, as the ass had poked its nose there before in quest of the apple.

"I see," said Parson Dale, soliloquising, "that if one don't give Justice the first place at the table, all the other Virtues eat up her share."

Indeed, the case was perplexing. Charity, like a forward, impudent baggage as she is, always thrusting herself in the way, and taking other people's apples to make her own little pie, had defrauded Lenny of his due; and now Susceptibility, who looks like a shy, blush-faced, awkward Virtue in her teens — but who, nevertheless, is always engaged in picking the pockets of her sisters, tried to filch from him his lawful recompense. The case was perplexing; for the Parson held Susceptibility in great honor, despite her hypocritical tricks, and did not like to give her a slap in the face, which might frighten her away for ever. So Mr. Dale stood irresolute, glancing from the sixpence to Lenny, and from Lenny to the sixpence.

"*Buon giorno*, Good-day to you," said a voice behind, in an accent slightly but unmistakably foreign, and a strange-looking figure presented itself at the stile

Imagine a tall and exceedingly meagre man, dressed in a rusty suit of black — the pantaloons tight at the calf and ankle, and there forming a loose gaiter over thick shoes, buckled high at the instep; — an old cloak, lined with red, was thrown over one shoulder, though the day was sultry; — a quaint, red, outlandish umbrella, with a carved brass handle, was thrust under one arm, though the sky was cloudless; — a profusion of raven hair, in waving curls that seemed as fine as silk, escaped from the sides of a straw hat of prodigious brim; a complexion sallow and swarthy, and features which, though not without considerable beauty to the eye of the artist, were not only unlike what we fair, well-fed, neat-faced Englishmen are wont to consider comely, but exceedingly like what we are disposed to regard as awful and Satanic — to wit, a long hooked nose, sunken cheeks, black eyes, whose piercing brilliancy took something wizard-like and mystical from the large spectacles through which they shone; a mouth round which played an ironical smile, and in which a physiognomist would have remarked singular shrewdness, and some closeness, complete the picture. Imagine this figure, grotesque, peregrinate, and to the eye of a peasant certainly diabolical; then perch it on the stile in the midst of those green English fields, and in sight of that primitive English village; there let it sit straddling, its long legs dangling down, a short German pipe emitting clouds from one corner of those sardonic lips, its dark eyes glaring through the spectacles full upon the Parson, yet askant upon Lenny Fairfield. Lenny Fairfield looked exceedingly frightened.

"Upon my word, Dr. Riccabocca," said Mr. Dale,

smiling, "you come in good time to solve a very nice question in casuistry;" and herewith the Parson explained the case, and put the question — "Ought Lenny Fairfield to have the sixpence, or ought he not?"

"*Cospetto!*" said the Doctor, "if the hen would but hold her tongue nobody would know that she had laid an egg."

CHAPTER V.

"GRANTED," said the Parson; "but what follows? The saying is good, but I don't see the application."

"A thousand pardons!" replied Dr. Riccabocca, with all the urbanity of an Italian; "but it seems to me that if you had given the sixpence to the *fanciullo* — that is, to this good little boy — without telling him the story about the donkey, you would never put him and yourself into this awkward dilemma."

"But, my dear sir," whispered the Parson mildly, as he inclined his lips to the Doctor's ear, "I should then have lost the opportunity of inculcating a moral lesson — you understand."

Dr. Riccabocca shrugged his shoulders, restored his pipe to his mouth, and took a long whiff. It was a whiff eloquent, though cynical — a whiff peculiar to your philosophical smoker—a whiff that implied the most absolute, but the most placid incredulity as to the effect of the Parson's moral lesson.

"Still you have not given us your decision," said the Parson, after a pause.

The Doctor withdrew his pipe. "*Cospetto!*" said he — "He who scrubs the head of an ass wastes his soap."

"If you scrubbed mine fifty times over with those enigmatical proverbs of yours," said the Parson, testily, "you would not make it any the wiser."

"My good sir," said the Doctor, bowing low from his perch on the stile, "I never presumed to say that there were more asses than one in the story; but I thought that I could not better explain my meaning, which is simply this — you scrubbed the ass's head, and therefore you must lose the soap. Let the *fanciullo* have the sixpence; and a great sum it is too, for a little boy, who may spend it all as pocket-money!"

"There, Lenny — you hear?" said the Parson, stretching out the sixpence. But Lenny retreated, and cast on the umpire a look of great aversion and disgust.

"Please, Master Dale," said he, obstinately, "I'd rather not."

"It is a matter of feeling, you see," said the Parson, turning to the umpire; "and I believe the boy is right."

"If it be a matter of feeling," replied Dr. Riccabocca, "there is no more to be said on it. When Feeling comes in at the door, Reason has nothing to do but to jump out of the window."

"Go, my good boy," said the Parson, pocketing the coin; "but stop! give me your hand first. *There* I understand you; — good-bye!"

Lenny's eyes glistened as the Parson shook him by the hand, and, not trusting himself to speak, he walked off sturdily. The Parson wiped his forehead, and sat himself down on the stile beside the Italian. The view before them was lovely, and both enjoyed it (though not equally) enough to be silent for some moments. On the other side the lane seen between gaps in the old oaks and chestnuts that hung over the moss-grown pales of Hazeldean Park, rose gentle, verdant slopes, dotted with sheep and herds of deer; a stately avenue stretched far away to the left, and ended at the right-hand, within a few yards of a ha-ha that divided the park from a level sward of table-land gay with shrubs and flower-pots, relieved by the shade of two mighty cedars. And on this platform, only seen in part, stood the Squire's old-fashioned house, red-brick, with stone mullions, gable-ends, and quaint chimney-pots. On this side the road, immediately facing the two gentlemen, cottage after cottage whitely emerged from the curves in the lane, while, beyond, the ground declining, gave an extensive prospect of woods and corn-fields, spires and farms. Behind, from a belt of lilacs and evergreens, you caught a peep of the parsonage-house, backed by woodlands, and a little noisy rill running in front. The birds were still in the hedge-rows, — only, as if from the very heart of the most distant woods, there came now and then the mellow note of the cuckoo.

"Verily," said Mr. Dale, softly, "my lot has fallen on a goodly heritage.

The Italian twitched his cloak over him, and sighed almost inaudibly. Perhaps he thought of his own Summer Land, and felt that, amidst all that fresh verdure of the North, there was no heritage for the stranger.

However, before the Parson could notice the sigh, or conjecture the cause, Dr. Riccabocca's thin lips took an expression almost malignant.

"*Per Bacco!*" said he; "in every country I observe that the rocks settle where the trees are the finest. I am sure that, when Noah first landed on Ararat, he must have found some gentleman in black already settled in the pleasantest part of the mountain, and waiting for his tenth of the cattle as they came out of the Ark."

The Parson fixed his meek eyes on the philosopher, and there was in them something so deprecating, rather than reproachful, that Dr. Riccabocca turned away his face, and refilled his pipe. Dr. Riccabocca abhorred priests; but though Parson Dale was emphatically a parson, he seemed at that moment so little of what Dr. Riccabocca understood by a priest, that the Italian's heart smote him for his irreverent jest on the cloth. Luckily at this moment there was a diversion to that untoward commencement of conversation, in the appearance of no less a personage than the donkey himself — I mean the donkey who ate the apple.

CHAPTER VI.

The Tinker was a stout swarthy fellow, jovial and musical withal, for he was singing a stave as he flourished his staff, and at the end of each *refrain* down came the staff on the quarters of the donkey. The Tinker went behind and sung, the donkey went before and was thwacked.

"Yours is a droll country," quoth Dr. Riccabocca; "in mine, it is not the ass that walks first in the procession that gets the blows."

The parson jumped from the stile, and looking over the hedge that divided the field from the road — "Gently, gently," said he; "the sound of the stick spoils the singing! O, Mr. Sprott, Mr. Sprott! a good man is merciful to his beast."

The donkey seemed to recognise the voice of its friend, for it stopped short, pricked one ear wistfully, and looked up.

The Tinker touched his hat, and looked up too. "Lord bless your reverence! he does not mind it, he likes it. I vould not hurt thee; vould I, Neddy?"

The donkey shook his head and shivered: perhaps a fly had settled on the sore, which the chestnut-leaves no longer protected.

"I am sure you did not mean to hurt him, Sprott," said the Parson, more politely I fear than honestly — for he had seen enough of that cross-grained thing called the human heart, even in the little world of a country parish, to know that it requires management, and coaxing, and flattering, to interfere successfully between a man and his own donkey—"I am sure you did not mean to hurt him; but he has already got a sore on his shoulder as big as my hand, poor thing!"

"Lord, love 'un! yes; that was done a-playing with the manger, the day I gave 'un oats!" said the Tinker.

Dr. Riccabocca adjusted his spectacles, and surveyed the ass. The ass pricked up his other ear, and surveyed Dr. Riccabocca. In that mutual survey of physical qualifications, each being regarded according to the average symmetry of its species, it may be doubted whether the advantage was on the side of the philosopher.

The Parson had a great notion of the wisdom of his friend, in all matters not purely ecclesiastical:

"Say a good word for the donkey!" whispered he.

"Sir," said the Doctor, addressing Mr. Sprott, with a respectful salutation, "there's a great kettle at my house — the Casino — which wants soldering: can you recommend me a tinker?"

"Why, that's all in my line," said Sprott, "and there ben't a tinker in the country that I vould recommend like myself, thof I say it."

"You jest, good sir," said the Doctor, smiling pleasantly. "A man who can't mend a hole in his own donkey, can never demean himself by patching up my great kettle."

"Lord, sir!" said the Tinker, archly, "if I had known that poor Neddy had had two sitch friends in court, I'd had seen he vas a gintleman, and treated him as sitch."

"*Corpo di Bacco!*" quoth the Doctor, "though that jest's not new, I think the Tinker comes very well out of it."

"True; but the donkey!" said the Parson; "I've a great mind to buy it."

"Permit me to tell you an anecdote in point," said Dr. Riccabocca.

"Well?" said the Parson, interrogatively.

"Once in a time," pursued Riccabocca, "the Emperor Adrian, going to the public baths, saw an old soldier, who had served under him, rubbing his back against the marble wall. The Emperor, who was a wise, and therefore a curious, inquisitive man, sent for the soldier, and asked him why he resorted to that sort of friction. 'Because,' answered the veteran, 'I am too poor to have slaves to rub me down.' The Emperor was touched, and gave him slaves and money. The next day, when Adrian went to the baths, all the old men in the city were to be seen rubbing themselves against the marble as hard as they could. The Emperor sent for them, and asked them the same question which he had put to the soldier: the cunning old rogues, of course, made the same answer. 'Friends,' said Adrian, 'since there are so many of you, you will just rub one another!' Mr. Dale, if you don't want to have all the donkeys in the country with holes in their shoulders, you had better not buy the Tinker's!"

"It is the hardest thing in the world to do the least bit of good," groaned the Parson, as he broke a twig off the hedge nervously, snapped it in two, and flung away the fragments: one of them hit the donkey on the nose. If the ass could have spoken Latin, he would have said, "*Et tu, Brute!*" As it was, he hung down his ears, and walked on.

"Gee hup!" said the Tinker; and he followed the ass. Then stopping, he looked over his shoulder, and seeing that the Parson's eyes were gazing mournfully on his *protégé*, "Never fear, your reverence," cried the Tinker, kindly; "I'll not spite 'un."

CHAPTER VII.

"Four o'clock," cried the Parson, looking at his watch; "half an hour after dinner-time, and Mrs. Dale particularly begged me to be punctual, because of the fine trout the Squire sent us. Will you venture on what our homely language calls 'pot luck,' Doctor?"

Now Riccabocca was a professed philosopher, and valued himself on his penetration into the motives of human conduct. And when the Parson thus invited him to pot luck, he smiled with a kind of lofty complacency; for Mrs. Dale enjoyed the reputation of having what her friends styled, "her little tempers." And, as well-bred ladies rarely indulge "little tempers" in the presence of a third person not of the family, so Dr. Riccabocca instantly concluded that he was invited to stand between the pot and the luck! Nevertheless — as he was fond of trout, and a much more good-natured man than he ought to have been according to his principles — he accepted the hospitality; but he did so with a sly look from over his spectacles, which brought a blush into the guilty cheeks of the Parson. Certainly Riccabocca had for once guessed right, in his estimate of human motives.

The two walked on, crossed a little bridge that spanned the rill, and entered the parsonage lawn. Two dogs, that seemed to have sate on watch for their master, sprang towards him, barking; and the sound drew the notice of Mrs. Dale, who, with parasol in hand, sallied out from the sash window which opened on the lawn. Now, O reader! I know that, in thy secret heart, thou art chuckling over the want of knowledge in the sacred arcana of the domestic hearth, betrayed by the author; thou art saying to thyself, "A pretty way to conciliate 'little tempers' indeed, to add to the offence of spoiling the fish the crime of bringing an unexpected friend to eat it. Pot luck, quotha, when the pot's boiled over this half hour!"

But, to thy utter shame and confusion, O reader! learn that both the author and Parson Dale knew very well what they were about.

Dr. Riccabocca was the special favorite of Mrs. Dale, and the only person in the whole county who never put her out, by dropping in. In fact, strange though it may seem at first glance, Dr. Riccabocca had that mysterious something about him, which we of his own sex can so little comprehend, but which always propitiates the other. He owed this, in part, to his own profound but hypocritical policy; for he looked upon woman as the natural enemy to man — against whom it was necessary to be always on the guard; whom it was prudent to disarm by every species of fawning servility and abject complaisance. He owed it also, in part, to the compassionate and heavenly nature of the angels whom his thoughts thus villanously traduced — for women like one whom they can pity without despising; and there was something in Signor Riccabocca's poverty, in his loneliness, in his exile, whether voluntary or compelled, that excited pity; while, despite the threadbare coat, the red umbrella, and the wild hair, he had, especially when addressing ladies, that air of gentleman and cavalier, which is or was more innate in an educated Italian, of whatever rank, than perhaps in the highest aristocracy of any other country in Europe. For, though I grant that nothing is more exquisite than the politeness of your French marquis of the old *régime* — nothing more frankly gracious than the cordial address of a high-bred English gentleman — nothing more kindly prepossessing than the genial good-nature of some patriarchal German, who will condescend to forget his sixteen quarterings in the pleasure of doing you a favor — yet these specimens of the suavity of their several nations are rare; whereas blandness and polish are common attributes with your Italian. They seem to have been immemorially handed down to him, from ancestors emulating the urbanity of Cæsar, and refined by the grace of Horace.

"Dr. Riccabocca consents to dine with us," cried the Parson, hastily.

"If Madame permit?" said the Italian, bowing over the hand extended to him, which, however, he forbore to take, seeing it was already full of the watch.

"I am only sorry that the trout must be quite spoiled," began Mrs. Dale, plaintively.

"It is not the trout one thinks of when one dines with Mrs. Dale," said the infamous dissimulator.

"But I see James coming to say that dinner is ready," observed the Parson.

"He said *that* three quarters of an hour ago, Charles dear," retorted Mrs. Dale, taking the arm of Dr. Riccabocca.

CHAPTER VIII.

While the Parson and his wife are entertaining their guest, I propose to regale the reader with a small treatise apropos of that "Charles dear," murmured by Mrs. Dale —a treatise expressly written for the benefit of The Domestic Circle.

It is an old jest that there is not a word in the language

that conveys so little endearment as the word "dear." But though the saying itself, like most truths, be trite and hackneyed, no little novelty remains to the search of the inquirer into the varieties of inimical import comprehended in that malign monosyllable. For instance, I submit to the experienced that the degree of hostility it betrays is in much proportioned to its collocation in the sentence. When, gliding indirectly through the rest of the period, it takes its stand at the close, as in that "Charles dear" of Mrs. Dale, it has spilt so much of its natural bitterness by the way that it assumes even a smile, "amara lento temperet risu." Sometimes the smile is plaintive, sometimes arch. *Ex. Gr.*

(*Plaintive.*)—"I know very well that whatever I do is wrong, Charles dear."

"Nay, I am very glad you amused yourself so much without me, Charles dear."

"Not quite so loud! If you had but my poor head, Charles dear," &c.

(*Arch.*)—"If you could spill the ink anywhere but on the best table-cloth, Charles dear!"

"But though you must always have your own way, you are not *quite faultless*, own, Charles dear," &c.

When the enemy stops in the middle of the sentence, its venom is naturally less exhausted. *Ex. gr.*

"Really, I must say, Charles dear, that you are the most fidgety person," &c.

"And if the house bills were so high last week, Charles

dear, I should just like to know whose fault it was — that's all."

"But you know, Charles dear, that you care no more for me and the children than —" &c.

But if the fatal word spring up, in its primitive freshness, at the head of the sentence, bow your head to the storm. It then assumes the majesty of "my" before it; it is generally more than objurgation — it prefaces a sermon. My candor obliges me to confess that this is the mode in which the hateful monosyllable is more usually employed by the marital part of the one flesh; and has something about it of the odious assumption of the Petruchian *pater-familias* — the head of the family — boding, not perhaps "peace and love, and quiet life," but certainly "awful rule and right supremacy." *Ex. gr.*

"My dear Jane — I wish you would just put by that everlasting crochet, and listen to me for a few moments," &c.

"My dear Jane — I wish you would understand me for once — don't think I am angry — no, but I am hurt. You must consider, &c.

"My dear Jane — I don't know if it is your intention to ruin me, but I only wish you would do as all other women do who care three straws for their husband's property," &c.

"My dear Jane — I wish you to understand that I am the last person in the world to be jealous; but I'll be d——d if that puppy, Captain Prettyman," &c.

Now, few so carefully cultivate the connubial garden,

as to feel much surprise at the occasional sting of a homely nettle or two; but who ever expected, before entering that garden, to find himself pricked and lacerated by an insidious exotical "dear," which he had been taught to believe only lived in a hothouse, along with myrtles and other tender and sensitive shrubs, which poets appropriate to Venus? Nevertheless Parson Dale, being a patient man, and a pattern to all husbands, would have found no fault with his garden, though there had not been a single specimen of "dear," whether the dear *humilis*, or the dear *superba;* the dear *pallida, rubra,* or *nigra;* the dear *suavis,* or the dear *horrida;* — no, not a single "dear" in the whole horticulture of matrimony, which Mrs. Dale had not brought to perfection. But this was far from being the case — Mrs. Dale, living much in retirement, was unaware of the modern improvements, in variety of color and sharpness of prickle, which have rewarded the persevering skill of our female florists.

CHAPTER IX.

In the cool of the evening Dr. Riccabocca walked home across the fields. Mr. and Mrs. Dale had accompanied him half-way; and as they now turned back to the parsonage, they looked behind to catch a glimpse of the tall, outlandish figure, winding slowly through the path amidst the waves of the green corn.

"Poor man!" said Mrs. Dale feelingly; "and the button was off his wristband! What a pity he has nobody to take care of him! He seems very domestic. Don't you think, Charles, it would be a great blessing if we could get him a good wife?"

"Um," said the Parson; "I doubt if he values the married state as he ought."

"What do you mean, Charles? I never saw a man more polite to ladies in my life."

"Yes, but—"

"But what? You are always so mysterious, Charles dear."

"Mysterious! No, Carry; but if you could hear what the Doctor says of the ladies sometimes."

"Ay, when you men get together, my dear. I know what that means—pretty things you say of us. But you are all alike; you know you are, love!"

"I am sure," said the Parson simply, "that I have good cause to speak well of the sex—when I think of you, and my poor mother."

Mrs. Dale, who, with all her "tempers," was an excellent woman, and loved her husband with the whole of her little heart, was touched. She pressed his hand, and did not call him *dear* all the way home.

Meanwhile the Italian passed the fields, and came upon the high-road about two miles from Hazeldean. On one side stood an old-fashioned solitary inn, such as English inns used to be before they became railway hotels—square, solid, old-fashioned, looking so hospitable and comfortable, with their great signs swinging from some elm-tree in front, and the long row of stables standing a little back, with a chaise or two in the yard, and the jolly landlord talking of the crops to some stout farmer, whose rough pony halts of itself at the well-known door. Opposite this inn, on the other side of the road, stood the habitation of Dr. Riccabocca.

A few years before the date of these annals, the stage-coach on its way to London from a seaport town stopped at the inn, as was its wont, for a good hour, that its passengers might dine like Christian Englishmen — not gulp down a basin of scalding soup, like everlasting heathen Yankees, with that cursed railway whistle shrieking like a fiend in their ears! It was the best dining-place on the whole road, for the trout in the neighboring rill were famous, and so was the mutton which came from Hazeldean Park.

From the outside of the coach had descended two passengers, who, alone insensible to the attractions of mutton and trout, refused to dine — two melancholy-looking foreigners, of whom one was Signor Riccabocca, much the same as we see him now, only that the black suit was less threadbare, the tall form less meagre, and he did not then wear spectacles; and the other was his servant. "They would walk about while the coach stopped." Now the Italian's eye had been caught by a mouldering, dismantled house on the other side of the road, which nevertheless was well situated; half-way up a green hill, with its aspect due south, a little cascade falling down artificial rock-work, a terrace with a balustrade, and a few broken urns and statues before its Ionic portico; while on the roadside stood a board, with characters already half-effaced, implying that the house was "To be let unfurnished, with or without land."

The abode that looked so cheerless, and which had so evidently hung long on hand, was the property of Squire Hazeldean. It had been built by his grandfather on the female side—a country gentleman who had actually been in Italy (a journey rare enough to boast of in those days), and who, on his return home, had attempted a miniature imitation of an Italian villa. He left an only daughter and sole heiress, who married Squire Hazeldean's father; and since that time, the house, abandoned by its proprietors for the larger residence of the Hazeldeans, had been uninhabited and neglected. Several tenants, indeed, had offered themselves; but your true country squire is slow in admitting upon his own property a rival neighbor. Some wanted shooting. "That," said the Hazeldeans, who were great sportsmen and strict preservers, "was quite out of the question." Others were fine folks from London. "London servants," said the Hazeldeans, who were moral and prudent people, "would corrupt their own, and bring London prices." Others, again, were retired manufacturers, at whom the Hazeldeans turned up their agricultural noses. In short, some were too grand, and others too vulgar. Some were refused because they were known so well: "Friends are best at a distance," said the Hazeldeans. Others because they were not known at all: "No good comes of strangers," said the Hazeldeans. And finally, as the house fell more and more into decay, no one would take it unless it was put into thorough repair: "As if one was made of money!" said the Hazeldeans. In short, there stood the house unoccupied and ruinous; and there, on its terrace, stood the two forlorn Italians, surveying it with a smile at each other, as for the first time since they set foot in England, they recognised, in dilapidated pilasters and broken statues, in a weed-grown terrace, and the remains of an orangery, something that reminded them of the land they had left behind.

On returning to the inn, Dr. Riccabocca took the occasion to learn from the innkeeper (who was indeed a tenant of the Squire's) such particulars as he could collect; and a few days afterwards Mr. Hazeldean received a letter from a solicitor of repute in London, stating that a very respectable foreign gentleman had commissioned him to treat for Clump Lodge, otherwise called the "Casino:" that the said gentleman did not shoot — lived in great seclusion—and, having no family, did not care about the repairs of the place, provided only it were made weather-proof — if the omission of more expensive reparations could render the rent suitable to his finances, which were very limited. The offer came at a fortunate moment — when the steward had just been representing to the Squire the necessity of doing something to keep the Casino from falling into positive ruin, and the Squire was cursing the fates which had put the Casino into an entail—so that he could not pull it down for the building materials. Mr. Hazeldean therefore caught at the proposal even as a fair lady, who has refused the best offers in the kingdom, catches, at last, at some battered old captain on half-pay, and replied that, as for rent, if the solicitor's client was a quiet, respectable man, he did not care for that, but that the gentleman might have it for the first year rent-free, on condition of paying the taxes and putting the place a little in order. If they suited each other, they could then come to terms. Ten days subsequently to this gracious reply, Signor Riccabocca and his servant arrived; and, before the year's end, the Squire was so contented with his tenant that he gave him a running lease of seven, fourteen, or twenty-one years, at a rent merely nominal, on condition that Signor Riccabocca would put and maintain the place in repair, barring the roof and fences, which the Squire generously renewed at his own expense. It was astonishing, by little and little, what a pretty place the Italian had made of it, and, what is more astonishing, how little it had cost him. He had, indeed, painted the walls of the hall, staircase, and the rooms appropriated to himself, with his own hands. His servant had done the greater part of the upholstery. The two between them had got the garden into order. The Italians seemed to have taken a joint love to the place, and to deck it as they would have done some favorite chapel to their Madonna.

It was long before the natives reconciled themselves to the odd ways of the foreign settlers—the first thing that offended them was the exceeding smallness of the household bills. Three days out of the seven, indeed, both man and master dined on nothing else but the vegetables in the garden, and the fishes in the neighboring rill: when no trout could be caught, they fried the minnows (and certainly, even in the best streams, minnows are more frequently caught than trouts). The next thing, which angered the natives quite as much, especially the female part of the neighborhood, was the very sparing employment the two he creatures gave to the sex usually deemed so indispensable in household matters. At first, indeed, they had no woman servant at all. But this created such horror, that Parson Dale ventured to hint upon the matter, which Riccabocca took in very good part, and an old woman was forthwith engaged, after some bargaining — at three shillings a week — to wash and scrub as much as she liked during the day-time. She always returned to her own cottage to sleep. The man-servant, who was styled in the neighborhood "Jackeymo," did all else for his master — smoothed his room, dusted his papers, prepared his coffee, cooked his dinner, brushed his clothes, and cleaned his pipes, of which Riccabocca had a large collection. But however close a man's character, it generally creeps out in driblets; and on many little occasions the Italian had shown acts of kindness, and, on some more rare occasions, even of generosity, which had served to silence his calumniators, and by degrees he had established a very fair reputation — suspected, it is true, of being a little inclined to the Black Art, and of a strange inclination to starve Jackeymo and himself, — in other respects harmless enough.

Signor Riccabocca had become very intimate, as we have seen, at the Parsonage. But not so at the hall. For though the Squire was inclined to be very friendly to all his neighbors, he was, like most country gentlemen, rather easily *huffed.* Riccabocca had, if with great politeness, still with great obstinacy, refused Mr. Hazeldean's earlier invitations to dinner; and when the Squire found that the Italian rarely declined to dine at the Parsonage, he was offended in one of his weak points — viz., his pride in the hospitality of Hazeldean Hall — and he ceased altogether invitations so churlishly rejected. Nevertheless, as it was impossible for the Squire, however huffed, to bear malice, he now and then reminded Riccabocca of his existence by presents of game, and would have called on him more often than he did, but that Riccabocca received him with such excessive politeness, that the blunt country gentleman felt shy and put out, and used to say that "to call on Rickeybockey was as bad as going to Court."

But we have left Dr. Riccabocca on the high-road. By this time he has ascended a narrow path that winds by the side of the cascade; he has passed a trellis-work covered with vines, from the which Jackeymo has positively succeeded in making what he calls *wine* — a liquid, indeed, that if the cholera had been popularly known in those days, would have soured the mildest member of the Board of Health; for Squire Hazeldean, though a robust man, who daily carried off his bottle of port with impunity, having once rashly tasted it, did not recover the effect till he had had a bill from the apothecary as long as his own arm. Passing this trellis, Dr. Riccabocca entered upon the terrace, with its stone pavement smoothed and trimmed as hands could make it. Here, on neat stands, all his favorite flowers were arranged; here four orange trees were in full blossom; here a kind of summer-house or Belvidere, built by Jackeymo and himself, made his chosen morning room from May till October; and from this Belvidere there was as beautiful an expanse of prospect as if our English Nature had hospitably spread on her green board all that she had to offer as a banquet to the exile.

A man without his coat, which was thrown over the balustrade, was employed in watering the flowers; a man with movements so mechanical, with a face so rigidly grave in its tawny hues, that he seemed like an automaton made out of mahogany.

"Giacomo," said Dr. Riccabocca, softly.

The automaton stopped its hand, and turned its head.

"Put by the watering-pot, and come hither," continued Riccabocca, in Italian; and moving towards the balustrade, he leaned over it. Mr. Mitford, the historian, calls Jean Jacques "*John James.*" Following that illustrious example, Giacomo shall be Anglified into Jackeymo. Jackeymo came to the balustrade also, and stood a little behind his master.

"Friend," said Riccabocca, "enterprises have not

always succeeded with us. Don't you think, after all, it is tempting our evil star to rent those fields from the landlord ?" Jackeymo crossed himself, and made some strange movement with a little coral charm which he wore set in a ring on his finger.

"If the Madonna send us luck, and we could hire a lad cheap?" said Jackeymo, doubtfully.

"*Più vale un presente che dui futuri,*" said Riccabocca ("A bird in the hand is worth two in the bush.")

"*Chi non fa quando può, non può fare quando vuole*"—("He who will not when he may, when he will it shall have nay"),—answered Jackeymo, as sententiously as his master. "And the Padrone should think in time that he must lay by for the dower of the poor signorina" (young lady.)

Riccabocca sighed, and made no reply.

"She must be *that* high now!" said Jackeymo, putting his hand on some imaginary line a little above the balustrade. Riccabocca's eyes, raised over the spectacles, followed the hand.

"If the Padrone could but see her here——"

"I thought I did!" muttered the Italian.

"He would never let her go from his side till she went to a husband's," continued Jackeymo.

"But this climate—she could never stand it," said Riccabocca, drawing his cloak round him, as the north wind took him in the rear.

"The orange-trees blossom even here with care," said

Jackeymo, turning back to draw down an awning where the orange-trees faced the north. "See!" he added, as he returned with a sprig in full bud.

Dr. Riccabocca bent over the blossom, and then placed it in his bosom.

"The *other* one should be there too," said Jackeymo.

"To die—as this does already!" answered Riccabocca. "Say no more."

Jackeymo shrugged his shoulders; and then, glancing at his master, drew his hand over his eyes.

There was a pause. Jackeymo was the first to break it.

"But, whether here or there, beauty without money is the orange-tree without shelter. If a lad could be got cheap, I would hire the land, and trust for the crop to the Madonna."

"I think I know of such a lad," said Riccabocca, recovering himself, and with his sardonic smile once more lurking about the corners of his mouth,—"a lad made for us."

"*Diavolo!*"

"No, not the *Diavolo!* Friend, I have this day seen a boy who—refused sixpence!"

"*Cosa stupenda!*"—(Stupendous thing!)—exclaimed Jackeymo, opening his eyes, and letting fall the watering-pot.

"It is true, my friend."

"Take him, Padrone, in Heaven's name, and the fields will grow gold."

"I will think of it, for it must require management to catch such a boy," said Riccabocca. "Meanwhile, light a candle in the parlor, and bring from my bed-room — that great folio of Machiaveli."

CHAPTER X

In my next chapter I shall present Squire Hazeldean in patriarchal state — not exactly under the fig-tree he has planted, but before the stocks he has reconstructed — Squire Hazeldean and his family on the village green! The canvas is all ready for the colors.

But in this chapter I must so far afford a glimpse into antecedents as to let the reader know that there is one member of the family whom he is not likely to meet at present, if ever, on the village green at Hazeldean.

Our Squire lost his father two years after his birth; his mother was very handsome — and so was her jointure; she married again at the expiration of her year of mourning; the object of her second choice was Colonel Egerton.

In every generation of Englishmen (at least since the lively reign of Charles II.) there are a few whom some elegant genius skims off from the milk of human nature, and reserves for the cream of society. Colonel Egerton was one of these *ter quaturque beati*, and dwelt apart on a top shelf in that delicate porcelain dish — not bestowed upon vulgar buttermilk — which persons of fashion call

The Great World. Mighty was the marvel of Pall Mall, and profound was the pity of Park Lane, when this super-eminent personage condescended to lower himself into a husband. But Colonel Egerton was not a mere gaudy butterfly; he had the provident instincts ascribed to the bee. Youth had passed from him, and carried off much solid property in its flight; he saw that a time was fast coming when a home, with a partner who could help to maintain it, would be conducive to his comforts, and an occasional hum-drum evening by the fireside beneficial to his health. In the midst of one season at Brighton, to which gay place he had accompanied the Prince of Wales, he saw a widow who, though in the weeds of mourning, did not appear inconsolable. Her person pleased his taste — the accounts of her jointure satisfied his understanding — he contrived an introduction, and brought a brief wooing to a happy close. The late Mr. Hazeldean had so anticipated the chance of the young widow's second espousals, that, in case of that event, he transferred, by his testamentary dispositions, the guardianship of his infant heir from the mother to two squires, whom he had named his executors. This circumstance combined with her new ties somewhat to alienate Mrs. Hazeldean from the pledge of her former loves; and when she had borne a son to Colonel Egerton, it was upon that child that her maternal affections gradually concentrated.

William Hazeldean was sent by his guardians to a large provincial academy, at which his forefathers had received their education time out of mind. At first he spent his holidays with Mrs. Egerton; but as she now resided either in London, or followed her lord to Brighton, to partake of the gaieties at the Pavilion — so, as he grew older, William, who had a hearty affection for country life, and of whose bluff manners and rural breeding Mrs. Egerton (having grown exceedingly refined) was openly ashamed, asked and obtained permission to spend his vacations either with his guardians or at the old Hall. He went late to a small college at Cambridge, endowed in the fifteenth century by some ancestral Hazeldean; and left it, on coming of age, without taking a degree. A few years afterwards he married a young lady, country born and bred like himself.

Meanwhile his half-brother, Audley Egerton, may be said to have begun his initiation into the *beau monde* before he had well cast aside his coral and bells; he had been fondled in the lap of duchesses, and had galloped across the room astride on the canes of ambassadors and princes. For Colonel Egerton was not only very highly connected — not only one of the *Dii majores* of fashion— but he had the still rarer good fortune to be an exceedingly popular man with all who knew him; so popular, that even the fine ladies whom he had adored and abandoned forgave him for marrying out of "the set," and continued to be as friendly as if he had not married at all. People who were commonly called heartless were never weary of doing kind things to the Egertons. When the time came for Audley to leave the preparatory school at which his infancy budded forth amongst the stateliest of the little lilies of the field, and go to Eton, half the fifth and sixth forms had been canvassed to be exceedingly civil to young Egerton. The boy soon showed that he inherited his father's talent for acquiring popularity, and that to this talent he added those which put popularity to use. Without achieving any scholastic distinction, he yet contrived to establish at Eton the most desirable reputation which a boy can obtain — namely, that among his own contemporaries, the reputation of a boy who was sure to do something when he grew to be a man. As a gentleman commoner at Christ Church, Oxford, he continued to sustain this high expectation, though he won no prizes, and took but an ordinary degree; and at Oxford the future "something" became more defined — it was "something in public life" that this young man was to do.

While he was yet at the university, both his parents died — within a few months of each other. And when Audley Egerton came of age, he succeeded to a paternal property which was supposed to be large, and indeed had once been so; but Colonel Egerton had been too lavish a man to enrich his heir, and about £1,500 a year was all that sales and mortgages left of an estate that had formerly approached a rental of £10,000.

Still, Audley was considered to be opulent, and he did not dispel that favorable notion by any imprudent exhibition of parsimony. On entering the world of London, the Clubs flew open to receive him, and he woke one morning to find himself, not indeed famous — but the fashion. To this fashion he at once gave a certain gravity and value — he associated as much as possible with public men and political ladies — he succeeded in confirming the notion that he was "born to ruin or to rule the State."

The dearest and most intimate friend of Audley Egerton was Lord L'Estrange, from whom he had been inseparable at Eton; and who now, if Audley Egerton was the fashion, was absolutely the rage in London.

Harley, Lord L'Estrange, was the only son of the Earl of Lansmere, a nobleman of considerable wealth, and allied, by intermarriages, to the loftiest and most powerful families in England. Lord Lansmere, nevertheless, was but little known in the circles of London. He lived chiefly on his estates, occupying himself with the various duties of a great proprietor, and when he came to the metropolis, it was rather to save than to spend; so that he could afford to give his son a very ample allowance, when Harley, at the age of sixteen (having already attained to the sixth form at Eton), left school for one of the regiments of the Guards.

Few knew what to make of Harley L'Estrange — and that was, perhaps, the reason why he was so much thought of. He had been by far the most brilliant boy of his time at Eton — not only the boast of the cricket-ground, but the marvel of the school-room; yet so full of whims and oddities, and seeming to achieve his triumphs with so little aid from steadfast application, that he had not left behind him the same expectations of solid eminence which his friend and senior, Audley Egerton, had excited. His eccentricities — his quaint sayings, and out-of-the-way actions, became as notable in the great world as they had been in the small one of a public school. That he was very clever there was no doubt, and that the cleverness was of a high order might be surmised, not only from the originality but the independence of his character. He dazzled the world, without seeming to care for its praise or its censure — dazzled it, as it were, because he could not help shining. He had some strange notions, whether political or social, which rather frightened his father. According to Southey, "A man should be no more ashamed of having been a republican than of having been young." Youth and extravagant opinions naturally go together. I don't know whether Harley L'Estrange was a republican at the age of eighteen; but there was no young man in London who seemed to care less for being heir to an illustrious name and some forty or fifty thousand pounds a year. It was a vulgar fashion in that day to play the exclusive, and cut persons who wore bad neckcloths, and called themselves Smith or Johnson. Lord L'Estrange never cut any one, and it was quite enough to slight some worthy man because of his neckcloth or his birth, to insure to the offender the pointed civilities of this eccentric successor to the Belforts and the Wildairs.

It was the wish of his father that Harley, as soon as he came of age, should represent the borough of Lansmere (which said borough was the single plague of the

Earl's life). But this wish was never realised. Suddenly, when the young idol of London still wanted some two or three years of his majority, a new whim appeared to seize him. He withdrew entirely from society — he left unanswered the most pressing three-cornered notes of inquiry and invitation that ever strewed the table of a young Guardsman; he was rarely seen anywhere in his former haunts — when seen, was either alone or with Egerton; and his gay spirits seemed wholly to have left him. A profound melancholy was written in his countenance, and breathed in the listless tones of his voice. About this time a vacancy happening to occur for the representation of Lansmere, Harley made it his special request to his father that the family interest might be given to Audley Egerton — a request which was backed by all the influence of his lady mother, who shared in the esteem which her son felt for his friend. The Earl yielded; and Egerton, accompanied by Harley, went down to Lansmere Park, which adjoined the borough, in order to be introduced to the electors. This visit made a notable epoch in the history of many personages who figure in my narrative; but at present I content myself with saying, that circumstances arose which, just as the canvass for the new election commenced, caused both L'Estrange and Audley to absent themselves from the scene of action, and that the last even wrote to Lord Lansmere expressing his intention of declining to contest the borough.

Fortunately for the parliamentary career of Audley Egerton, the election had become to Lord Lansmere not only a matter of public importance, but of personal feeling. He resolved that the battle should be fought out, even in the absence of the candidate, and at his own expense. Hitherto the contest for this distinguished borough had been, to use the language of Lord Lansmere, "conducted in the spirit of gentlemen,"—that is to say, the only opponents to the Lansmere interest had been found in one or the other of two rival families in the same county; and as the Earl was a hospitable, courteous man, much respected and liked by the neighboring gentry, so the hostile candidate had always interlarded his speeches with profuse compliments to his Lordship's high character, and civil expressions as to his Lordship's candidate. But, thanks to successive elections, one of these two families had come to an end, and its actual representative was now residing within the Rules of the Bench; the head of the other family was the sitting member, and, by an amicable agreement with the Lansmere interest, he remained as neutral as it is in the power of any sitting member to be amidst the passions of an intractable committee. Accordingly, it had been hoped that Egerton would come in without opposition, when, the very day on which he had abruptly left the place, a handbill, signed "Haverill Dashmore, Captain R.N., Baker Street, Portman Square," announced, in very spirited language, the intention of that gentleman "to emancipate the borough from the unconstitutional domination of an oligarchical faction, not with a view to his own political aggrandisement — indeed, at great personal inconvenience — but actuated solely by abhorrence to tyranny, and patriotic passion for the purity of election."

This announcement was followed, within two hours, by the arrival of Captain Dashmore himself, in a carriage and four, covered with yellow favors, and filled, inside and out, with harum-scarum-looking friends, who had come down with him to share the canvass and partake the fun.

Captain Dashmore was a thorough sailor, who had, however. conceived a disgust to the profession from the date in which a minister's nephew had been appointed to the command of a ship to which the Captain considered himself unquestionably entitled. It is just to the minister to add, that Captain Dashmore had shown as little regard for orders from a distance, as had immortalised Nelson himself; but then the disobedience had not achieved the same redeeming success as that of Nelson, and Captain Dashmore ought to have thought himself fortunate in escaping a severer treatment than the loss of promotion. But no man knows when he is well off; and retiring on half-pay, just as he came into unexpected possession of some forty or fifty thousand pounds, bequeathed by a distant relation, Captain Dashmore was seized with a vindictive desire to enter parliament, and inflict oratorical chastisement on the Administration.

A very few hours sufficed to show the sea-captain to be a most capital electioneerer for a popular but not enlightened constituency. It is true that he talked the saddest nonsense ever heard from an open window; but then his jokes were so broad, his manner so hearty, his voice so big, that in those dark days, before the schoolmaster was abroad, he would have beaten your philosophical Radical and moralising Democrat hollow. Moreover, he kissed all the women, old and young, with the zest of a sailor who has known what it is to be three years at sea without sight of a beardless lip; he threw open all the public houses, asked a numerous committee every day to dinner, and, chucking his purse up in the air, declared "he would stick to his guns while there was a shot in his locker." Till then, there had been but little political difference between the candidate supported by Lord Lansmere's interest and the opposing parties — for country gentlemen, in those days, were pretty much of the same way of thinking, and the question had been really local — viz.: whether the Lansmere interest should or should not prevail over that of the two squirearchical families who had alone, hitherto, ventured to oppose it. But though Captain Dashmore was really a very loyal man, and much too old a sailor to think that the State (which, according to established metaphor, is a vessel *par excellence*) should admit Jack upon quarter-deck, yet, what with talking against lords and aristocracy, jobs and abuses, and searching through no very refined vocabulary for the strongest epithets to apply to those irritating nouns-substantive, his bile had got the better of his understanding, and he became fuddled, as it were, by his own eloquence. Thus, though as innocent of Jacobinical designs as he was incapable of setting the Thames on fire, you would have guessed him, by his speeches, to be one of the most determined incendiaries that ever applied a match to the combustible materials of a contested election; while, being by no means accustomed to respect his adversaries, he could not have treated the Earl of Lansmere with less ceremony if his Lordship had been a Frenchman. He usually designated that respectable nobleman, who was still in the prime of life, by the title of "Old Pompous;" and the Mayor, who was never seen abroad but in top-boots, and the solicitor, who was of a large build, received from his irreverent wit the joint *sobriquet* of "Tops and Bottoms!" Hence the election had now become, as I said before, a personal matter with my Lord, and, indeed, with the great heads of the Lansmere interest. The Earl seemed to consider his very coronet at stake in the question. "The Man from Baker Street," with his preternatural audacity, appeared to him a being ominous and awful—not so much to be regarded with resentment as with superstitious terror: he felt as felt the dignified Montezuma, when that ruffianly Cortez, with his handful of Spanish rapscallions, bearded him in his own capital, and in the midst of his Mexican splendor. The gods were menaced if man could be so insolent! wherefore, said my Lord, tremulously—"The Constitution is gone if the Man from Baker Street comes in for Lansmere!"

But, in the absence of Audley Egerton, the election looked extremely ugly, and Captain Dashmore gained ground hourly, when the Lansmere solicitor happily bethought him of a notable proxy for the missing candidate. The Squire of Hazeldean, with his young wife, had been invited by the earl in honor of Audley; and in the Squire, the solicitor beheld the only mortal who could cope with the sea-captain — a man with a voice as burly and a face as bold — a man who, if permitted for the nonce by Mrs. Hazeldean, would kiss all the women no less heartily than the captain kissed them; and who was, moreover, a taller, and a handsomer, and a younger man — all three great recommendations in the kissing department of a contested election. Yes, to canvass the borough, and to speak from the windows, Squire Hazeldean would be even more popularly presentable than the London-bred and accomplished Audley Egerton himself.

The Squire, applied to and urged on all sides, at first said bluntly, "that he would do anything in reason to serve his brother, but that he did not like, for his own part, appearing, even in proxy, as a lord's nominee; and moreover, if he was to be sponsor for his brother, why, he must promise and vow, in his name, to be staunch and true to the land they lived by! And how could he tell that Audley, when once he got into the House, would not forget the land, and then he, William Hazeldean, would be made a liar, and look like a turncoat!"

But these scruples being overruled by the arguments of the gentlemen, and the entreaties of the ladies, who took in the election that intense interest which those gentle creatures usually do take in all matters of strife and contest, the Squire at length consented to confront the Man from Baker Street, and went accordingly into the thing with that good heart and old English spirit with which he went into everything whereon he had once made up his mind.

The expectations formed of the Squire's capacities for popular electioneering were fully realised. He talked quite as much nonsense as Captain Dashmore on every subject except the landed interest; there he was great, for he knew the subject well — knew it by the instinct that comes with practice, and compared to which all your showy theories are mere cobwebs and moonshine.

The agricultural outvoters — many of whom, not living under Lord Lansmere, but being small yeomen, had hitherto prided themselves on their independence, and gone against my Lord — could not in their hearts go against one who was every inch the farmer's friend. They began to share in the Earl's personal interest against the Man from Baker Street; and big fellows, with legs bigger round than Captain Dashmore's tight little body, and huge whips in their hands, were soon seen entering the shops, "intimidating the electors," as Captain Dashmore indignantly declared.

These new recruits made a great difference in the muster-roll of the Lansmere books; and when the day for polling arrived, the result was a fair question for even betting. At the last hour, after a neck-and-neck contest, Mr. Audley Egerton beat the Captain by two votes. And the names of these voters were John Avenel, resident freeman, and his son-in-law, Mark Fairfield, an outvoter, who, though a Lansmere freeman, had settled in Hazeldean, where he had obtained the situation of head carpenter on the Squire's estate.

These votes were unexpected; for, though Mark Fairfield had come to Lansmere on purpose to support the Squire's brother, and though the Avenels had been always staunch supporters of the Lansmere Blue interest, yet a severe affliction (as to the nature of which, not desiring to sadden the opening of my story, I am considerately silent) had befallen both these persons, and they had left the town on the very day after Lord L'Estrange and Mr. Egerton had quitted Lansmere Park.

Whatever might have been the gratification of the Squire, as a canvasser and a brother, at Mr. Egerton's triumph, it was much damped when, on leaving the dinner given in honor of the victory at the Lansmere Arms, and about, with no steady step, to enter the carriage which was to convey him to his lordship's house, a letter was put into his hands by one of the gentlemen who had accompanied the Captain to the scene of action; and the perusal of that letter, and a few whispered words from the bearer thereof, sent the Squire back to Mrs. Hazeldean a much soberer man than she had ventured to hope for. The fact was, that on the day of nomination, the Captain having honored Mr. Hazeldean with many poetical and figurative appellations — such as "Prize Ox," "Tony Lumpkin," "Blood-sucking Vampire," and "Brotherly Warming-pan," the Squire had retorted by a joke about "Salt-water Jack;" and the Captain, who, like all satirists, was extremely susceptible and thin-skinned, could not consent to be called "Salt-water Jack" by a "Prize Ox" and a "Blood-sucking Vampire."

The letter, therefore, now conveyed to Mr. Hazeldean by a gentleman, who, being from the Sister Country, was deemed the most fitting accomplice in the honorable destruction of a brother mortal, contained nothing more nor less than an invitation to single combat; and the bearer thereof, with the suave politeness enjoined by etiquette on such well-bred homicidal occasions, suggested the expediency of appointing the place of meeting in the neighborhood of London, in order to prevent interference from the suspicious authorities of Lansmere.

The natives of some countries — the warlike French in particular — think little of that formal operation which goes by the name of DUELLING. Indeed, they seem rather to like it than otherwise. But there is nothing your thorough-paced Englishman — a Hazeldean of Hazeldean — considers with more repugnance and aversion, than that same cold-blooded ceremonial. It is not within the range of an Englishman's ordinary habits of thinking. He prefers going to law — a much more destructive proceeding of the two. Nevertheless, if an Englishman must fight, why, he will fight. He says "it is very foolish;" he is sure "it is most unchristianlike;" he agrees with all that Philosophy, Preacher, and Press have laid down on the subject; but he makes his will, says his prayers, and goes out — like a heathen.

It never, therefore, occurred to the Squire to show the

white feather upon this unpleasant occasion. The next day, feigning excuse to attend the sale of a hunting stud at Tattersall's, he ruefully went up to London, after taking a peculiarly affectionate leave of his wife. Indeed, the Squire felt convinced that he should never return home except in a coffin. "It stands to reason," said he to himself, "that a man who has been actually paid by the King's Government for shooting people ever since he was a little boy in a midshipman's jacket, must be a dead hand at the job. I should not mind if it was with double-barrelled Mantons and small shot; but, ball and pistol! they aren't human nor sportsmanlike!" However, the Squire, after settling his worldly affairs, and hunting up an old college friend who undertook to be his second, proceeded to a sequestered corner of Wimbledon Common, and planted himself, not sideways, as one ought to do in such encounters (the which posture the Squire swore was an unmanly way of shirking,) but full front to the mouth of his adversary's pistol, with such sturdy composure, that Captain Dashmore, who, though an excellent shot, was at bottom as good-natured a fellow as ever lived, testified his admiration by letting off his gallant opponent with a ball in the fleshy part of the shoulder, after which he declared himself perfectly satisfied. The parties then shook hands, mutual apologies were exchanged, and the Squire, much to his astonishment to find himself still alive, was conveyed to Limmer's Hotel, where, after a considerable amount of anguish, the ball was extracted and the wound healed. Now it was all over, the Squire felt very much raised in his own conceit: and when he was in a humor more than ordinarily fierce, that perilous event became a favorite allusion with him.

He considered, moreover, that his brother had incurred at his hand the most lasting obligations; and that, having procured Audley's return to Parliament, and defended his interests at risk of his own life, he had an absolute right to dictate to that gentleman how to vote — upon all matters, at least, connected with the landed interest. And when, not very long after Audley took his seat in Parliament (which he did not do for some months,) he thought proper both to vote and to speak in a manner wholly belying the promises the Squire had made on his behalf, Mr. Hazeldean wrote him such a trimmer that it could not but produce an unconciliatory reply. Shortly afterwards, the Squire's exasperation reached the culminating point; for having to pass through Lansmere on a market-day, he was hooted by the very farmers whom he had induced to vote for his brother; and justly imputing the disgrace to Audley, he never heard the name of that traitor to the land mentioned without a heightened color and an indignant expletive. Monsieur de Ruqueville — who was the greatest wit of his day — had, like the Squire, a half-brother, with whom he was not on the best of terms, and of whom he always spoke as his "*frère de loin!*" Audley Egerton was thus Squire Hazeldean's "*distant brother!*" — Enough of these explanatory antecedents — let us return to the Stocks.

CHAPTER XI.

The Squire's carpenters were taken from the park pales, and set to work at the Parish Stocks. Then came the painter and colored them a beautiful dark blue, with white border — and a white rim round the holes — with an ornamental flourish in the middle. It was the gayest public edifice in the whole village — though the village possessed no less than three other monuments of the Vitruvian genius of the Hazeldeans — to wit, the alms-house, the school, and the parish pump.

A more elegant, enticing, coquettish pair of stocks never gladdened the eye of a justice of the peace.

And Squire Hazeldean's eye was gladdened. In the pride of his heart he brought all the family down to look at the stocks. The Squire's family (omitting the *frère de loin*) consisted of Mrs. Hazeldean, his wife; next, of Miss Jemima Hazeldean, his first-cousin; thirdly, of Mr. Francis Hazeldean, his only son; and fourthly, of Captain Barnabas Higginbotham, a distant relation — who, indeed, strictly speaking, was not of the family, but only a visitor ten months in the year. Mrs. Hazeldean was every inch the lady — the lady of the parish. In her comely, florid, and somewhat sunburnt countenance, there was an equal expression of majesty and benevolence; she had a blue eye that invited liking, and an aquiline nose that commanded respect. Mrs. Hazeldean had no affectation of fine airs — no wish to be greater and handsomer and cleverer than she was. She knew herself, and her station, and thanked heaven for it. There was about her speech and manner something of the shortness and bluntness which often characterise royalty: and if the lady of a parish is not a queen in her own circle, it is never the fault of a parish. Mrs. Hazeldean dressed her part to perfection. She wore silks that seemed heirlooms — so thick were they, so substantial and imposing. And over these, when she was in her own domain, the whitest of aprons; while at her waist was seen no fiddle-faddle *chatelaine*, with *breloques* and trumpery, but a good honest gold watch to mark the time, and a long pair of scissors to cut off the dead leaves from her flowers — for she was a great horticulturist. When occasion needed, Mrs. Hazeldean, could, however, lay by her more sumptuous and imperial raiment for a stout riding-habit, of blue Saxony, and canter by her husband's side to see the hounds throw off. Nay, on the days on which Mr. Hazeldean drove his famous fast-trotting cob to the market-town, it was rarely that you did not see his wife on the left side of the gig. She cared as little as her lord did for wind and weather, and in the midst of some pelting shower, her pleasant face peeped over the collar and capes of a stout dreadnough, expanding into smiles and bloom as some frank rose, that opens from its petals, and rejoices in the dews. It was easy to see that the worthy couple had married for love; they were as little apart as they could help it. And still, on the first of September, if the house was not full of company which demanded her cares, Mrs. Hazeldean "stepped out" over the stubbles by her husband's side, with as light a tread and as blithe an eye as when, in the first bridal year, she had enchanted the Squire by her genial sympathy with his sports.

So there now stands Harriet Hazeldean, one hand leaning on the Squire's broad shoulder, the other thrust into her apron, and trying her best to share her husband's enthusiasm for his own public-spirited patriotism, in the renovation of the parish stocks. A little behind, with two fingers resting on the thin arm of Captain Barnabas, stood Miss Jemima, the orphan daughter of the Squire's uncle, by a runaway imprudent marriage with a young lady who belonged to a family which had been at war with the Hazeldeans since the reign of Charles the First, respecting a right of way to a small wood (or rather spring) of about an acre, through a piece of furze land, which was let to a brickmaker at twelve shillings a-year. The wood belonged to the Hazeldeans, the furze land to the Sticktorights (an old Saxon family, if ever there was one). Every twelfth year, when the faggots and timber were felled, this feud broke out afresh; for the Sticktorights refused to the Hazeldeans the right to cart off the said faggots and timber through the only way by which a cart could possibly pass. It is just to the Hazeldeans to say that they had offered to buy the land at ten times its value. But the Sticktorights, with equal magnanimity, had declared that they would not "alienate the family property for the convenience of the best squire that ever stood upon shoe-leather." Therefore, every twelfth year, there was always a great breach of the peace on the part of both Hazeldeans and Sticktorights, magistrates and deputy-lieutenants though they were. The question was fairly fought out by their respective dependants, and followed by various actions for assault and trespass. As the legal question of right was extremely obscure, it never had been properly decided; and, indeed, neither party wished it to be decided, each at heart having some doubt of the propriety of its own claim. A marriage beween a younger son of the Hazeldeans, and a younger daughter of the Sticktorights, was viewed with equal indignation by both families; and the consequence had been that the runaway couple, unblessed and unforgiven, had scrambled through life as they could, upon the scanty pay of the husband, who was in a marching regiment, and the interest of £1,000, which was the wife's fortune independent of her parents. They died and left an only daughter (upon whom the maternal £1,000 had been settled), about the time that the Squire came of age and into possession of his estates. And though he inherited all the ancestral hostility towards the Sticktorights, it was not in his nature to be unkind to a poor orphan, who was, after all, the child of a Hazeldean. Therefore, he had educated and fostered Jemima with as much tenderness as if she had been his sister; put out her £1,000 at nurse, and devoted, from the ready money which had accrued from the rents during his minority, as much as made her fortune (with her own accumulated at compound interest), no less than £4,000, the ordinary marriage portion of the daughters of Hazeldean. On her coming of age, he transferred this sum to her absolute disposal, in order that she might feel herself independent, see a little more of the world than she could at Hazeldean, have candidates to choose from if she deigned to marry; or enough to live upon, if she chose to remain single. Miss Jemima had somewhat availed herself of this liberty, by occasional visits to Cheltenham and other watering-places. But her grateful affection to the Squire was such, that she could never bear to be long away from the Hall. And this was the more praise to her heart, inasmuch as she was far from taking kindly to the prospect of being an old maid. And there were so few bachelors in the neighborhood of Hazeldean, that she could not but have that prospect before her eyes whenever she looked out of the Hall windows. Miss Jemima was indeed one of the most kindly and affectionate of beings feminine; and if she disliked the thought of single blessedness, it really was from those innocent and womanly instincts towards the tender charities of hearth and home, without which a lady, however otherwise estimable, is little better than a Minerva in bronze. But whether or not, despite her fortune and her face, which last, though not strictly handsome, was pleasing, and would have been positively pretty if she had laughed more often (for when she laughed, there appeared three charming dimples, invisible when she was grave) —

whether or not, I say, it was the fault of our insensibility or her own fastidiousness, Miss Jemima approached her thirtieth year, and was still Miss Jemima. Now, therefore, that beautifying laugh of hers was very rarely heard, and she had of late become confirmed in two opinions, not at all conducive to laughter. One was a conviction not at all conducive to laughter. One was a conviction of the general and progressive wickedness of the male sex, and the other was a decided and lugubrious belief that the world was coming to an end. Miss Jemima was now accompanied by a small canine favorite, true Blenheim, with a snub nose. It was advanced in life, and somewhat obese. It sate on its haunches, with its tongue out of its mouth, except when it snapped at the flies. There was a strong platonic friendship between Miss Jemima and Captain Barnabas Higginbotham; for he too was unmarried, and he had the same ill opinion of your sex, my dear madam, that Miss Jemima had of ours. The Captain was a man of a slim and elegant figure; — the less said about the face the better, a truth of which the Captain himself was sensible, for it was a favorite maxim of his — "that in a man, everything is a slight, gentleman-like figure." Captain Barnabas did not absolutely deny that the world was coming to an end, only he thought it would last his time.

Quite apart from all the rest, with the nonchalant survey of virgin dandyism, Francis Hazeldean looked over one of the high starched neckcloths which were then the fashion — a handsome lad, fresh from Eton for the summer holidays, but at that ambiguous age, when one disdains the sports of the boy, and has not yet arrived at the resources of the man.

"I should be glad, Frank," said the Squire, suddenly turning round to his son, "to see you take a little more interest in duties which, one day or the other, you may be called upon to discharge. I can't bear to think that the property should fall into the hands of a fine gentleman, who will let things go to rack and ruin, instead of keeping them up as I do."

And the Squire pointed to the stocks.

Master Frank's eye followed the direction of the cane, as well as his cravat would permit; and he said drily—

"Yes, sir; but how came the stocks to be so long out of repair?"

"Because one can't see to everything at once," retorted the Squire, tartly. "When a man has got eight thousand acres to look after, he must do a bit at a time."

"Yes," said Captain Barnabas. "I know that by experience."

"The deuce you do!" cried the Squire, bluntly. "Experience in eight thousand acres!'

"No; in my apartments in the Albany—No. 3 A. I have had them ten years, and it was only last Christmas that I bought my Japan cat."

"Dear me," said Miss Jemima; "a Japan cat! that must be very curious. What sort of a creature is it?"

"Don't you know? Bless me, a thing with three legs,

and holds toast! I never thought of it, I assure you, till my friend Cosey said to me, one morning when he was breakfasting at my rooms — 'Higginbotham, how is it that you, who like to have things comfortable about you, don't have a cat?' 'Upon my life,' said I, 'one can't think of everything at a time;' just like you, Squire."

"Pshaw," said Mr. Hazeldean, gruffly — "not at all like me. And I'll thank you another time, Cousin Higginbotham, not to put me out, when I am speaking on matters of importance; poking your cat into my stocks! They look something like now, my stocks — don't they, Harry? I declare that the whole village seems more respectable. It is astonishing how much a little improvement adds to the — to the ——"

"Charm of the landscape," put in Miss Jemima, sentimentally.

The Squire neither accepted nor rejected the suggested termination; but, leaving his sentence uncompleted, broke suddenly off with —

"And if I had listened to Parson Dale ——"

"You would have done a very wise thing," said a voice behind, as the Parson presented himself in the rear.

"Wise thing! Why, surely, Mr. Dale," said Mrs. Hazeldean, with spirit, for she always resented the least contradiction to her lord and master — perhaps as an interference with her own special right and prerogative! — "why, surely if it is necessary to have stocks, it is necessary to repair them."

"That's right — go it, Harry!" cried the Squire, chuckling, and rubbing his hands as if he had been setting his terrier at the Parson: "St — St — at him! Well, Master Dale, what do you say to that?"

"My dear ma'am," said the Parson, replying in preference to the lady, "there are many institutions in the country which are very old, look very decayed, and don't seem of much use; but I would not pull them down for all that."

"You would reform them, then," said Mrs. Hazeldean, doubtfully, and with a look at her husband, as much as to say, "He is on politics now — that's your business."

"No, I would not, ma'am," said the Parson, stoutly.

"What on earth would you do, then?" quoth the Squire.

"Just let 'em alone," said the Parson. "Master Frank, there's a Latin maxim which was often in the mouth of Sir Robert Walpole, and which they ought to put into the Eton grammar — '*Quieta non movere.*' If things are quiet, let them be quiet! I would not destroy the stocks, because that might seem to the ill-disposed like a license to offend; and I would not repair the stocks, because that puts it into people's heads to get into them."

The Squire was a staunch politician of the old school, and he did not like to think that, in repairing the stocks, he had perhaps been conniving at revolutionary principles.

"This constant desire of innovation," said Miss Jemima,

suddenly mounting the more funereal of her two favorite hobbies, "is one of the great symptoms of the approaching crash. We are altering, and mending, and reforming, when in twenty years at the utmost the world itself may be destroyed!" The fair speaker paused, and —

Captain Barnabas said thoughtfully—"Twenty years! — the insurance offices rarely compute the best life at more than fourteen." He struck his hand on the stocks as he spoke, and added, with his usual consolatory conclusion — "The odds are, that it will last our time, Squire."

But whether Captain Barnabas meant the stocks or the world, he did not clearly explain, and no one took the trouble to inquire.

"Sir," said Master Frank to his father, with that furtive spirit of quizzing, which he had acquired amongst other polite accomplishments at Eton — "sir, it is no use now considering whether the stocks should or should not have been repaired. The only question is, whom you will get to put into them?"

"True," said the Squire, with much gravity.

"Yes, there it is!" said the Parson, mournfully. "If you would but learn '*non quieta movere!*'"

"Don't spout your Latin at me, Parson!" cried the Squire, angrily; "I can give you as good as you bring, any day.

> 'Propria quæ maribus tribuuntur mascula dicas. —
> As in præsenti, perfectum format in avi.'

There," added the Squire, turning triumphantly towards his Harry, who looked with great admiration at this unprecedented burst of learning on the part of Mr. Hazeldean — "there, two can play at that game! And now that we have all seen the stocks, we may as well go home, and drink tea. Will you come up and play a rubber, Dale? No! — hang it, man, I've not offended you — you know my ways."

"That I do, and they are among the things I would not have altered," cried the Parson — holding out his hand cheerfully. The Squire gave it a hearty shake, and Mrs. Hazeldean hastened to do the same.

"Do come; I am afraid we've been very rude; we are sad blunt folks. Do come; that's a dear good man; and of course, poor Mrs. Dale too." Mrs. Hazeldean's favorite epithet for Mrs. Dale was *poor*, and that for reasons to be explained hereafter.

"I fear my wife has got one of her bad headaches, but I will give her your kind message, and at all events you may depend upon me."

"That's right," said the Squire; "in half-an-hour, eh? — How dy'e do, my little man?" as Lenny Fairfield, on his way home from some errand in the village, drew aside and pulled off his hat with both hands. "Stop — you see those stocks — eh? Tell all the bad boys in the parish to take care how they get into them — a sad disgrace — you'll never be in such a quandary?"

"That at least I will answer for," said the Parson.

"And I too," added Mrs. Hazeldean, patting the boy's

curly head. "Tell your mother I shall come and have a good chat with her to-morrow evening."

And so the party passed on, and Lenny stood still on the road, staring hard at the stocks, which stared back at him from its four great eyes.

But Lenny did not remain long alone. As soon as the great folks had fairly disappeared, a large number of small folks emerged timorously from the neighboring cottages, and approached the site of the stocks with much marvel, fear, and curiosity.

In fact, the renovated appearance of this monster — *à propos de bottes*, as one may say — had already excited considerable sensation among the population of Hazeldean. And even as when an unexpected owl makes his appearance in broad daylight, all the little birds rise from tree and hedgerow, and cluster round their ominous enemy, so now gathered all the much-excited villagers round the intrusive and portentous phenomenon.

"D'ye know what the diggins the Squire did it for, Gaffer Solomons?" asked one many-childed matron, with a baby in arms, an urchin of three years old clinging fast to her petticoat, and her hand maternally holding back a more adventurous hero of six, who had a great desire to thrust his head into one of the grisly apertures. All eyes turned to a sage old man, the oracle of the village, who, leaning both hands on his crutch, shook his head bodingly.

"Maw be," said Gaffer Solomons, "some of the boys ha' been robbing the orchards."

"Orchards!" cried a big lad, who seemed to think himself personally appealed to — "why, the bud's scarce off the trees yet!"

"No more it in't!" said the dame with many children, and she breathed more freely.

"Maw be," said Gaffer Solomons, "some o' ye has been sitting snares."

"What for?" said a stout, sullen-looking young fellow, whom conscience possibly pricked to reply —"what for, when it bean't the season? And if a poor man did find a hear in his pocket i' the hay-time, I should like to know if ever a Squire in the world would let un off with the stocks — eh?"

This last question seemed a settler, and the wisdom of Gaffer Solomons went down fifty per cent. in the public opinion of Hazeldean.

"Maw be," said the Gaffer — this time with a thrilling effect, which restored his reputation —"maw be some o' ye ha' been getting drunk, and making beestises o' yoursels!"

There was a dead pause, for this suggestion applied too generally to be met with a solitary response. At last one of the women said, with a meaning glance at her husband, "God bless the Squire; he'll make some on us happy women, if that's all!"

There then arose an almost unanimous murmur of approbation among the female part of the audience; and the men looked at each other, and then at the phenomenon, with a very hang-dog expression of countenance.

"Or, maw be," resumed Gaffer Solomons, encouraged to a fourth suggestion by the success of its predecessor — "maw be some o' the Misseses ha' been making a rumpus, and scolding their goodmen. I heard say in my granfeythir's time, that arter old Mother Bang nigh died o' the ducking-stool, them 'ere stocks were first made for the women, out o' compassion like! And every one knows the Squire is a koind-hearted man, God bless un!"

"God bless un!" cried the men heartily; and they gathered lovingly round the phenomenon, like heathens of old round a tutelary temple. But then there rose one shrill clamor among the females, as they retreated with involuntary steps towards the verge of the green, whence they glared at Solomons and the phenomenon with eyes so sparkling, and pointed at both with gestures so menacing, that Heaven only knows if a morsel of either would have remained much longer to offend the eyes of the justly-enraged matronage of Hazeldean, if fortunately Master Stirn, the Squire's right-hand man, had not come up in the nick of time.

Master Stirn was a formidable personage — more formidable than the Squire himself — as, indeed, a Squire's right hand is generally more formidable than the head can pretend to be. He inspired the greater awe, because, like the stocks, of which he was deputed guardian, his powers were undefined and obscure, and he had no particular place in the out-of-door establishment. He was not the steward, yet he did much of what ought to be the steward's work; he was not the farm-bailiff, for the Squire called himself his own farm-bailiff; nevertheless, Mr. Hazeldean sowed and ploughed, cropped and stocked, bought and sold, very much as Mr. Stirn condescended to advise. He was not the park-keeper, for he neither shot the deer nor superintended the preserves; but it was he who always found out who had broken a park-pale or snared a rabbit. In short, what may be called all the harsher duties of a large landed proprietor, devolved, by custom and choice, upon Mr. Stirn. If a laborer was to be discharged, or a rent enforced, and the Squire knew that he should be talked over and that the steward would be as soft as himself, Mr. Stirn was sure to be the avenging ἄγγελος or messenger, to pronounce the words of fate; so that he appeared to the inhabitants of Hazeldean like the Poet's *Sæva Necessitas,* a vague incarnation of remorseless power, armed with whips, nails, and wedges. The very brute creation stood in awe of Mr. Stirn. The calves knew that it was he who singled out which should be sold to the butcher, and huddled up into a corner with beating hearts at his grim footstep; the sow grunted, the duck quacked, the hen bristled her feathers and called to her chicks when Mr. Stirn drew near. Nature had set her stamp upon him. Indeed, it may be questioned whether the great M. de Chambray himself, surnamed the brave, had an aspect so awe-inspiring as that of Mr. Stirn; albeit the face of that hero was so terrible, that a man who had been his lackey, seeing his portrait after he had been dead twenty years, fell a trembling all over like a leaf!

"And what the plague are you all doing here?" said

Mr. Stirn, as he waved and smacked a great cart-whip which he held in his hand, "making such a hullabaloo, you women, you! that I suspect the Squire will be sending out to know if the village is on fire. Go home, will ye? High time indeed to have the stocks ready, when you get squalling and conspiring under the very nose of a justice of the peace, just as the French revolutioners did afore they cut off their king's head; my hair stands on end to look at ye." But already, before half this address was delivered, the crowd had dispersed in all directions — the women still keeping together, and the men sneaking off towards the ale-house. Such was the beneficent effect of the fatal stocks, on the first day of their resuscitation!

However, in the break-up of every crowd there must always be one who gets off the last; and it so happened that our friend Lenny Fairfield, who had mechanically approached close to the stocks, the better to hear the oracular opinions of Gaffer Solomons, had no less mechanically, on the abrupt appearance of Mr. Stirn, crept, as he hoped, out of sight behind the trunk of the elm-tree which partially shaded the stocks; and there now, as if fascinated, he still cowered, not daring to emerge in full view of Mr. Stirn, and in immediate reach of the cart-whip—when the quick eye of the right-hand man detected his retreat.

"Hallo you, sir — what the deuce, laying a mine to blow up the stocks! just like Guy Fox and the Gunpowder Plot, I declares! What ha' you got in your willanous little fist there?"

"Nothing, sir," said Lenny, opening his palm.

"Nothing — um!" said Mr. Stirn, much dissatisfied; and then, as he gazed more deliberately, recognising the pattern boy of the village, a cloud yet darker gathered over his brow — for Mr. Stirn, who valued himself much on his learning — and who, indeed, by dint of more knowledge as well as more wit than his neighbors, had attained his present eminent station of life—was extremely anxious that his only son should also be a scholar; that wish

"The gods dispersed in empty air."

Master Stirn was a notable dunce at the Parson's school, while Lenny Fairfield was the pride and boast of it; therefore Mr. Stirn was naturally, and almost justifiably, ill-disposed towards Lenny Fairfield, who had appropriated to himself the praises which Mr. Stirn had designed for his own son.

"Um!" said the right-hand man, glowering on Lenny malignantly, "you are the pattern boy of the village, are you? Very well, sir—then I put these here stocks under your care — and you'll keep off the other boys from sitting on 'em, and picking off the paint, and playing three-holes and chuck-farthing, as I declare they've been a doing, just in front of the elewation. Now, you knows your 'sponsibilities, little boy — and a great honor they are too, for the like o' you. If any damage be done, it is to you I shall look; d'ye understand? — and that's what the Squire says to me. So you sees what it is to be a pattern boy, Master Lenny!"

With that Mr. Stirn gave a loud crack of the cart-whip, by way of military honors, over the head of the vicegerent he had thus created, and strode off to pay a visit to two young unsuspectiug pups, whose ears and tails he had graciously promised their proprietor to crop that evening. Nor, albeit few charges could be more obnoxious than that of deputy-governor or *chargé-d'affaires extraordinaires* to the Parish Stocks, nor one more likely to render Lenny Fairfield odious to his contemporaries, ought he to have been insensible to the signal advantage of his condition over that of the two sufferers, against whose ears and tails Mr. Stirn had no special motives of resentment. To every bad there is a worse—and fortunately for little boys, and even for grown men, whom the Stirns of the world regard malignly, the majesty of law protects their ears, and the merciful forethought of nature deprived their remote ancestors of the privilege of entailing tails upon them. Had it been otherwise — considering what handles tails would have given to the oppressor, how many traps envy would have laid for them, how often they must have been scratched and mutilated by the briars of life, how many good excuses would have been found for lopping, docking, and trimming them—I fear that only the lap-dogs of Fortune would have gone to the grave tail-whole.

CHAPTER XII.

THE card-table was set out in the drawing-room at Hazeldean Hall; though the little party were still lingering in the deep recess of the large bay window — which (in itself of dimensions that would have swallowed up a moderate-sized London parlor) held the great round tea-table, with all appliances and means to boot — for the beautiful summer moon shed on the sward so silvery a lustre, and the trees cast so quiet a shadow, and the flowers and new-mown hay sent up so grateful a perfume, that, to close the windows, draw the curtains, and call for other lights than those of heaven, would have been an abuse of the prose of life which even Captain Barnabas, who regarded whist as the business of town and the holiday of the country, shrank from suggesting. Without, the scene, beheld by the clear moonlight, had the beauty peculiar to the garden-ground round those old-fashioned country residences which, though a little modernised, still preserve their original character: the velvet lawn, studded with large plots of flowers, shaded and scented — here, to the left, by lilacs, laburnums, and rich seringas — there, to the right, giving glimpses, over low-clipped yews, of a green bowling-alley, with the white columns of a summer-house built after the Dutch taste, in the reign of William III.; and in front — stealing away under covert of those still cedars, into the wilder landscape of the well-wooded undulating park. Within, viewed by the placid glimmer of the moon, the scene was no less characteristic of the abodes of that race which has no parallel in other lands, and which, alas! is somewhat losing its native idiosyncrasies in this — the stout country gentleman, not the fine gentleman of the country — the country gentleman somewhat softened and civilised from the mere sportsman or farmer, but still plain and homely, relinquishing the old hall for the drawing-room, and with books not three months old on his table, instead of *Fox's Martyrs* and *Baker's Chronicle* — yet still retaining many a sacred old prejudice, that, like the knots in his native oak, rather adds to the ornament of the grain than takes from the strength of the tree. Opposite to the window, the high chimney-piece rose to the heavy cornice of the ceiling, with dark pannels glistening against the moonlight. The broad and rather clumsy chintz sofas and settees of the reign of George III., contrasted at intervals with the tall-backed chairs of a far more distant generation, when ladies in fardingales and gentlemen in trunk hose seem never to have indulged in horizontal positions. The walls, of shining wainscot, were thickly covered, chiefly with family pictures; though now and then some Dutch fair, or battle-piece, showed that a former proprietor had been less exclusive in his taste for the arts. The pianoforte stood open near the fire-place; a long dwarf bookcase, at the far end, added its sober smile to the room. That bookcase contained what was called "The Lady's Library," a collection commenced by the Squire's grandmother, of pious memory, and completed by his mother, who had more taste for the lighter letters, with but little addition from the bibliomaniac tendencies of the present Mrs. Hazeldean, who, being no great reader, contented herself with subscribing to the Book Club. In this feminine Bodleian, the sermons collected by Mrs. Hazeldean, the grandmother, stood cheek-by-jowl beside the novels purchased by Mrs. Hazeldean, the mother.

"Mixtaque ridenti colocasia fundet acantho!"

But, to be sure, the novels, in spite of very inflammatory titles, such as "Fatal Sensibility," "Errors of the Heart," &c., were so harmless, that I doubt if the sermons could have had much to say against their next-door neighbors —and that is all that can be expected by the best of us.

A parrot dozing on his perch — some gold-fish fast asleep in their glass bowl—two or three dogs on the rug, and Flimsey, Miss Jemima's spaniel, curled into a ball on the softest sofa — Mrs. Hazeldean's work-table rather in disorder, as if it had been lately used — the *St. James's Chronicle* dangling down from a little tripod near the Squire's arm-chair — a high screen of gilt and stamped leather fencing off the card-table: all these, dispersed about a room large enough to hold them all and not seem crowded, offered many a pleasant resting-place for the eye, when it turned from the world of nature to the home of man.

But see, Captain Barnabas, fortified by his fourth cup of tea, has at length summoned courage to whisper to Mrs. Hazeldean, "Don't you think the Parson will be impatient for his rubber?" Mrs. Hazeldean glanced at the Parson, and smiled; but she gave the signal to the Captain, and the bell was rung, lights were brought in, the curtains let down; in a few moments more, the group had collected round the card-table. The best of us are but human — that is not a new truth, I confess, but yet people forget it every day of their lives — and I dare say there are many who are charitably thinking at this very moment, that my Parson ought not to be playing at whist. All I can say to those rigid disciplinarians is, "Every man has his favorite sin: whist was Parson Dale's! — ladies and gentlemen, what is yours?" In truth, I must not set up my poor parson now-a-days, as a pattern parson — it is enough to have one pattern in a village no bigger than Hazeldean, and we all know that Lenny Fairfield has bespoken that place, and got the patronage of the stocks for his emoluments! Parson Dale was ordained, not indeed so very long ago, but still at a time when churchmen took it a great deal more easily than they do now. The elderly parson of that day played his rubber as a matter of course, the middle-aged parson was sometimes seen riding to cover (I knew a schoolmaster, a doctor of divinity, and an excellent man, whose pupils were chiefly taken from the highest families in England, who hunted regularly three times a-week during the season), and the young parson would often sing a capital song — not composed by David — and join in those rotatory dances, which certainly David never danced before the ark.

Does it need so long an exordium to excuse thee, poor Parson Dale, for turning up that ace of spades with so triumphant a smile at thy partner? I must own that nothing which could well add to the Parson's offence was wanting. In the first place, he did not play charitably, and merely to oblige other people. He delighted in the game — he rejoiced in the game — his whole heart was in the game — neither was he indifferent to the mammon of the thing, as a Christian pastor ought to have been. He looked very sad when he took his shillings out of his purse, and exceedingly pleased when he put the shillings that had just before belonged to other people into it. Finally, by one of those arrangements common with married people, who play at the same table, Mr. and Mrs. Hazeldean were invariably partners, and no two people could play worse; while Captain Barnabas, who had played at Graham's with honor and profit, necessarily became partner to Parson Dale, who himself played a good steady, parsonic game. So that, in strict truth, it was hardly fair play — it was almost swindling — the combination of these two great dons against that innocent married couple! Mr. Dale, it is true, was aware of this disproportion of force, and had often proposed, either to change partners or to give odds — propositions always scornfully scouted by the Squire and his lady, so that the Parson was obliged to pocket his conscience, together with the ten points which made his average winnings.

The strangest thing in the world is the different way in which whist affects the temper. It is no test of temper, as some pretend — not at all! The best-tempered people in the world grow snappish at whist; and I have seen the most testy and peevish in the ordinary affairs of life bear their losses with the stoicism of Epictetus. This was notably manifested in the contrast between the present adversaries of the Hall and the Rectory. The Squire, who was esteemed as choleric a gentleman as most in the country, was the best-humored fellow you could imagine when you set him down to whist opposite the sunny face of his wife. You never heard one of those incorrigible blunderers scold each other; on the contrary, they only laughed when they threw away the game, with four by honors in their hands. The utmost that was ever said was a "Well, Harry, that was the oddest trump of yours. Ho — ho — ho!" or "Bless me, Hazeldean — why, they made three tricks in clubs, and you had the ace in your hand all the time! Ha — ha — ha!"

Upon which occasions Captain Barnabas, with great good-humor, always echoed both the Squire's Ho—ho—ho! and Mrs. Hazeldean's Ha — ha — ha.

Not so the Parson. He had so keen and sportsman-like an interest in the game, that even his adversaries' mistakes ruffled him. And you would hear him, with elevated voice and agitated gestures, laying down the law, quoting Hoyle, appealing to all the powers of memory and common sense against the very delinquencies by which he was enriched — a waste of eloquence that always heightened the hilarity of Mr. and Mrs. Hazeldean. While these four were thus engaged, Mrs. Dale, who had come with her husband despite her headache, sate on the sofa beside Miss Jemima, or rather beside Miss Jemima's Flimsey, which had already secured the centre of the sofa, and snarled at the very idea of being disturbed. And Master Frank — at a table by himself — was employed sometimes in looking at his pumps, and sometimes at Gilray's Caricatures, which his mother had provided for his intellectual requirements. Mrs. Dale, in her heart liked Miss Jemima better than Mrs. Hazeldean, of whom she was rather in awe, notwithstanding they had been little girls together, and occasionally still called each other Harry and Carry. But those tender diminutives belonged to the "Dear" genus, and were rarely employed by the ladies, except at times when — had they been little girls still, and the governess out of the way, they would have slapped and pinched each other. Mrs. Dale was still a very pretty woman, as Mrs. Hazeldean was still a very fine woman. Mrs. Dale painted in water colors, and sang, and made card-racks and pen-holders, and was called an "elegant, accomplished woman." Mrs. Hazeldean cast up the Squire's accounts, wrote the best part of his letters, kept a large establishment in excellent order, and was called "a clever, sensible woman." Mrs. Dale had headaches and nerves, Mrs. Hazeldean had neither nerves nor headaches. Mrs. Dale said, "Harry had no real harm in her, but was certainly very masculine." Mrs. Hazeldean said, "Carry would be a good creature but for her airs and graces. Mrs. Dale said, Mrs. Hazeldean was "just made to be a country squire's lady." Mrs. Hazeldean said, "Mrs. Dale was the last person in the world who ought to have been a parson's wife." Carry, when she spoke of Harry to a third person, said, "Dear Mrs. Hazeldean." Harry, when she referred incidentally to Carry, said, "Poor Mrs. Dale." And now the reader knows why Mrs. Hazeldean called Mrs. Dale "poor," at least as well as I do. For, after all, the word belonged to that class in the female vocabulary which may be called "obscure significants," resembling the Konx Ompax, which hath so puzzled the inquirers into the Eleusinian Mysteries; the application is rather to be illustrated than the meaning to be exactly explained.

"That's really a sweet little dog of yours, Jemima," said Mrs. Dale, who was embroidering the word CAROLINE on the border of a cambric pocket-handkerchief, but edging a little farther off, as she added, "he'll not bite, will he?"—"Dear me, no!" said Miss Jemima; but (she added in a confidential whisper) "don't say *he*—'tis a lady dog!" "Oh," said Mrs. Dale, edging off still farther, as if that confession of the creature's sex did not serve to allay her apprehensions—"Oh, then, you carry your aversion to the gentlemen even to lap-dogs—that is being consistent, indeed, Jemima!"

MISS JEMIMA.—I had a gentleman dog once—a pug!—pugs are getting very scarce now.—I thought he was so fond of me—he snapped at every one else—the battles I fought for him! Well, will you believe—I had been staying with my friend, Miss Smilecox, at Cheltenham. Knowing that William is so hasty, and his boots are so thick, I trembled to think what a kick might do. So, on coming here, I left Buff — that was his name — with Miss Smilecox. (A pause.)

Mrs. Dale (looking up languidly).—Well, my love ?

Miss Jemima.—Will you believe it, I say, when I returned to Cheltenham, only three months afterwards, Miss Smilecox had seduced his affections from me, and the ungrateful creature did not even know me again. A pug, too — yet people *say* pugs are faithful ! ! ! I am sure they ought to be, nasty things. I have never had a gentleman dog since — they are all alike, believe me, heartless, selfish creatures.

Mrs. Dale.— Pugs ? I dare say they are !

Miss Jemima (with spirit).— Men ! — I told you it was a gentleman dog !

Mrs. Dale (apologetically).— True, my love, but the whole thing was so mixed up !

Miss Jemima. — You saw that cold-blooded case of Breach of Promise of Marriage in the papers — an old wretch, too, of sixty-four. No age makes them a bit better. And when one thinks that the end of all flesh is approaching, and that ——

Mrs. Dale (quickly, for she prefers Miss Jemima's other hobby to that black one upon which she is preparing to precede the bier of the universe).—Yes, my love, we'll avoid that subject, if you please. Mr. Dale has his own opinions, and it becomes me, you know, as a parson's wife (said smilingly: Mrs. Dale has as pretty a dimple as any of Miss Jemima's, and makes more of that one than Miss Jemima of three), to agree with him — that is in theology.

Miss Jemima (earnestly). — But the thing is so clear, if you will but look into ——

Mrs. Dale (putting her hand on Miss Jemima's lips playfully). — Not a word more. Pray, what do you think of the Squire's tenant at the Casino, Signor Riccabocca? An interesting creature, is not he?

Miss Jemima. — Interesting! not to me. Interesting? Why is he interesting?

Mrs. Dale is silent, and turns her handkerchief in her pretty little white hands, appearing to contemplate the R. in Caroline.

Miss Jemima (half pettishly, half coaxingly). — Why is he interesting? I scarcely ever looked at him; they say he smokes, and never eats. Ugly, too!

Mrs. Dale. — Ugly — no. A fine head — very like Dante's — but what is beauty?

Miss Jemima. — Very true: what is it, indeed? Yes, as you say, I think there *is* something interesting about him; he looks melancholy, but that may be because he is poor.

Mrs. Dale. — It is astonishing how little one feels poverty when one loves. Charles and I were very poor once — before the Squire —— (Mrs. Dale paused, looked towards the Squire, and murmured a blessing, the warmth of which brought tears into her eyes). — Yes, (she added, after a pause), we were very poor, but we were happy even then — more thanks to Charles than to me (and tears from a new source again dimmed those quick, lively eyes, as the little woman gazed fondly on her husband, whose brows were knit into a black frown over a bad hand).

MISS JEMIMA.— It is only those horrid men who think of money as a source of happiness. I should be the last person to esteem a gentleman less because he was poor.

MRS. DALE.— I wonder the Squire does not ask Signor Riccabocca here more often. Such an acquisition *we* find him!

The Squire's voice from the card-table. — "Whom ought I to ask more often, Mrs. Dale?"

Parson's voice, impatiently.—"Come — come — come, Squire: play to my queen of diamonds — do!"

SQUIRE. — There, I trump it — pick up the trick, Mrs. H.

PARSON.— Stop! stop! trump my diamond?

The CAPTAIN (solemnly). — Trick turned; play on, Squire.

SQUIRE. — The king of diamonds.

MRS. HAZELDEAN. — Lord! Hazeldean; why, that's the most barefaced revoke — ha — ha — ha! trump the queen of diamonds and play out the king! well I never — ha — ha — ha!

CAPTAIN BARNABAS (in tenor). — Ha, ha, ha!

SQUIRE.— Ho — ho — ho! bless my soul; ho, ho, ho!

CAPTAIN BARNABAS (in base).— Ho — ho — ho!

Parson's voice raised, but drowned by the laughter of his adversaries and the firm, clear tone of Captain Barnabas — "Three to our score! — game!"

SQUIRE (wiping his eyes). — No help for it, Harry — deal for me! Whom ought I to ask, Mrs. Dale? (waxing angry). First time I ever heard the hospitality of Hazeldean called in question!

MRS. DALE. — My dear sir, I beg a thousand pardons, but listeners — you know the proverb.

SQUIRE (growling like a bear). — I hear nothing but proverbs ever since we had that Mounseer among us. Please to speak plainly, ma'am.

MRS. DALE (sliding into a little temper at being thus roughly accosted). — It was of Mounseer, as you call him, that I spoke, Mr. Hazeldean.

SQUIRE. — What! Rickeybockey?

MRS. DALE (attempting the pure Italian accentuation). — Signor Riccabocca.

PARSON (slapping his cards on the table in despair). — Are we playing at whist, or are we not?

The Squire, who is fourth player, drops the king to Captain Higginbotham's lead of the ace of hearts. Now the Captain has left queen, knave, and two other hearts — four trumps to the queen and nothing to win a trick with in the two other suits. This hand is therefore precisely one of those in which, especially after the fall of that king of hearts in the adversary's hand, it becomes a matter of reasonable doubt whether to lead trumps or not. The Captain hesitates, and not liking to play out his good hearts with the certainty of their being trumped by the Squire, nor, on the other hand, liking to open the other suits, in which he has not a card that can assist his partner, resolves, as becomes a military man, in such dilemma, to make a bold push and lead out trumps, in the chance of finding his partner strong, and so bringing in his long suit.

SQUIRE (taking advantage of the much meditating pause made by the Captain).—Mrs. Dale, it is not my fault. I have asked Rickeybockey—time out of mind. But I suppose I am not fine enough for those foreign chaps. He'll not come—that's all I know.

PARSON (aghast at seeing the Captain play out trumps, of which he, Mr. Dale, has only two, wherewith he expects to ruff the suit of spades of which he has only one—the cards all falling in suits—while he has not a single other chance of a trick in his hand).—Really, Squire, we had better give up playing if you put out my partner in this extraordinary way—jabber—jabber—jabber!

SQUIRE.—Well, we must be good children, Harry. What!—trumps, Barney? Thank ye for that! And the Squire might well be grateful, for the unfortunate adversary has led up to ace king knave—with two other trumps. Squire takes the Parson's ten with his knave, and plays out ace king; then, having cleared all the trumps except the Captain's queen and his own remaining two, leads off tierce major in that very suit of spades of which the Parson has only one—and the Captain, indeed, but two—forces out the Captain's queen, and wins the game in a canter.

PARSON (with a look at the Captain which might have become the awful brows of Jove, when about to thunder). — That, I suppose, is the new-fashioned London play! In my time the rule was, "First save the game, then try to win it."

CAPTAIN. — Could not save it, sir.

PARSON (exploding).— Not save it! — two ruffs in my own hand — two tricks certain till you took them out! Monstrous! The rashest trump. — Seizes the cards — spreads them on the table, lip quivering, hands trembling —tries to show how five tricks could have been gained— (N. B. It is *short* whist, which Captain Barnabas had introduced at the Hall) can't make out more than four— Captain smiles triumphantly — Parson in a passion, and not at all convinced, mixes all the cards together again, and falling back in his chair, groans, with tears in his voice—"The cruelest trump! the most wanton cruelty!"

The Hazeldeans in chorus. — "Ho — ho — ho! Ha — ha — ha!"

The Captain, who does not laugh this time, and whose turn it is to deal, shuffles the cards for the conquering game of the rubber with as much caution and prolixity as Fabius might have employed in posting his men. The Squire gets up to stretch his legs, and, the insinuation against his hospitality recurring to his thoughts, calls out to his wife — "Write to Rickeybockey to-morrow yourself, Harry, and ask him to come and spend two or three days here. There, Mrs. Dale, you hear me?"

"Yes," said Mrs. Dale, putting her hands to her ears in implied rebuke at the loudness of the Squire's tone. "My dear sir, do remember that I'm a sad nervous creature."

"Beg pardon," muttered Mr. Hazeldean, turning to his son, who, having got tired of the caricatures, had fished out for himself the great folio County History, which was the only book in the library that the Squire much valued, and which he usually kept under lock and key, in his study, together with the field-books and steward's accounts, but which he had reluctantly taken into the drawing-room that day, in order to oblige Captain Higginbotham. For the Higginbothams — an old Saxon family, as the name evidently denotes — had once possessed lands in that very county. And the Captain, during his visits to Hazeldean Hall, was regularly in the habit of asking to look into the County History, for the purpose of refreshing his eyes, and renovating his sense of ancestral dignity, with the following paragraph therein: — "To the left of the village of Dunder, and pleasantly situated in a hollow, lies Botham Hall, the residence of the ancient family of Higginbotham, as it is now commonly called. Yet it appears by the county rolls, and sundry old deeds, that the family formerly styled itself Higges, till the Manor House lying in Botham, they gradually assumed the appellation of Higges-in-Botham, and in process of time, yielding to the corruptions of the vulgar, Higginbotham."

"What, Frank! my County History!" cried the Squire. "Mrs. H., he has got my County History!"

"Well, Hazeldean, it is time he should know something about the County."

"Ay, and History too," said Mrs. Dale, malevolently, for the little temper was by no means blown over.

FRANK. — I'll not hurt it, I assure you, sir. But I'm very much interested just at present.

The CAPTAIN (putting down the cards to cut). — You've got hold of that passage about Botham Hall, page 706, eh?

FRANK. — No; I was trying to make out how far it is to Mr. Leslie's place, Rood Hall. Do you know, mother?

MRS. HAZELDEAN. — I can't say I do. The Leslies don't mix with the country; and Rood lies very much out of the way.

FRANK. — Why don't they mix with the country?

MRS. HAZELDEAN. — I believe they are poor, and therefore I suppose they are proud: they are an old family.

PARSON (thrumming on the table with great impatience). — Old fiddledee! — talking of old families when the cards have been shuffled this half-hour!

CAPTAIN BARNABAS. — Will you cut for your partner, ma'am?

SQUIRE (who has been listening to Frank's inquiries with a musing air). — Why do you want to know the distance to Rood Hall?

FRANK (rather hesitatingly).—Because Randal Leslie is there for the holidays, sir.

PARSON. — Your wife has cut for you, Mr. Hazeldean.

I don't think it was quite fair; and my partner has turned up a deuce — deuce of hearts. Please to come and play, if you *mean* to play.

The Squire returns to the table, and in a few minutes the game is decided by a dexterous finesse of the Captain against the Hazeldeans. The clock strikes ten; the servants enter with a tray; the Squire counts up his own and his wife's losings; and the Captain and Parson divide sixteen shillings between them.

SQUIRE. — There, Parson, I hope now you'll be in a better humor. You win enough out of us to set up a coach-and-four.

"Tut!" muttered the Parson; "at the end of the year, I'm not a penny the richer for it all."

And indeed, monstrous as that assertion seemed, it was perfectly true, for the Parson portioned out his gains into three divisions. One-third he gave to Mrs. Dale, for her own special pocket-money: what became of the second third he never owned even to his better half; but certain it was, that every time the Parson won seven-and-sixpence, half-a-crown, which nobody could account for, found its way to the poor-box; while the remaining third the Parson, it is true, openly and avowedly retained; but I have no manner of doubt that, at the year's end, it got to the poor quite as safely as if it had been put into the box.

The party had now gathered round the tray, and were helping themselves to wine and water, or wine without water—except Frank, who still remained poring over the map in the County History, with his head leaning on his hands, and his fingers plunged in his hair.

"Frank," said Mrs. Hazeldean, "I never saw you so studious before."

Frank started up and colored, as if ashamed of being accused of too much study in anything.

The SQUIRE (with a little embarrassment in his voice). — Pray, Frank, what do you know of Randal Leslie?

"Why, sir, he is at Eton."

"What sort of a boy is he?" asked Mrs. Hazeldean.

Frank hesitated, as if reflecting, and then answered,— "They say he is the cleverest boy in the school. But then he saps."

"In other words," said Mr. Dale, with proper parsonic gravity, "he understands that he was sent to school to learn his lessons, and he learns them. You call that sapping, — I call it doing his duty. But, pray, who and what is this Randal Leslie, that you look so discomposed, Squire?"

"Who and what is he?" repeated the Squire, in a low growl. "Why, you know, Mr. Audley Egerton married Miss Leslie, the great heiress; and this boy is a relation of hers. I may say," added the Squire, "that he is a near relation of mine, for his grandmother was a Hazeldean. But all I know about the Leslies is, that Mr. Egerton, as I am told, having no children of his own, took up young Randal (when his wife died, poor woman), pays for his schooling, and has, I suppose, adopted the boy as his heir. Quite welcome. Frank and I want nothing from Mr. Audley Egerton, thank Heaven!"

"I can well believe in your brother's generosity to his wife's kindred," said the Parson, sturdily, "for I am sure Mr. Egerton is a man of strong feeling."

"What the deuce do you know about Mr. Egerton? I don't suppose you could ever have even spoken to him."

"Yes," said the Parson, coloring up, and looking confused, "I had some conversation with him once;" and observing the Squire's surprise, he added,—"when I was curate at Lansmere, and about a painful business connected with the family of one of my parishioners."

"Oh! one of your parishioners at Lansmere, — one of the constituents Mr. Audley Egerton threw over, after all the pains I had taken to get him his seat. Rather odd you should never have mentioned this before, Mr. Dale!"

"My dear sir," said the Parson, sinking his voice, and in a mild tone of conciliatory expostulation, "you are so irritable whenever Mr. Egerton's name is mentioned at all."

"Irritable!" exclaimed the Squire, whose wrath had long been simmering, and now fairly boiled over. "Irritable, sir! — I should think so: a man for whom I stood godfather at the hustings, Mr. Dale! — a man for whose sake I was called a 'prize ox,' Mr. Dale! — a man for whom I was hissed in a market-place, Mr. Dale! — a man for whom I was shot at, in cold blood, by an officer in his Majesty's service, who lodged a ball in my right shoulder, Mr. Dale! — a man who had the ingratitude, after all this, to turn his back on the landed interest,— to deny that there was any agricultural distress in a year which broke three of the best farmers I ever had, Mr. Dale! — a man, sir, who made a speech on the Currency, which was complimented by Ricardo, a Jew! Good Heavens! a pretty parson you are, to stand up for a fellow complimented by a Jew! Nice ideas you must have of Christianity. Irritable, sir!" now fairly roared the Squire, adding to the thunder of his voice the cloud of a brow which evinced a menacing ferocity that might have done honor to Bussy d'Amboise or Fighting Fitzgerald. "Sir, if that man had not been my own half-brother, I'd have called him out. I have stood my ground before now. I have had a ball in my right shoulder. Sir, I'd have called him out."

"Mr. Hazeldean! — Mr. Hazeldean! I'm shocked at you," cried the Parson; and, putting his lips close to the Squire's ear, he went on in a whisper, — "What an example to your son! You'll have him fighting duels one of these days, and nobody to blame but yourself."

This warning cooled Mr. Hazeldean; and muttering, "Why the deuce did you set me off?" he fell back into his chair, and began to fan himself with his pocket-handkerchief.

The Parson skilfully and remorselessly pursued the advantage he had gained. "And now, that you may have it in your power to show civility and kindness to a boy whom Mr. Egerton has taken up, out of respect to his wife's memory — a kinsman, you say, of your own, — and who has never offended you, — a boy whose diligence in his studies proves him to be an excellent companion to your son — Frank (here the Parson raised his voice,) I suppose you would like to call on young Leslie, as you were studying the country map so attentively?"

"Why, yes," answered Frank, rather timidly, "if my father does not object to it. Leslie has been very kind to me, though he is in the sixth form, and, indeed, almost the head of the school."

"Ah!" said Mrs. Hazeldean, "one studious boy has a fellow-feeling for another; and though you enjoy your holidays, Frank, I am sure you read hard at school."

Mrs. Dale opened her eyes very wide, and stared in astonishment.

Mrs. Hazeldean retorted that look with great animation. "Yes, Carry," said she, tossing her head, "though *you* may not think Frank clever, his masters find him so. He got a prize last half. That beautiful book, Frank — hold up your head, my love, — what did you get it for?"

FRANK (reluctantly). — Verses, ma'am.

MRS. HAZELDEAN (with triumph). — Verses! — there, Carry, verses!

FRANK (in a hurried tone). — Yes, but Leslie wrote them for me.

MRS. HAZELDEAN (recoiling). — O Frank! a prize for what another did for you — that was mean.

FRANK (ingenuously). — You can't be more ashamed, mother, than I was when they gave me the prize.

MRS. DALE (though previously provoked at being snubbed by Harry, now showing the triumph of generosity over temper).—I beg your pardon, Frank. Your mother must be as proud of that shame as she was of the prize.

Mrs. Hazeldean puts her arm round Frank's neck, smiles beamingly on Mrs. Dale, and converses with her son in a low tone about Randal Leslie. Miss Jemima now approached Carry, and said in an "aside,"—"But we are forgetting poor Mr. Riccabocca. Mrs. Hazeldean, though the dearest creature in the world, has such a blunt way of inviting people—don't you think if you were to say a word to him, Carry?"

Mrs. Dale (kindly, as she wraps her shawl round her).—Suppose you write the note yourself. Meanwhile, I shall see him, no doubt.

Parson (putting his hand on the Squire's shoulder).—You forgive my impertinence, my kind friend. We parsons, you know, are apt to take strange liberties, when we honor and love folks, as I do.

"Pish," said the Squire; but his hearty smile came to his lips in spite of himself.—"You always get your own way, and I suppose Frank must ride over and see this pet of my—"

"*Brother's*," quoth the Parson, concluding the sentence in a tone which gave to the sweet word so sweet a sound that the Squire would not correct the Parson, as he had been about to correct himself.

Mr. Dale moved on; but as he passed Captain Barnabas, the benignant character of his countenance changed sadly.

"The cruelest trump, Captain Higginbotham!" said he sternly, and stalked by—majestic.

The night was so fine that the Parson and his wife, as

they walked home, made a little *détour* through the shrubbery.

MRS. DALE. — I think I have done a good piece of work to-night.

PARSON (rousing himself from a reverie). — Have you, Carry? — it will be a very pretty handkerchief.

MRS. DALE. — Handkerchief!—nonsense, dear. Don't you think it would be a very happy thing for both, if Jemima and Signor Riccabocca could be brought together?

PARSON. — Brought together!

MRS. DALE. — You do snap up one so, my dear — I mean, if I could make a match of it.

PARSON. — I think Riccabocca is a match already, not only for Jemima, but yourself into the bargain.

MRS. DALE (smiling loftily). — Well, we shall see. Was not Jemima's fortune about £4,000?

PARSON (dreamily, for he is relapsing fast into his interrupted reverie). — Ay — ay — I dare say.

MRS. DALE. — And she must have saved! I dare say it is nearly £6,000 by this time; — eh! Charles dear, you really are so — good gracions, what's that!

As Mrs. Dale made this exclamation, they had just emerged from the shrubbery into the village green.

PARSON. — What's what?

MRS. DALE (pinching her husband's arm very nippingly). — That thing — there — there!

PARSON.—Only the new stocks, Carry; I don't wonder they frighten you, for you are a very sensible woman. I only wish they would frighten the Squire.

CHAPTER XIII

SUPPOSED TO BE A LETTER FROM MRS. HAZELDEAN TO A. RICCABOCCA, ESQ., THE CASINO; BUT EDITED, AND INDEED COMPOSED, BY MISS JEMIMA HAZELDEAN.

"DEAR SIR, — To a feeling heart it must always be painful to give pain to another, and (though I am sure unconsciously) you have given the *greatest* pain to poor Mr. Hazeldean and myself, indeed to *all* our little circle, in so cruelly refusing our attempts to become better acquainted with a gentleman we so highly ESTEEM. Do, pray, dear sir, make us the *amende honorable*, and give us the *pleasure* of your company for a few days at the Hall! May we expect you Saturday next? — our dinner hour is six o'clock.

"With the best compliments of Mr. and Miss Jemima Hazeldean,

"Believe me, my dear Sir, yours truly,

"H. H.

"Hazeldean Hall."

Miss Jemima having carefully sealed this note, which Mrs. Hazeldean had very willingly deputed her to write, riding with more than his usual dandyism, came into the yard, calling for his pony in a loud voice, and singling out the very groom whom Miss Jemima was addressing — for, indeed, he was the smartest of all in the Squire's stables — told him to saddle the grey pad, and accompany the pony.

"No, Frank," said Miss Jemima, "you can't have George; your father wants him to go on a message — you can take Mat."

"Mat, indeed!" said Frank, grumbling with some reason; for Mat was a surly old fellow, who tied a most indefensible neckcloth, and always contrived to have a great patch in his boots; — besides, he called Frank "Master," and obstinately refused to trot down hill; — "Mat, indeed! — let Mat take the message, and George go with me."

But Miss Jemima had also her reasons for rejecting Mat. Mat's foible was not servility, and he always showed true English independence in all houses where he was not invited to take his ale in the servants' hall. Mat might offend Signor Riccabocca, and spoil all. An animated altercation ensued, in the midst of which the Squire and his wife entered the yard, with the intention of driving in the conjugal gig to the market-town. The matter was referred to the natural umpire by both the contending parties.

The Squire looked with great contempt on his son. "And what did you want a groom at all for? Are you afraid of tumbling off the pony?"

Frank. — No, sir; but I like to go as a gentleman, when I pay a visit to a gentleman!

Squire (in high wrath).—You precious puppy! I think I'm as good a gentleman as you any day, and I should like to know when you ever saw me ride to call on a neighbor with a fellow jingling at my heels, like that upstart Ned Spankie, whose father kept a cotton-mill. First time I ever heard of a Hazeldean thinking a livery-coat was necessary to prove his gentility!

Mrs. Hazeldean (observing Frank coloring, and about to reply). — Hush, Frank, never answer your father — and you are going to call on Mr. Leslie?

"Yes, ma'am, and I am very much obliged to my father for letting me," said Frank, taking the Squire's hand.

"Well, but Frank," continued Mrs. Hazeldean, "I think you heard that the Leslies were very poor."

Frank. — Eh, mother?

Mrs. Hazeldean.—And would you run the chance of wounding the pride of a gentleman, as well born as yourself, by affecting any show of being richer than he is?

Squire (with great admiration). — Harry, I'd give ten pounds to have said that!

Frank (leaving the Squire's hand to take his mother's). — You're quite right, mother — nothing could be more *snobbish!*

Squire. — Give us your fist, too, sir; you'll be a chip of the old block, after all.

Frank smiled, and walked off to his pony.

Mrs. Hazeldean (to Miss Jemima).— Is that the note you were to write for me?

Miss Jemima.—Yes; I supposed you did not care about seeing it, so I have sealed it, and given it to George.

Mrs. Hazeldean.— But Frank will pass close by the Casino on his way to the Leslies'. It may be more civil if he leaves the note himself.

Miss Jemima (hesitatingly).— Do you think so?

Mrs. Hazeldean.—Yes, certainly. Frank — Frank — as you pass by the Casino, call on Mr. Riccabocca, give this note, and say we shall be heartily glad if he will come.

Frank nods.

"Stop a bit," cried the Squire. "If Rickeybockey's at home, 'tis ten to one if he don't ask you to take a glass of wine! If he does, mind, 'tis worse than asking you to take a turn on the rack. Faugh! you remember, Harry? — I thought it was all up with me."

"Yes," cried Mrs. Hazeldean; "for Heaven's sake, not a drop. Wine, indeed!"

"Don't talk of it," cried the Squire, making a wry face.

"I'll take care, sir!" said Frank, laughing as he disappeared within the stable, followed by Miss Jemima, who now coaxingly makes it up with him, and does not leave off her admonitions to be extremely polite to the poor foreign gentleman till Frank gets his foot into the stirrup, and the pony, who knows whom he has got to deal with, gives a preparatory plunge or two, and then darts out of the yard.

BOOK SECOND.

INITIAL CHAPTER.

INFORMING THE READER HOW THIS WORK CAME TO HAVE INITIAL CHAPTERS.

"THERE can't be a doubt," said my father, "that to each of the main divisions of your work — whether you call them Books or Parts — you should prefix an Initial or Introductory Chapter."

PISISTRATUS. — Can't be a doubt, sir! Why so?

MR. CAXTON. — Fielding lays it down as an indispensable rule, which he supports by his example; and Fielding was an artistical writer, and knew what he was about.

PISISTRATUS. — Do you remember any of his reasons, sir?

MR. CAXTON. — Why, indeed, Fielding says very justly, that he is not bound to assign any reason; but he does assign a good many, here and there — to find which, I refer you to *Tom Jones*. I will only observe, that one of his reasons, which is unanswerable, runs to the effect that thus, in every Part or Book, the reader has the advantage of beginning at the fourth or fifth page instead of the first—" a matter by no means of trivial consequence," saith Fielding, "to persons who read books with no other view than to say they have read them — a more general motive to reading than is commonly imagined; and from which not only law books and good books, but the pages of Homer and Virgil, of Swift and Cervantes, have been often turned over." There, cried my father triumphantly, I will lay a shilling to twopence that I have quoted the very words.

Mrs. Caxton. — Dear me! that only means skipping: I don't see any great advantage in writing a chapter, merely for people to skip it.

Pisistratus. — Neither do I.

Mr. Caxton (dogmatically). — It is the repose in the picture — Fielding calls it "contrast" — (still more dogmatically) I say there can't be a doubt about it. Besides (added my father after a pause), besides, this usage gives you opportunities to explain what has gone before, or to prepare for what's coming; or, since Fielding contends, with great truth, that some learning is necessary for this kind of historical composition, it allows you, naturally and easily, the introduction of light and pleasant ornaments of that nature. At each flight in the terrace, you may give the eye the relief of an urn or a statue. Moreover, when so inclined, you create proper pausing places for reflection; and complete by a separate, yet harmonious ethical department, the design of a work, which is but a mere Mother Goose's tale if it does not embrace a general view of the thoughts and actions of mankind.

PISISTRATUS. — But then, in these initial chapters, the author thrusts himself forward; and just when you want to get on with the *dramatis personæ*, you find yourself face to face with the poet himself.

MR. CAXTON. — Pooh! you can contrive to prevent that! Imitate the chorus of the Greek stage, who fill up the intervals between the action by saying what the author would otherwise say in his own person.

PISISTRATUS (slily). — That's a good idea, sir; and I have a chorus, and a choregus too, already in my eye.

MR. CAXTON (unsuspectingly).—Aha! you are not so dull a fellow as you would make yourself out to be; and, even if an author did thrust himself forward, what objection is there to that? It is a mere affectation to suppose that a book can come into the world without an author. Every child has a father—one father at least, as the great Condé says very well in his poem.

PISISTRATUS. — The great Condé a poet! — I never heard that before.

MR. CAXTON. — I don't say he was a poet, but he sent a poem to Madame de Montansier. Envious critics think that he must have paid somebody else to write it; but there is no reason why a great captain should not write a poem; I don't say a good poem, but a poem. I wonder, Roland, if the Duke ever tried his hand at "Stanzas to Mary," or "Lines to a sleeping babe."

CAPTAIN ROLAND. — Austin, I'm ashamed of you. Of

course, the Duke could write poetry if he pleased — something, I dare say, in the way of the great Condé; that is, something warlike and heroic, I'll be bound. Let's hear!

Mr. Caxton (reciting) —

> "Telle est du Ciel la loi sévère
> Qu'il faut qu'un enfant ait un père;
> On dit même quelque fois
> Tel enfant en a jusqu'à trois." *

Captain Roland (greatly disgusted). Condé write such stuff! — I don't believe it.

Pisistratus. — I do, and accept the quotation; you and Roland shall be joint fathers to my child as well as myself.

> "Tel enfant en a jusqu'à trois."

Mr. Caxton (solemnly). — I refuse the proffered paternity; but so far as administering a little wholesome castigation, now and then, I have no objection to join in the discharge of a father's duty.

Pisistratus. — Agreed. Have you anything to say against the infant hitherto?

Mr. Caxton.—He is in long clothes at present; let us wait till he can walk.

Blanche.—But pray, whom do you mean for a hero? — and is Miss Jemima your heroine?

---

* Paraphrase; —

> "That each child has a father
> Is Nature's decree;
> But, to judge by a rumor,
> Some children have three."

CAPTAIN ROLAND.—There is some mystery about the—

PISISTRATUS (hastily). Hush, uncle: no letting the cat out of the bag yet. Listen all of you! I left Frank Hazeldean on his way to the Casino.

CHAPTER II.

"IT is a sweet, pretty place," thought Frank, as he opened the gate which led across the fields to the Casino, that smiled down upon him with its plaster pilasters. "I wonder, though, that my father, who is so particular in general, suffers the carriage-road to be so full of holes and weeds. Mounseer does not receive many visits, I take it."

But when Frank got into the ground immediately before the house, he saw no cause of complaint as to want of order and repair. Nothing could be kept more neatly. Frank was ashamed of the dint made by the pony's hoofs in the smooth gravel: he dismounted, tied the animal to the wicket, and went on foot towards the glass-door in front.

He rang the bell once, twice, but nobody came, for the old woman-servant, who was hard of hearing, was far away in the yard, searching for any eggs which the hen might have scandalously hidden from culinary purposes; and Jackeymo was fishing for the sticklebacks and minnows, which were, when caught, to assist the eggs, when found, in keeping together the bodies and souls of himself and his master. The old woman had been lately put upon board-wages — lucky old woman! Frank rang a third time, and with the impetuosity of his age. A face peeped from the Belvidere on the terrace. "Diavolo!" said Dr. Riccabocca to himself. "Young cocks crow hard on their own dunghill; it must be a cock of a high race to crow so loud at another's."

Therewith he shambled out of the summer-house, and appeared suddenly before Frank, in a very wizard-like dressing-robe of black serge, a red cap on his head, and a cloud of smoke coming rapidly from his lips, as a final consolatory whiff, before he removed the pipe from them. Frank had indeed seen the Doctor before, but never in so scholastic a costume, and he was a little startled by the apparition at his elbow, as he turned round.

"Signorino" (young gentleman), said the Italian, taking off his cap with his usual urbanity, "pardon the negligence of my people—I am too happy to receive your commands in person."

"Dr. Rickeybockey?" stammered Frank, much confused by this polite address, and the low, yet stately, bow with which it was accompanied. "I — I have a note from the Hall. Mamma — that is, my mother—and aunt Jemima beg their best compliments, and hope you will come, sir."

The Doctor took the note with another bow, and, opening the glass door, invited Frank to enter.

The young gentleman, with a schoolboy's usual bluntness, was about to say that he was in a hurry, and had rather not; but Dr. Riccabocca's grand manner awed him, while a glimpse of the hall excited his curiosity—so he silently obeyed the invitation.

The hall, which was of an octagon shape, had been originally panelled off into compartments, and in these the Italian had painted landscapes, rich with the warm sunny light of his native climate. Frank was no judge of the art displayed; but he was greatly struck with the scenes depicted: they were all views of some lake, real or imaginary—in all, dark-blue shining waters reflected dark-blue placid skies. In one, a flight of steps descended to the lake, and a gay group was seen feasting on the margin; in another, sunset threw its rose-hues over a vast villa or palace, backed by Alpine hills, and flanked by long arcades of vines, while pleasure-boats skimmed over the waves below. In short, throughout all the eight compartments, the scene, though it differed in details, preserved the same general character, as if illustrating some favorite locality. The Italian did not, however, evince any desire to do the honors of his own art, but, preceding Frank across the hall, opened the door of his usual sitting-room, and requested him to enter. Frank did so, rather reluctantly, and seated himself with unwonted bashfulness on the edge of a chair. But here new specimens of the Doctor's handicraft soon riveted attention. The room had been originally papered; but Riccabocca had stretched canvas over the walls, and painted thereon sundry satirical devices, each separated from the other by scroll-works of fantastic arabesques. Here a Cupid was trundling a wheel-barrow full of hearts, which he appeared to be selling to an ugly old fellow, with a money-bag in his hand—probably Plutus. There Diogenes might be seen walking through a market-place, with his lantern in his hand, in search of an honest man, whilst the children jeered at him, and the curs snapped at his heels. In another place, a lion was seen half dressed in a fox's hide, while a wolf in a sheep's mask was conversing very amicably with a young lamb. Here again might be seen the geese stretching out their necks from the Roman Capitol in full cackle, while the stout invaders were beheld in the distance, running off as hard as they could. In short, in all these quaint entablatures some pithy sarcasm was symbolically conveyed; only over the mantelpiece was the design graver and more touching. It was the figure of a man in a pilgrim's garb, chained to the earth by small, but innumerable ligaments, while a phantom likeness of himself, his shadow, was seen hastening down what seemed an interminable vista; and underneath were written the pathetic words of Horace—

> "Patriæ quis exul
> Se quoque fugit?"

("What exile from his country can also fly from himself?") The furniture of the room was extremely simple, and somewhat scanty; yet it was arranged so as to impart an air of taste and elegance to the room. Even a few plaster busts and statues, though bought but of some humble itinerant, had their classical effect, glistening from out stands of flowers that were grouped around them, or backed by graceful screen-works formed from twisted osiers, which, by the simple contrivance of trays at the bottom, filled with earth, served for living parasitical plants, with gay flowers contrasting thick ivy leaves, and gave to the whole room the aspect of a bower.

"May I ask your permission?" said the Italian, with his finger on the seal of the letter.

"Oh yes," said Frank with *naïveté*.

Riccabocca broke the seal, and a slight smile stole over his countenance. Then he turned a little aside from Frank, shaded his face with his hand, and seemed to muse. "Mrs. Hazeldean," said he at last, "does me very great honor. I hardly recognise her hand-writing, or I should have been more impatient to open the letter." The dark eyes were lifted over the spectacles, and went right into Frank's unprotected and undiplomatic heart. The doctor raised the note, and pointed to the characters with his forefinger.

"Cousin Jemima's hand," said Frank, as directly as if the question had been put to him.

The Italian smiled. "Mr. Hazeldean has company staying with him?"

"No; that is, only Barney—the Captain. There's seldom much company before the shooting season," added Frank with a slight sigh; "and then, you know, the holidays are over. For my part, I think we ought to break up a month later."

The Doctor seemed re-assured by the first sentence in

Frank's reply, and, seating himself at the table, wrote his answer — not hastily, as we English write, but with care and precision, like one accustomed to weigh the nature of words — in that stiff Italian hand, which allows the writer so much time to think while he forms his letters. He did not, therefore, reply at once to Frank's remark about the holidays, but was silent till he had concluded his note, read it three times over, sealed it by the taper he slowly lighted, and then, giving it to Frank, he said —

"For your sake, young gentleman, I regret that your holidays are so early; for mine, I must rejoice, since I accept the kind invitation you have rendered doubly gratifying by bringing it yourself."

"Deuce take the fellow and his fine speeches! One don't know which way to look," thought English Frank.

The Italian smiled again, as if this time he had read the boy's heart, without need of those piercing black eyes, and said, less ceremoniously than before, "You don't care much for compliments, young gentleman?"

"No, I don't indeed," said Frank heartily.

"So much the better for you, since your way in the world is made; it would be so much the worse, if you had to make it!"

Frank looked puzzled: the thought was too deep for him — so he turned to the pictures.

"Those are very funny," said he: "they seem capitally done. Who did 'em?"

"Signorino Hazeldean, you are giving me what you refused yourself"

"Eh?" said Frank inquiringly.

"Compliments!"

"Oh — I — no; but they are well done: ar'n't they, sir?"

"Not particularly: you speak to the artist."

"What! *you* painted them?"

"Yes."

"And the pictures in the hall?"

"Those too."

"Taken from nature, eh?"

"Nature," said the Italian sententiously, perhaps evasively, "lets nothing be taken from her."

"Oh!" said Frank, puzzled again. "Well, I must wish you good morning, sir; I am very glad you are coming."

"Without compliment?"

"Without compliment."

"*A rivedersi* — good-by for the present, my young Signorino. This way," observing Frank made a bolt towards the wrong door.

"Can I offer you a glass of wine! — it is pure, of our own making."

"No, thank you, indeed, sir," cried Frank, suddenly recollecting his father's admonition. "Good-by, don't trouble yourself, sir; I know my way now."

But the bland Italian followed his guest to the wicket, where Frank had left the pony. The young gentleman, afraid lest so courteous a host should hold the stirrup for him, twitched off the bridle, and mounted in haste, not even staying to ask if the Italian could put him in the way to Rood Hall, of which way he was profoundly ignorant. The Italian's eye followed the boy as he rode up the ascent in the lane, and the Doctor sighed heavily. "The wiser we grow," said he to himself, "the more we regret the age of our follies: it is better to gallop with a light heart up the stony hill than sit in the summer-house and cry 'How true!' to the stormy truths of Machiavelli!"

With that he turned back into the Belvidere; but he could not resume his studies. He remained some minutes gazing on the prospect, till the prospect reminded him of the fields which Jackeymo was bent on his hiring, and the fields reminded him of Lenny Fairfield. He returned to the house, and in a few moments re-emerged in his out-of-door trim, with cloak and umbrella, re-lighted his pipe, and strolled towards Hazeldean village.

Meanwhile Frank, after cantering on for some distance, stopped at a cottage, and there learned that there was a short cut across the fields to Rood Hall, by which he could save nearly three miles. Frank, however, missed the short cut, and came out into the high road: a turnpike keeper, after first taking his toll, put him back again into the short cut; and finally, he got into some green lanes, where a dilapidated finger-post directed him to Rood. Late at noon, having ridden fifteen miles in the desire to reduce ten to seven, he came suddenly upon a wild and primitive piece of ground, that seemed half chase, half common, with crazy tumbledown cottages of villanous aspect scattered about in odd nooks and corners; idle, dirty children were making mud pies on the road; slovenly-looking women were plaiting straw at the thresholds; a large but forlorn and decayed church, that seemed to say that the generation which saw it built was more pious than the generation which now resorted to it, stood boldly and nakedly out by the roadside.

"Is this the village of Rood?" asked Frank of a stout young man breaking stones on the road—sad sign that no better labor could be found for him!

The man sullenly nodded, and continued his work.

"And where's the Hall—Mr. Leslie's?"

The man looked up in stolid surprise, and this time touched his hat.

"Be you going there?"

"Yes, if I can find out where it is."

"I'll show your honor," said the boor alertly.

Frank reined in the pony, and the man walked by his side.

Frank was much of his father's son, despite the difference of age, and that more fastidious change of manner which characterises each succeeding race in the progress of civilisation. Despite all his Eton finery, he was familiar with peasants, and had the quick eye of one country-born as to country matters.

"You don't seem very well off in this village, my man?" said he, knowingly.

"Noa; there be a deal of distress here in the winter

time, and summer too, for that matter; and the parish ben't much help to a single man."

"But, surely, the farmers want work here as well as elsewhere?"

"'Deed, and there ben't much farming work here — most o' the parish be all wild ground loike."

"The poor have a right of common, I suppose," said Frank, surveying a large assortment of vagabond birds and quadrupeds.

"Yes; neighbor Timmins keeps his geese on the common, and some has a cow — and them be neighbor Jowlas's pigs. I don't know if there's a right, loike; but the folks at the Hall does all they can to help us, and that ben't much: they ben't as rich as some folks; but," added the peasant proudly, "they be as good blood as any in the shire."

"I'm glad to see you like them, at all events."

"Oh yes, I loikes them well eno'; mayhap you are at school with the young gentleman?"

'Yes," said Frank.

"Ah! I heard the clergyman say as how Master Randal was a mighty clever lad, and would get rich some day. I'se sure I wish he would, for a poor squire makes a poor parish. There's the Hall, sir."

CHAPTER III.

FRANK looked right ahead, and saw a square house that, in spite of modern sash-windows, was evidently of remote antiquity; a high conical roof; a stack of tall quaint chimney-pots of red baked clay (like those at Sutton Place, in Surrey) dominating over isolated vulgar smoke-conductors, of the ignoble fashion of present times; a dilapidated groin-work, encasing within a Tudor arch a door of the comfortable date of George III., and the peculiarly dingy and weather-stained appearance of the small finely-finished bricks, of which the habitation was built — all showed the abode of former generations adapted with tasteless irreverence to the habits of descendants unenlightened by Pugin, or indifferent to the poetry of the past. The house had emerged suddenly upon Frank out of the gloomy waste land, for it was placed in a hollow, and sheltered from sight by a disorderly group of ragged, dismal, valetudinarian fir-trees, until an abrupt turn of the road cleared that screen, and left the desolate abode bare to the discontented eye. Frank dismounted; the man held his pony; and after smoothing his cravat, the smart Etonian sauntered up to the door, and startled the solitude of the place with a loud peal from the modern brass knocker — a knock which instantly brought forth an astonished starling who had built under the eaves of the gable roof, and called up a cloud of sparrows, tomtits, and yellow-hammers, who had been regaling themselves amongst the litter of a slovenly farm-yard that lay in full sight to the right of the house, fenced off by a primitive, paintless wooden rail. In process of time a sow, accompanied by a thriving and inquisitive family, strolled up to the gate of the fence, and, leaning her nose on the lower bar of the gate, contemplated the visitor with much curiosity and some suspicion.

While Frank is still without, impatiently swingeing his white trousers with his whip, we will steal a hurried glance towards the respected members of the family within. Mr. Leslie, the *pater-familias*, is in a little room called his "study," to which he regularly retires every morning after breakfast, rarely re-appearing till one o'clock, which is his unfashionable hour for dinner. In what mysterious occupations Mr. Leslie passes those hours, no one ever formed a conjecture. At the present moment he is seated before a little rickety bureau, one leg of which (being shorter than the other) is propped up by sundry old letters and scraps of newspapers; and the bureau is open, and reveals a great number of pigeon-holes and divisions, filled with various odds and ends, the collection of many years. In some of these compartments are bundles of letters, very yellow, and tied in packets with faded tape; in another, all by itself, is a fragment of plum-pudding stone, which Mr. Leslie has picked up in his walks, and considered a rare mineral. It is neatly labelled, "Found in Hollow Lane, May 21st, 1804, by Maunder Slugge Leslie, Esq." The next division holds several bits of iron in the shape of nails, fragments of horse-shoes, &c., which Mr. Leslie has also met with in his rambles, and according to a harmless popular superstition, deemed it highly unlucky not to pick up, and, once picked up, no less unlucky to throw away. *Item*, in the adjoining pigeon-hole, a goodly collection of pebbles with holes in them, preserved for the same reason. In company with a crooked sixpence: *item*, neatly arranged in fanciful mosaics, several periwinkles, Blackamoor's teeth (I mean the shell so called), and other specimens of the conchiferous ingenuity of Nature, partly inherited from some ancestral spinster, partly amassed by Mr. Leslie himself in a youthful excursion to the sea-side. There were the farm-bailiff's accounts, several files of bills, an old stirrup, three sets of knee and shoe buckles, which had belonged to Mr. Leslie's father, a few seals tied together by a shoestring, a shagreen tooth-pick case, a tortoise-shell magnifying-glass to read with, his eldest son's first copybooks, his second son's ditto, his daughter's ditto, and a lock of his wife's hair arranged in a true lover's knot, framed and glazed. There were also a small mouse-trap; a patent cork-screw, too good to be used in common; fragments of a silver tea-spoon, that had, by natural decay, arrived at a dissolution of its parts, a small brown Holland bag, containing half-pence of various dates, as far back as Queen Anne, accompanied by two French *sous*, and a

German *silber gros;* — the which miscellany Mr. Leslie magniloquently called "his coins," and had left in his will as a family heir-loom. There were many other curiosities of a congenial nature and equal value — *quæ nunc describere longum est.* Mr. Leslie was engaged at this time in what is termed "putting things to rights" — an occupation he performed with exemplary care once a-week. This was his day; and he had just counted his coins, and was slowly tying them up again in the brown Holland bag, when Frank's knock reached his ears.

Mr. Maunder Slugge Leslie paused, shook his head as if incredulously, and was about to resume his occupation, when he was seized with a fit of yawning which prevented the bag being tied for full two minutes.

While such the employment of the study, let us turn to the recreations in the drawing-room, or rather parlor. A drawing-room there was on the first-floor, with a charming look-out, not on the dreary fir-trees, but on the romantic undulating forest-land; but the drawing-room had not been used since the death of the last Mrs. Leslie. It was deemed too good to sit in, except when there was company: there never being company, it was never sate in. Indeed, now the paper was falling off the walls with the damp, and the rats, mice, and moths — those "*edaces rerum*" — had eaten, between them, most of the chair-bottoms and a considerable part of the floor. Therefore, the parlor was the sole general sitting-room; and being breakfasted in, dined and supped in, and, after supper, smoked in by Mr. Leslie to the accompaniment of rum-and-water, it is impossible to deny that it had what is called "a smell"—a comfortable, wholesome family smell—speaking of numbers, meals, and miscellaneous social habitation. There were two windows: one looked full on the fir-trees; the other on the farm-yard, with the pig-sty closing the view. Near the fir-tree window sate Mrs. Leslie; before her, on a high stool, was a basket of the children's clothes that wanted mending. A work-table of rose-wood inlaid with brass, which had been a wedding-present, and was a costly thing originally, but in that peculiar taste which is vulgarly called "Bramagen," stood at hand: the brass had started in several places, and occasionally made great havoc in the children's fingers and in Mrs. Leslie's gown; in fact, it was the liveliest piece of furniture in the house, thanks to that petulant brass-work, and could not have been more mischievous if it had been a monkey. Upon the work-table lay a housewife and a thimble, and scissors, and skeins of worsted and thread, and little scraps of linen and cloth for patches. But Mrs. Leslie was not actually working—she was preparing to work; she had been preparing to work for the last hour and a half. Upon her lap she supported a novel, by a lady who wrote much for a former generation, under the name of "Mrs. Bridget Blue Mantle." She had a small needle in her left hand, and a very thick piece of thread in her right; occasionally she applied the end of the said thread to her lips, and then—her eyes fixed on the novel—made a blind, vacillating attack at the eye of the needle. But a camel would have gone through it with quite as much ease. Nor did the novel alone engage Mrs. Leslie's attention, for ever and anon she interrupted herself to scold the children, to inquire "what o'clock it was;" to observe that "Sarah would never suit;" and to wonder "why Mr. Leslie would not see that the work-table was mended." Mrs. Leslie has been rather a pretty woman. In spite of a dress at once slatternly and economical, she has still the air of a lady — rather too much so, the hard duties of her situation considered. She is proud of the antiquity of her family on both sides; her mother was of the venerable stock of the Daudles of Daudle Place, a race that existed before the Conquest. Indeed, one has only to read our earliest chronicles, and to glance over some of those long-winded moralising poems which delighted the thanes and ealdermen of old, in order to see that the Daudles must have been a very influential family before William the First turned the country topsy-turvy. While the mother's race was thus indubitably Saxon, the father's had not only the name but the peculiar idiosyncrasy of the Normans, and went far to establish that crotchet of the brilliant author of *Sibyl, or the Two Nations*, as to the continued distinction between the conquering and conquered populations. Mrs. Leslie's father boasted the name of Montfydget; doubtless of the same kith and kin as those great barons Montfichet, who once owned such broad lands and such turbulent castles. A high-nosed thin, nervous, excitable progeny, those same Montfydgets, as the most troublesome Norman could pretend to be. This fusion of race was notable to the most ordinary physiognomist in the *physique* and in the *morale* of Mrs. Leslie. She had the speculative blue eye of the Saxon, and the passionate high nose of the Norman; she had the musing do-nothingness of the Daudles, and the reckless have-at-every-thingness of the Montfydgets. At Mrs. Leslie's feet, a little girl with her hair about her ears (and beautiful hair it was too) was amusing herself with a broken-nosed doll. At the far end of the room, before a high desk, sate Frank's Eton school-fellow, the eldest son. A minute or two before Frank's alarum had disturbed the tranquillity of the household, he had raised his eyes from the books on the desk to glance at a very tattered copy of the Greek Testament, in which his brother Oliver had found a difficulty that he came to Randal to solve. As the young Etonian's face was turned to the light, your first impression, on seeing it, would have been melancholy, but respectful, interest — for the face had already lost the joyous character of youth — there was a wrinkle between the brows; and the lines that speak of fatigue were already visible under the eyes and about the mouth: the complexion was sallow, the lips were pale. Years of study had already sown in the delicate organization the seeds of many an infirmity and many a pain: but if your look had rested longer on that countenance, gradually your compassion might have given place to some feeling uneasy and sinister — a feeling akin to fear. There was in the whole expression so much of cold, calm force, that it belied the debility of the frame. You saw there the evidence of a mind that was cultivated, and you felt that in that cultivation there was something formidable. A notable contrast to this countenance, prematurely worn, and eminently intelligent, was the round healthy face of Oliver, with slow blue eyes fixed hard on the penetrating orbs of his brother, as if trying with might and main to catch from them a gleam of that knowledge with which they shone clear and frigid as a star.

At Frank's knock, Oliver's slow blue eyes sparkled into animation, and he sprang from his brother's side. The little girl flung back the hair from her face, and stared at her mother with a look which spoke wonder and affright.

The young student knit his brows, and then turned wearily back to the books on his desk.

"Dear me," cried Mrs. Leslie, "who can that possibly be? Oliver, come from the window, sir, this instant; you will be seen! Juliet, run — ring the bell — no, go to the head of the kitchen stairs, and call out to Jenny, 'Not at home.' Not at home on any account," repeated Mrs. Leslie, nervously, for the Montfydget blood was now in full flow.

In another minute or so, Frank's loud, boyish voice was distinctly heard at the outer door.

Randal slightly started.

"Frank Hazeldean's voice," said he; "I should like to see him, mother."

"See him," repeated Mrs. Leslie, in amaze; "see him! and the room in this state!"

—Randal might have replied that the room was in no worse state than usual; but he said nothing. A slight flush came and went over his pale face; and then he leaned his cheek on his hand, and compressed his lips firmly.

The outer door closed with a sullen, inhospitable jar, and a slip-shod female servant entered with a card between her finger and thumb.

"Who is that for?—give it to me, Jenny," cried Mrs. Leslie.

But Jenny shook her head, laid the card on the desk beside Randal, and vanished without saying a word.

"Oh look, Randal, look up," cried Oliver, who had again rushed to the window; "such a pretty grey pony!"

Randal did look up; nay, he went deliberately to the window, and gazed a moment on the high-mettled pony, and the well-dressed, spirited rider. In that moment changes passed over Randal's countenance more rapidly than clouds over the sky in a gusty day. Now envy and discontent, with the curled lip and the gloomy scowl; now hope and proud self-esteem, with the clearing brow and the lofty smile; and then again all became cold, firm, and close, as he walked back to his books, seated himself resolutely, and said, half aloud—

"Well, KNOWLEDGE IS POWER.

CHAPTER IV.

MRS. LESLIE came up in fidget and in fuss; she leaned over Randal's shoulder and read the card. Written in pen and ink, with an attempt at imitation of printed Roman character, there appeared first "MR. FRANK HAZELDEAN;" but just over these letters, and scribbled hastily and less legibly in pencil, was—

"Dear Leslie—sorry you were out—come and see us—*Do!*"

"You will go, Randal?" said Mrs. Leslie, after a pause.

"I'm not sure."

"Yes, *you* can go; *you* have clothes like a gentleman: *you* can go anywhere, not like those children;" and Mrs. Leslie glanced almost spitefully at poor Oliver's coarse threadbare jacket, and little Juliet's torn frock.

"What I have I owe at present to Mr. Egerton, and I should consult his wishes; he is not on good terms with these Hazeldeans." Then turning towards his brother, who looked mortified, he added, with a strange sort of haughty kindness, "What I may have hereafter, Oliver, I shall owe to myself; and then if I rise, I will raise my family."

"Dear Randal," said Mrs. Leslie, fondly kissing him on the forehead, "what a good heart you have!"

"No, mother; my books don't tell me that it is a good heart that gets on in the world: it is a hard head," replied Randal, with a rude and scornful candor. "But I can read no more just now; come out, Oliver."

So saying, he slid from his mother's hand, and left the room.

When Oliver joined him, Randal was already on the common; and, without seeming to notice his brother, he continued to walk quickly, and with long strides, in profound silence. At length he paused under the shade of an old oak, that, too old to be of value save for firewood, had escaped the axe. The tree stood on a knoll, and the spot commanded a view of the decayed house — the dilapidated church — the dreary village.

"Oliver," said Randal, between his teeth, so that his voice had the sound of a hiss, "it was under this tree that I first resolved to ——"

He paused.

"What, Randal?"

"Read hard: knowledge is power!"

"But you are so fond of reading."

"I!" cried Randal. "Do you think, when Wolsey and Thomas-à-Becket became priests, they were fond of telling their beads and pattering aves? I fond of reading!"

Oliver stared; the historical allusions were beyond his comprehension.

"You know," continued Randal, "that we Leslies were not always the beggarly poor gentlemen we are now.

You know that there is a man who lives in Grosvenor Square, and is very rich—very. His riches come to him from a Leslie; that man is my patron, Oliver, and he — is very good to me."

Randal's smile was withering as he spoke. "Come on," he said, after a pause — "come on." Again the walk was quick, and the brothers were silent.

They came at length to a little shallow brook, across which some large stones had been placed at short intervals, so that the boys walked over the ford dry-shod. "Will you pull down that bough, Oliver?" said Randal, abruptly, pointing to a tree. Oliver obeyed mechanically; and Randal, stripping the leaves, and snapping off the twigs, left a fork at the end; with this he began to remove the stepping-stones.

"What are you about, Randal?" asked Oliver, wonderingly.

"We are on the other side of the brook now, and we shall not come back this way. We don't want the stepping-stones any more! — away with them!"

CHAPTER V.

THE morning after this visit of Frank Hazeldean's to Rood Hall, the Right Honorable Audley Egerton, member of parliament, privy councillor, and minister of a high department in the state—just below the rank of the cabinet — was seated in his library, awaiting the delivery of the post, before he walked down to his office. In the meanwhile, he sipped his tea, and glanced over the newspapers with that quick and half-disdainful eye with which your practical man in public life is wont to regard the abuse or the eulogium of the Fourth Estate.

There is very little likeness between Mr. Egerton and his half-brother; none, indeed, except that they are both of tall stature, and strong, sinewy, English build. But even in this last they do not resemble each other; for the Squire's athletic shape is already beginning to expand into that portly *embonpoint* which seems the natural development of contented men as they approach middle life. Audley, on the contrary, is inclined to be spare; and his figure, though the muscles are as firm as iron, has enough of the slender to satisfy metropolitan ideas of elegance. His dress, his look — his *tout ensemble* — are those of the London man. In the first, there is more attention to fashion than is usual amongst the busy members of the House of Commons; but then Audley Egerton has always been something more than a mere busy member of the House of Commons. He has always been a person of mark in the best society; and one secret of his success in life has been his high reputation as "a gentleman."

As he now bends over the journals, there is an air of distinction in the turn of the well-shaped head, with the dark brown hair — dark in spite of a reddish tinge — cut close behind, and worn away a little towards the crown, so as to give additional height to a commanding forehead. His profile is very handsome, and of that kind of beauty which imposes on men if it pleases women; and is, therefore, unlike that of your mere pretty fellows, a positive advantage in public life. It is a profile with large features clearly cut, masculine, and somewhat severe. The expression of his face is not open, like the Squire's; nor has it the cold closeness which accompanies the intellectual character of young Leslie's; but it is reserved and dignified, and significant of self-control, as should be the physiognomy of a man accustomed to think before he speaks. When you look at him, you are not surprised to learn that he is not a florid orator nor a smart debater—he is a "weighty speaker." He is fairly read, but without any great range either of ornamental scholarship or constitutional lore. He has not much humor; but he has that kind of wit which is essential to grave and serious irony. He has not much imagination, nor remarkable subtlety in reasoning; but if he does not dazzle, he does not *bore*: he is too much of the man of the world for that. He is considered to have sound sense and accurate judgment. Withal, as he now lays aside the journals, and his face relaxes its austerer lines, you will not be astonished to hear that he is a man who is said to have been greatly beloved by women, and still to exercise much influence in drawing-rooms and boudoirs. At least, no one was surprised when the great heiress, Clementina Leslie, kinswoman and ward to Lord Lansmere—a young lady who had refused three earls and the heir-apparent to a dukedom—was declared by her dearest friends to be dying of love for Audley Egerton. It had been the natural wish of the Lansmeres that this lady should marry their son, Lord L'Estrange. But that young gentleman, whose opinions on matrimony partook of the eccentricity of his general character, could never be induced to propose, and had, according to the *on-dits* of town, been the principal party to make up the match between Clementina and his friend Audley; for the match required making-up, despite the predilections of the young heiress. Mr. Egerton had had scruples of delicacy. He avowed, for the first time, that his fortune was much less than had been generally supposed, and he did not like the idea of owing all to a wife, however highly he might esteem and admire her. Now, Lord L'Estrange (not long after the election at Lansmere, which had given to Audley his first seat in parliament) had suddenly exchanged from the battalion of the Guards to which he belonged, and which was detained at home, into a cavalry regiment on active service in the Peninsula. Nevertheless, even abroad, and amidst the distractions of war, his interest in all that could forward Egerton's career was unabated; and, by letters to his father, and to his cousin Clementina, he assisted in the negotiations for the marriage between Miss Leslie and his friend; and, before the year in which Audley was returned for Lansmere had expired, the young senator received the hand of the great heiress. The settlement of her fortune, which was chiefly in the funds, had been unusually advantageous to the husband; for though the capital was tied up so long as both survived — for the benefit of any children they might have — yet, in the event of one of the parties dying without issue by the marriage, the whole passed without limitation to the survivor. Miss Leslie, in spite of all remonstrance from her own legal adviser, had settled this clause with Egerton's confidential solicitor, one Mr. Levy, of whom we shall see more hereafter; and Egerton was to be kept in ignorance of it till after the marriage. If in this Miss Leslie showed a generous trust in Mr. Egerton, she still inflicted no positive wrong on her relations, for she had none sufficiently near to her to warrant their claim to the succession. Her nearest kinsman, and therefore her natural heir, was Harley L'Estrange; and if he was contented, no one had a right to complain. The tie of blood between herself and the Leslies of Rood Hall was, as we shall see presently, extremely distant.

It was not till after his marriage that Mr. Egerton took an active part in the business of the House of Commons. He was then at the most advantageous starting-point for the career of ambition. His words on the state of the country took importance from his stake in it. His talents from accessories in the opulence of Grosvenor Square, the dignity of a princely establishment, the respectability of one firmly settled in life, the reputation of a fortune in reality very large, and which was magnified by popular report into the revenues of a Crœsus. Audley Egerton succeeded in Parliament beyond the early expectations formed of him. He took, from the first, that station in the House which it requires tact to establish, and great knowledge of the world to free from the charge of impracticability and crotchet, but which, once established, is peculiarly imposing from the rarity of its independence; that is to say, the station of the moderate man, who belongs sufficiently to a party to obtain its support, but is yet sufficiently disengaged from a party to make his vote and word, on certain questions, matter of anxiety and speculation.

Professing Toryism (the word Conservative, which would have suited him better, was not then known), he separated himself from the country party, and always avowed great respect for the opinions of the large towns. The epithet given to the views of Audley Egerton was "enlightened." Never too much in advance of the passion of the day, yet never behind its movement, he had that shrewd calculation of odds which a consummate mastery of the world sometimes bestows upon politicians, —perceived the chances for and against a certain question being carried within a certain time, and nicked the question between wind and water. He was so good a barometer of that changeful weather called Public Opinion, that he might have had a hand in the *Times* newspaper. He soon quarrelled, and purposely, with his Lansmere constituents; nor had he ever revisited that borongh, — perhaps because it was associated with unpleasant reminiscences in the shape of the Squire's epistolary trimmer, and in that of his own effigies which his agricultural constituents had burned in the corn-market. But the speeches that produced such indignation at Lansmere had delighted one of the greatest of our commercial towns, which at the next general election honored him with its representation. In those days, before the Reform Bill, great commercial towns chose men of high mark for their members; and a proud station it was for him who was delegated to speak the voice of the princely merchants of England.

Mrs. Egerton survived her marriage but a few years; she left no children; two had been born, but died in their first infancy. The property of the wife, therefore, passed without control or limit to the husband.

Whatever might have been the grief of the widower, he disdained to betray it to the world. Indeed, Audley Egerton was a man who had early taught himself to conceal emotion. He buried himself in the country, none knew where, for some months. When he returned, there was a deep wrinkle on his brow; but no change in his habits and avocations, except that shortly afterwards he accepted office, and thus became more busy than ever.

Mr. Egerton had always been lavish and magnificent in money matters. A rich man in public life has many claims on his fortune, and no one yielded to those claims with an air so regal as Audley Egerton. But amongst his many liberal actions there was none which seemed more worthy of panegyric than the generous favor he extended to the son of his wife's poor and distant kinsfolk, the Leslies, of Rood Hall.

Some four generations back, there had lived a certain

Squire Leslie, a man of large acres and active mind. He had cause to be displeased with his eldest son, and though he did not disinherit him, he left half his property to a younger.

The younger had capacity and spirit, which justified the parental provision. He increased his fortune, lifted himself into notice and consideration by public services and a noble alliance. His descendants followed his example, and took rank among the first commoners in England, till the last male, dying, left his sole heiress and representative in one daughter, Clementina, afterwards married to Mr. Egerton.

Meanwhile the elder son of the forementioned squire had muddled and sotted away much of his share in the Leslie property, and by low habits and mean society, lowered in repute his representation of the name.

His successors imitated him, till nothing was left to Randal's father, Mr. Maunder Slugge Leslie, but the decayed house, which was what the Germans call the *stamm schloss* or "stem hall" of the race, and the wretched lands immediately around it.

Still, though all intercourse between the two branches of the family had ceased, the younger had always felt a respect for the elder, as the head of the house. And it was supposed that, on her death-bed, Mrs. Egerton had recommended her impoverished namesakes and kindred to the care of her husband; for, when he returned to town, after Mrs. Egerton's death, Audley had sent to Mr. Maunder Slugge Leslie the sum of £5,000, which he said his wife, leaving no written will, had orally bequeathed as a legacy to that gentleman; and he requested permission to charge himself with the education of the eldest son.

Mr. Maunder Slugge Leslie might have done great things for his little property with those £5,000, or even (kept in the Three per Cents) the interest would have afforded a material addition to his comforts. But a neighboring solicitor, having caught scent of the legacy, hunted it down into his own hands, on pretence of having found a capital investment in a canal. And when the solicitor had got possession of the £5,000, he went off with them to America.

Meanwhile Randal, placed by Mr. Egerton at an excellent preparatory school, at first gave no signs of industry or talent; but just before he left it, there came to the school, as classical tutor, an ambitious young Oxford man; and his zeal — for he was a capital teacher — produced a great effect generally on the pupils, and especially on Randal Leslie. He talked to them much in private on the advantages of learning, and shortly afterwards he exhibited those advantages in his own person; for, having edited a Greek play with much subtle scholarship, his college, which some slight irregularities of his had displeased, recalled him to its venerable bosom by the presentation of a fellowship. After this he took orders, became a college tutor, distinguished himself yet more by a treatise on the Greek accent, got a capital living, and was considered on the high road to a bishopric. This young man, then, communicated to Randal the thirst for knowledge; and when the boy went afterwards to Eton, he applied with such earnestness and resolve, that his fame soon reached the ears of Audley; and that person, who had the sympathy for talent, and yet more for purpose, which often characterises ambitious men, went to Eton to see him. From that time Audley evinced great and almost fatherly interest in the brilliant Etonian; and Randal always spent with him some days in each vacation.

I have said that Egerton's conduct, with respect to this boy, was more praiseworthy than most of those generous actions for which he was renowned, since to this the world gave no applause. What a man does within the range of his family connexions does not carry with it that *éclat* which invests a munificence exhibited on public occasions. Either people care nothing about it, or tacitly suppose it to be but his duty. It was true, too, as the Squire had observed, that Randal Leslie was even less distantly related to the Hazeldeans than to Mrs. Egerton, since Randal's grandfather had actually married a Miss Hazeldean (the highest worldly connexion that branch of the family had formed since the great split I have commemorated). But Audley Egerton never appeared aware of that fact. As he was not himself descended from the Hazeldeans, he did not trouble himself about their genealogy; and he took care to impress it upon the Leslies that his generosity on their behalf was solely to be ascribed to his respect for his wife's memory and kindred. Still the Squire had felt as if his "distant brother" implied a rebuke on his own neglect of these poor Leslies, by the liberality Audley evinced towards them; and this had made him doubly sore when the name of Randal Leslie was mentioned. But the fact really was, that the Leslies of Rood had so shrunk out of all notice that the Squire had actually forgotten their existence, until Randal became thus indebted to his brother; and then he felt a pang of remorse that any one save himself, the head of the Hazeldeans, should lend a helping hand to the grandson of a Hazeldean.

But having thus, somewhat too tediously, explained the position of Audley Egerton, whether in the world or in relation to his young *protégé*, I may now permit him to receive and to read his letters.

CHAPTER VI.

Mr. Egerton glanced over the pile of letters placed beside him, and first he tore up some, scarcely read, and threw them into the waste-basket. Public men have such odd, out-of-the-way letters, that their waste-baskets are never empty: letters from amateur financiers proposing new ways to pay off the National Debt; letters from America (never free), asking for autographs; letters from fond mothers in country villages, recommending some miracle of a son for a place in the King's service; letters from free-thinkers in reproof of bigotry; letters from bigots in reproof of free-thinkers; letters signed Brutus Redivivus, containing the agreeable information that the writer has a dagger for tyrants, if the Danish claims are not forthwith adjusted; letters signed Matilda or Caroline, stating that Caroline or Matilda has seen the public man's portrait at the Exhibition, and that a heart sensible to its attractions may be found at No. —, Piccadilly; letters from beggars, impostors, monomaniacs, speculators, jobbers — all food for the waste-basket.

From the correspondence thus winnowed, Mr. Egerton first selected those on business, which he put methodically together in one division of his pocket-book; and secondly, those of a private nature, which he as carefully put into another. Of these last there were but three — one from his steward, one from Harvey L'Estrange, one from Randal Leslie. It was his custom to answer his correspondence at his office; and to his office, a few minutes afterwards, he slowly took his way. Many a passenger turned back to look again at the firm figure, which, despite the hot summer day, was buttoned up to the throat; and the black frock-coat thus worn well became the erect air, and the deep, full chest of the handsome senator. When he entered Parliament Street, Audley Egerton was joined by one of his colleagues, also on his way to the cares of office.

After a few observations on the last debate, this gentleman said —

"By the way, can you dine with me next Saturday, to meet Lansmere? He comes up to town to vote for us on Monday."

"I had asked some people to dine with me," answered Egerton, "but I will put them off. I see Lord Lansmere too seldom to miss any occasion to meet a man whom I respect so much."

"So seldom! True, he is very little in town; but why don't you go and see him in the country? Good shooting — pleasant, old-fashioned house."

"My dear Westbourne, his house is '*nimium vicina Cremonæ*,' close to a borough in which I have been burned in effigy."

"Ha — ha — yes — I remember you first came into Parliament for that snug little place; but Lansmere himself never found fault with your votes, did he?"

"He behaved very handsomely, and said he had not presumed to consider me his mouthpiece; and then, too, I am so intimate with L'Estrange."

"Is that queer fellow ever coming back to England?"

"He comes, generally, every year, for a few days, just to see his father and mother, and then returns to the Continent."

"I never met him."

"He comes in September or October, when you, of course, are not in town, and it is in town that the Lansmeres meet him."

"Why does he not go to them?"

"A man in England but once a year, and for a few days, has so much to do in London, I suppose?"

"Is he as amusing as ever?"

Egerton nodded.

"So distinguished as he might be!" remarked Lord Westbourne.

"So distinguished as he is!" said Egerton formally; "an officer selected for praise, even in such fields as Quatre Bras and Waterloo; a scholar, too, of the finest taste; and as an accomplished gentleman, matchless!"

"I like to hear one man praise another so warmly in these ill-natured days," answered Lord Westbourne. "But still, though L'Estrange is doubtless all you say, don't you think he rather wastes his life—living abroad?"

"And trying to be happy, Westbourne? Are you sure it is not we who waste our lives? but I can't stay to hear your answer. Here we are at the door of my prison."

"On Saturday, then?"

"On Saturday. Good day."

For the next hour, or more, Mr. Egerton was engaged on the affairs of the state. He then snatched an interval of leisure (while awaiting a report, which he had instructed a clerk to make him), in order to reply to his letters. Those on public business were soon despatched; and throwing his replies aside, to be sealed by a subordinate hand, he drew out the letters which he had put apart as private.

He attended first to that of his steward: the steward's letter was long, the reply was contained in three lines. Pitt himself was scarcely more negligent of his private interests and concerns than Audley Egerton—yet, withal, Audley Egerton was said by his enemies to be an egotist.

The next letter he wrote was to Randal, and that, though longer, was far from prolix: it ran thus—

"Dear Mr. Leslie,—I appreciate your delicacy in consulting me whether you should accept Frank Hazeldean's invitation to call at the Hall. Since you are asked, I can see no objection to it. I should be sorry if you appeared to force yourself there; and for the rest, as a general rule, I think a young man who has his own way to make in life had better avoid all intimacy with those of his own age who have no kindred objects nor congenial pursuits.

"As soon as this visit is paid, I wish you to come to London. The report I receive of your progress at Eton renders it unnecessary, in my judgment, that you should return there. If your father has no objection, I propose that you should go to Oxford at the ensuing term. Meanwhile, I have engaged a gentleman, who is a fellow of Baliol, to read with you. He is of opinion, judging only by your high repute at Eton, that you may at once obtain a scholarship in that college. If you do so, I shall look upon your career in life as assured.

"Your affectionate friend, and sincere well-wisher,

"A. E."

The reader will remark that, in this letter, there is a certain tone of formality. Mr. Egerton does not call his *protégé* "Dear Randal," as would seem natural, but coldly and stiffly, "Dear Mr. Leslie." He hints, also, that the boy has his own way to make in life. Is this meant to guard against too sanguine notions of inheritance, which his generosity may have excited?

The letter to Lord L'Estrange was of a very different

kind from the others. It was long, and full of such little scraps of news and gossip as may interest friends in a foreign land; it was written gaily, and as with a wish to cheer his friend; you could see that it was a reply to a melancholy letter; and in the whole tone and spirit there was an affection, even to tenderness, of which those who most liked Audley Egerton would have scarcely supposed him capable. Yet, notwithstanding, there was a kind of constraint in the letter, which perhaps only the fine tact of a woman would detect. It had not the *abandon*, that hearty self-outpouring, which you might expect would characterise the letters of two such friends, who had been boys at school together, and which did breathe indeed in all the abrupt rambling sentences of his correspondent. But where was the evidence of the constraint? Egerton is off-hand enough where his pen runs glibly through paragraphs that relate to others; it is simply that he says nothing about himself—that he avoids all reference to the inner world of sentiment and feeling. But perhaps, after all, the man has no sentiment and feeling! How can you expect that a steady personage in practical life, whose mornings are spent in Downing-street, and whose nights are consumed in watching Government bills through a committee, can write in the same style as an idle dreamer amidst the pines of Ravenna, or on the banks of Como?

Audley had just finished this epistle, such as it was, when the attendant in waiting announced the arrival of a deputation from a provincial trading town, the members of which deputation he had appointed to meet at two o'clock. There was no office in London at which deputations were kept waiting less than at that over which Mr. Egerton presided.

The deputation entered — some score or so of middle-aged, comfortable-looking persons, who, nevertheless, had their grievance — and considered their own interests, and those of the country, menaced by a certain clause in a bill brought in by Mr. Egerton.

The Mayor of the town was the chief spokesman, and he spoke well — but in a style to which the dignified official was not accustomed. It was a slap-dash style — unceremonious, free, and easy—an American style. And, indeed, there was something altogether in the appearance and bearing of the Mayor which savored of residence in the Great Republic. He was a very handsome man, but with a look sharp and domineering — the look of a man who did not care a straw for president or monarch, and who enjoyed the liberty to speak his mind and "wallop his own nigger!"

His fellow-burghers evidently regarded him with great respect; and Mr. Egerton had penetration enough to perceive that Mr. Mayor must be a rich man, as well as an eloquent one, to have overcome those impressions of soreness or jealousy which his tone was calculated to create to the self-love of his equals.

Mr. Egerton was far too wise to be easily offended by mere manner; and, though he stared somewhat haughtily when he found his observations actually pooh-poohed, he was not above being convinced. There was much sense and much justice in Mr. Mayor's arguments, and the statesman civilly promised to take them into full consideration.

He then bowed out the deputation; but scarcely had the door closed before it opened again, and Mr. Mayor presented himself alone, saying aloud to his companions in the passage, "I forgot something I had to say to Mr. Egerton — wait below for me."

"Well, Mr. Mayor," said Audley, pointing to a seat, "what else would you suggest?"

The Mayor looked round to see that the door was closed; and then, drawing his chair close to Mr. Egerton's, laid his forefinger on that gentleman's arm, and said, "I think I speak to a man of the world, sir?"

Mr. Egerton bowed, and made no reply by word, but he gently removed his arm from the touch of the forefinger.

MR. MAYOR.—You observe, sir, that I did not ask the members whom we return to Parliament to accompany us. Do better without 'em. You know they are both in Opposition — out-and-outers.

MR. EGERTON. — It is a misfortune which the Government cannot remember, when the question is whether the trade of the town itself is to be served or injured.

MR. MAYOR.—Well, I guess you speak handsome, sir. But you'd be glad to have two members to support Ministers after the next election.

MR. EGERTON (smiling).—Unquestionably, Mr. Mayor.

MR. MAYOR. — And I can do it, Mr. Egerton. I may say I have the town in my pocket; so I ought—I spend a great deal of money in it. Now, you see, Mr. Egerton, I have passed a part of my life in a land of liberty—the United States—and I come to the point when I speak to a man of the world. I'm a man of the world myself, sir. And so, if the Government will do something for me, why, I'll do something for the Government. Two votes for a free and independent town like ours — that's something, isn't it?

MR. EGERTON (taken by surprise). — Really, I ——

MR. MAYOR (advancing his chair still nearer, and interrupting the official).—No nonsense, you see, on one side or the other. The fact is, that I've taken it into my head that I should like to be knighted. You may well look surprised, Mr. Egerton — trumpery thing enough, I dare say; still, every man has his weakness, and I should like to be Sir Richard. Well, if you can get me made Sir Richard, you may just name your two members for the next election — that is, if they belong to your own set, enlightened men, up to the times. That's speaking fair and manful, isn't it?

MR. EGERTON (drawing himself up). — I am at a loss to guess why you should select me, sir, for this very extraordinary proposition.

MR. MAYOR (nodding good-humoredly). — Why, you see, I don't go along with the Government; you're the best of the bunch. And may be you'd like to strengthen your own party. This is quite between you and me, you understand; honor's a jewel!

MR. EGERTON (with great gravity).—Sir, I am obliged

by your good opinion; but I agree with my colleagues in all the great questions that affect the government of the country, and ——

MR. MAYOR (interrupting him). — Ah, of course, you must say so; very right. But I guess things would go differently if you were Prime Minister. However, I have another reason for speaking to you about my little job. You see you were member for Lansmere once, and I think you only came in by a majority of two, eh?

MR. EGERTON. — I know nothing of the particulars of that election; I was not present.

MR. MAYOR. — No; but luckily for you, two relations of mine were, and they voted for you. Two votes, and you came in by two. Since then, you have got into very snug quarters here, and I think we have a claim on you ——

MR. EGERTON. — Sir, I acknowledge no such claim; I was and am a stranger to Lansmere; and, if the electors did me the honor to return me to Parliament, it was in compliment rather to ——

MR. MAYOR (again interrupting the official).—Rather to Lord Lansmere, you were going to say; unconstitutional doctrine that, I fancy. Peer of the realm. But never mind, I know the world; and I'd ask Lord Lansmere to do my affair for me, only he is a pompous sort of man; might be qualmish: antiquated notions. Not up to snuff like you and me.

MR. EGERTON (in great disgust, and settling his papers before him). — Sir, it is not in my department to recommend to his Majesty candidates for the honor of knighthood, and it is still less in my department to make bargains for seats in Parliament.

MR. MAYOR.—Oh, if that's the case you'll excuse me; I don't know much of the etiquette in these matters. But I thought that, if I put two seats in your hands, for your own friends, you might contrive to take the affair into your department, whatever it was. But, since you say you agree with your colleagues, perhaps it comes to the same thing. Now, you must not suppose I want to sell the town, and that I can change and chop my politics for my own purpose. No such thing! I don't like the sitting members; I'm all for progressing, but they go *too* much ahead for me; and, since the Government is disposed to move a little, why, I'd as lief support them as not. But, in common gratitude, you see (added the Mayor, coaxingly), I ought to be knighted! I can keep up the dignity, and do credit to his Majesty.

MR. EGERTON (without looking up from his papers). —I can only refer you, sir, to the proper quarter.

MR. MAYOR (impatiently). — Proper quarter! Well, since there is so much humbug in this old country of ours, that one must go through all the forms and get at the job regularly, just tell me whom I ought to go to.

MR. EGERTON (beginning to be amused as well as indignant). — If you want a knighthood, Mr. Mayor, you must ask the Prime Minister; if you want to give the Government information relative to seats in Parliament, you must introduce yourself to Mr. ——, the Secretary of the Treasury.

MR. MAYOR. — And if I go to the last chap, what do you think he'll say?

MR. EGERTON (the amusement preponderating over the indignation).—He will say, I suppose, that you must not put the thing in the light in which you have put it to me; that the Government will be very proud to have the confidence of yourself and your brother electors; and that a gentleman like you, in the proud position of Mayor, may well hope to be knighted on some fitting occasion, but that you must not talk about the knighthood just at present, and must confine yourself to converting the unfortunate political opinions of the town.

MR. MAYOR. — Well, I guess that chap there would want to do me! Not quite so green, Mr. Egerton. Perhaps I had better go at once to the fountain-head. How do you think the Premier would take it?

MR. EGERTON (the indignation preponderating over the amusement). — Probably just as I am about to do.

Mr. Egerton rang the bell; the attendant appeared.

"Show Mr. Mayor the way out," said the Minister.

The Mayor turned round sharply, and his face was purple. He walked straight to the door: but suffering the attendant to precede him along the corridor, he came back with a rapid stride, and clenching his hands, and with a voice thick with passion, cried, "Some day or other I will make you smart for this, as sure as my name's Dick Avenel!"

"Avenel!" repeated Egerton, recoiling — "Avenel!"

But the Mayor was gone.

Audley fell into a deep and musing reverie, which seemed gloomy, and lasted till the attendant announced that the horses were at the door.

He then looked up, still abstractedly, and saw his letter to Harley L'Estrange open on the table. He drew it towards him, and wrote, "A man has just left me, who calls himself Aven—" In the middle of the name his pen stopped. "No, no," muttered the writer, "what folly to re-open the old wounds *there*," and he carefully erased the words.

Audley Egerton did not ride in the Park that day, as was his wont, but dismissed his groom; and, turning his horse's head towards Westminster Bridge, took his solitary way into the country. He rode at first slowly, as if in thought; then fast, as if trying to escape from thought. He was later than usual at the House that evening, and he looked pale and fatigued. But he had to speak, and he spoke well.

CHAPTER VII.

In spite of all his Machiavellian wisdom, Dr. Riccabocca had been foiled in his attempt to seduce Leonard Fairfield into his service, even though he succeeded in partially winning over the widow to his views. For to her he represented the worldly advantages of the thing. Lenny would learn to be fit for more than a day-laborer; he would learn gardening in all its branches — rise some day to be a head gardener. "And," said Riccabocca, "I will take care of his book-learning, and teach him whatever he has a head for."

"He has a head for everything," said the widow.

"Then," said the wise man, "everything shall go into it."

The widow was certainly dazzled; for, as we have seen, she highly prized scholarly distinction, and she knew that the Parson looked upon Riccabocca as a wondrous learned man. But still Riccabocca was said to be a Papist, and suspected to be a conjurer. Her scruples on both these points the Italian, who was an adept in the art of talking over the fair sex, would no doubt have dissipated, if there had been any use in it; but Lenny put a dead stop to all negotiations. He had taken a mortal dislike to Riccabocca: he was very much frightened by him — and the spectacles, the pipe, the cloak, the long hair, and the red umbrella; and said so sturdily, in reply to every overture — "Please, sir, I'd rather not; I'd rather stay along with mother," — that Riccabocca was forced to suspend all further experiments in his Machiavellian diplomacy. He was not at all cast down, however, by his first failure; on the contrary, he was one of those men whom opposition stimulates. And what before had been but a suggestion of prudence, became an object of desire. Plenty of other lads might no doubt be had, on as reasonable terms as Lenny Fairfield; but the moment Lenny presumed to baffle the Italian's designs upon him, the special acquisition of Lenny became of paramount importance in the eyes of Signor Riccabocca.

Jackeymo, however, lost all his interest in the traps, snares, and gins which his master proposed to lay for Leonard Fairfield, in the more immediate surprise that awaited him on learning that Dr. Riccabocca had accepted an invitation to pass a few days at the Hall.

"There will be no one there but the family," said Riccabocca. "Poor Giacomo, a little chat in the servants' hall will do you good; and the Squire's beef is more nourishing, after all, than the stickle-backs and minnows. It will lengthen your life."

"The Padrone jests," said Jackeymo, statelily; "as if any one could starve in his service."

"Um," said Riccabocca. "At least, faithful friend, you have tried that experiment as far as human nature will permit;" and he extended his hand to his fellow-exile with that familiarity which exists between servant and master in the usages of the Continent. Jackeymo bent low, and a tear fell upon the hand he kissed.

"*Cospetto!*" said Dr. Riccabocca, "a thousand mock pearls do not make up the cost of a single true one! The tears of women — we know their worth; but the tear of an honest man — Fie, Giacomo! — at least I can never repay you this! Go and see to our wardrobe."

So far as his master's wardrobe was concerned, that order was pleasing to Jackeymo; for the Doctor had in his drawers suits which Jackeymo pronounced to be as good as new, though many a long year had passed since they left the tailor's hands. But when Jackeymo came to examine the state of his own clothing department, his face grew considerably longer. It was not that he was without other clothes than those on his back — quantity was there, but the quality! Mournfully he gazed on two suits, complete in the three separate members of which man's raiments are composed: the one suit extended at length upon his bed, like a veteran stretched by pious hands after death; the other brought piecemeal to the invidious light — the *torso* placed upon a chair, the limbs dangling down from Jackeymo's melancholy arm. No bodies long exposed at the Morgue could evince less sign of resuscitation than those respectable defuncts! For, indeed, Jackeymo had been less thrifty of his apparel — more *profusus sui* — than his master. In the earliest days of their exile, he preserved the decorous habit of dressing for dinner — it was a respect due to the Padrone — and that habit had lasted till the two habits on which it necessarily depended had evinced the first symptoms of decay; then the evening clothes had been taken into morning wear, in which hard service they had breathed their last.

The Doctor, notwithstanding his general philosophical abstraction from such household details, had more than once said, rather in pity to Jackeymo than with an eye to that respectability which the costume of the servant reflects on the dignity of the master, "Giacomo, thou wantest clothes; fit thyself out of mine!"

And Jackeymo had bowed his gratitude, as if the donation had been accepted; but the fact was, that that same fitting-out was easier said than done. For though — thanks to an existence mainly upon stickle backs and minnows — both Jackeymo and Riccabocca had arrived at that state which the longevity of misers proves to be most healthful to the human frame — viz.: skin and bone — yet the bones contained in the skin of Riccabocca all took longitudinal directions; while those in the skin of Jackeymo spread out latitudinally. And you might as well have made the bark of a Lombardy poplar serve for the trunk of some dwarfed and pollarded oak — in whose hollow the Babes of the Wood could have slept at their ease — as have fitted out Jackeymo from the garb of Riccabocca. Moreover, if the skill of the tailor could have accomplished that undertaking, the faithful Jackeymo would never have had the heart to avail himself of the generosity of his master. He had a sort of religious sentiment, too, about those vestments of the Padrone. The ancients, we know, when escaping from shipwreck, suspended in the votive temple the garments in which they had struggled through the wave. Jackeymo looked on those relics of the past with a kindred superstition. "This coat the Padrone wore on such an occasion. I remember the very evening the Padrone last put on those pantaloons!" And coat and pantaloons were tenderly dusted, and carefully restored to their sacred rest.

But now, after all, what was to be done? Jackeymo was much too proud to exhibit his person to the eyes of the Squire's butler, in habiliments discreditable to himself and the Padrone. In the midst of his perplexity the bell rang, and he went down into the parlor.

Riccabocca was standing on the hearth, under his symbolical representation of the "Patriæ Exul."

"Giacomo," quoth he, "I have been thinking that thou hast never done what I told thee, and fitted thyself out from my superfluities. But we are going now into the great world: visiting once begun, Heaven knows where it may stop! Go to the nearest town, and get thyself clothes. Things are dear in England. Will this suffice?" And Riccabocca extended a £5 note.

Jackeymo, we have seen, was more familiar with his master than we formal English permit our domestics to be with us. But in his familiarity he was usually respectful. This time, however, respect deserted him.

"The Padrone is mad!" he exclaimed; "he would fling away his whole fortune if I would let him. Five pounds English, or a hundred and twenty-six pounds Milanese! * Santa Maria! Unnatural father! And what is to become of the poor Signorina? Is this the way you are to marry her in the foreign land?"

"Giacomo," said Riccabocca, bowing his head to the storm; "the Signorina to-morrow; to-day the honor of the house. Thy small-clothes, Giacomo. Miserable man, thy small-clothes!"

"It is just," said Jackeymo, recovering himself, and with humility; "and the Padrone does right to blame

---

* By the pounds Milanese, Giacomo means the Milanese lira.

me, but not in so cruel a way. It is just — the Padrone lodges and boards me, and gives me handsome wages, and he has a right to expect that I should not go in this figure."

"For the board and the lodgment, good," said Riccabocca. "For the handsome wages, they are the visions of thy fancy!"

"They are no such things," said Jackeymo, "they are only in arrear. As if the Padrone could not pay them some day or other — as if I was demeaning myself by serving a master who did not intend to pay his servants! And can't I wait? Have I not my savings too? But be cheered, be cheered; you shall be contented with me. I have two beautiful suits still. I was arranging them when you rang for me. You shall see, you shall see."

And Jackeymo hurried from the room, hurried back into his own chamber, unlocked a little trunk which he kept at his bed head, tossed out a variety of small articles, and from the deepest depth extracted a leather purse. He emptied the contents on the bed. They were chiefly Italian coins, some five-franc pieces, a silver medallion, enclosing a little image of his patron saint — San Giacomo — one solid English guinea, and somewhat more than a pound's worth in English silver. Jackeymo put back the foreign coins, saying, prudently, "One will lose on them here:" he seized the English coins, and counted them out. "But are you enough, you rascals!" quoth he, angrily, giving them a good shake. His eye caught sight of the medallion — he paused; and after eyeing the tiny representation of the saint with great deliberation, he added, in a sentence which he must have picked up from the proverbial aphorisms of his master —

"What's the difference between the enemy who does not hurt me, and the friend who does not serve me? *Monsignore San Giacomo*, my patron saint, you are of very little use to me in the leather bag. But if you help me to get into a new pair of small-clothes on this important occasion, you will be a friend indeed. *Alla bisogna, Monsignore.*" Then, gravely kissing the medallion, he thrust it into one pocket, the coins into the other, made up a bundle of the two defunct suits, and muttering to himself, "Beast, miser, that I am, to disgrace the Padrone, with all these savings in his service!" ran downstairs into his pantry, caught up his hat and stick, and in a few moments more was seen trudging off to the neighboring town of L——.

Apparently the poor Italian succeeded, for he came back that evening in time to prepare the thin gruel which made his master's supper, with a suit of black — a little threadbare, but still highly respectable — two shirt fronts, and two white cravats. But, out of all this finery, Jackeymo held the small-clothes in especial veneration; for, as they had cost exactly what the medallion had sold for, so it seemed to him that San Giacomo had heard his prayer in that quarter to which he had more exclusively directed the saint's attention. The other habiliments came to him in the merely human process of sale and barter; the small-clothes were the personal gratuity of San Giacomo!

CHAPTER VIII.

LIFE has been subjected to many ingenious comparisons; and if we do not understand it any better, it is not for want of what is called "reasoning by illustration." Amongst other resemblances, there are moments when, to a quiet contemplator, it suggests the image of one of those rotatory entertainments commonly seen in fairs, and known by the name of "whirligigs or roundabouts," in which each participator of the pastime, seated on his hobby, is always apparently in the act of pursuing some one before him, while he is pursued by some one behind. Man, and woman too, are naturally animals of chase; the greatest still find something to follow, and there is no one too humble not to be an object of prey to another. Thus, confining our view to the village of Hazeldean, we behold in this whirligig Dr. Riccabocca spurring his hobby after Lenny Fairfield; and Miss Jemima, on her decorous side-saddle, whipping after Dr. Riccabocca. Why, with so long and intimate a conviction of the villany of our sex, Miss Jemima should resolve upon giving the male animal one more chance of redeeming itself in her eyes, I leave to the explanation of those gentlemen who profess to find "their only books in woman's looks." Perhaps it might be from the over-tenderness and clemency of Miss

Jemima's nature; perhaps it might be that, as yet, she had only experienced the villany of man born and reared in these cold northern climates; and in the land of Petrarch and Romeo, of the citron and myrtle, there was reason to expect that the native monster would be more amenable to gentle influences, less obstinately hardened in his iniquities. Without entering further into these hypotheses, it is sufficient to say, that, on Signor Riccabocca's appearance in the drawing-room at Hazeldean, Miss Jemima felt more than ever rejoiced that she had relaxed in his favor her general hostility to men. In truth, though Frank saw something quizzical in the old-fashioned and outlandish cut of the Italian's sober dress; in his long hair, and the *chapeau bras*, over which he bowed so gracefully, and then pressed it, as if to his heart, before tucking it under his arm, after the fashion in which the gizzard reposes under the wing of a roasted pullet; yet it was impossible that even Frank could deny to Riccabocca that praise which is due to the air and manner of an unmistakable gentleman. And certainly as, after dinner, conversation grew more familiar, aud the Parson and Mrs. Dale, who had been invited to meet their friend, did their best to draw him out, his talk, though sometimes a little too wise for his listeners, became eminently animated and agreeable. It was the conversation of a man who, besides the knowledge which is acquired from books and life, had studied the art which becomes a gentleman—that of pleasing in polite society.

The result was, that all were charmed with him; and

that even Captain Barnabas postponed the whist-table for a full hour after the usual time. The Doctor did not play — he thus became the property of the two ladies, Miss Jemima and Mrs. Dale.

Seated between the two, in the place rightfully appertaining to Flimsey, who this time was fairly dislodged, to her great wonder and discontent, the Doctor was the emblem of true Domestic Felicity, placed between Friendship and Love.

Friendship, as became her, worked quietly at the embroidered pocket-handkerchief, and left Love to more animated operations. "You must be very lonely at the Casino," said Love, in a sympathising tone.

"Madam," replied Riccabocca, gallantly, "I shall think so when I leave you."

Friendship cast a sly glance at Love — Love blushed or looked down on the carpet, — which comes to the same thing. "Yet," began Love again — "yet solitude to a feeling heart——"

Riccabocca thought of the note of invitation, and involuntarily buttoned his coat, as if to protect the individual organ thus alarmingly referred to.

"Solitude, to a feeling heart, has its charms. It is so hard even for us poor ignorant women to find a congenial companion — but for *you!*" Love stopped short, as if it had said too much, and smelt confusedly at its bouquet.

Dr. Riccabocca cautiously lowered his spectacles, and darted one glance, which, with the rapidity and comprehensiveness of lightning, seemed to envelop and take in, as it were, the whole inventory of Miss Jemima's personal attractions. Now, Miss Jemima, as I have before observed, had a mild and pensive expression of countenance, and she would have been positively pretty had the mildness looked a little more alert, and the pensiveness somewhat less lackadaisical. In fact, though Miss Jemima was constitutionally mild, she was not *de naturâ* pensive; she had too much of the Hazeldean blood in her veins for that sullen and viscid humor called melancholy, and therefore this assumption of pensiveness really spoiled her character of features, which only wanted to be lighted up by a cheerful smile to be extremely prepossessing. The same remark might apply to the figure, which — thanks to the same pensiveness — lost all the undulating grace which movement and animation bestow on the fluent curves of the feminine form. The figure was a good figure, examined in detail — a little thin, perhaps, but by no means emaciated — with just and elegant proportions, and naturally light and flexible. But that same unfortunate pensiveness gave to the whole a character of inertness and languor; and when Miss Jemima reclined on the sofa, so complete seemed the relaxation of nerve and muscle that you would have thought she had lost the use of her limbs. Over her face and form, thus defrauded of the charms Providence had bestowed on them, Dr. Riccabocca's eye glanced rapidly; and then moving nearer to Mrs. Dale — "Defend me" (he stopped a moment, and added) — "from the charge of not being able to appreciate congenial companionship."

"Oh, I did not say that!" cried Miss Jemima.

"Pardon me," said the Italian, "if I am so dull as to misunderstand you. One may well lose one's head, at least, in such a neighborhood as this." He rose as he spoke, and bent over Frank's shoulder to examine some Views of Italy, which Miss Jemima (with what, if wholly unselfish, would have been an attention truly delicate) had extracted from the library in order to gratify the guest.

"Most interesting creature, indeed," sighed Miss Jemima, "but too — too flattering."

"Tell me," said Mrs. Dale gravely, "do you think, love, that you could put off the end of the world a little longer, or must we make haste in order to be in time?"

"How wicked you are!" said Miss Jemima, turning aside.

Some few minutes afterwards, Mrs. Dale contrived it so that Dr. Riccabocca and herself were in a further corner of the room, looking at a picture said to be by Wouvermans.

MRS. DALE.—She is very amiable, Jemima, is she not?

RICCABOCCA.—Exceedingly so. Very fine battle-piece!

MRS. DALE. — So kind-hearted.

RICCABOCCA. — All ladies are. How naturally that warrior makes his desperate cut at the runaway!

MRS. DALE.— She is not what is called regularly handsome, but she has something very winning.

RICCABOCCA (with a smile). — So winning, that it is strange she is not won. That grey mare in the foreground stands out very boldly!

Mrs. Dale (distrusting the smile of Riccabocca, and throwing in a more effective grape charge). — Not won yet; and it *is* strange! she will have a very pretty fortune.

Riccabocca. — Ah!

Mrs. Dale. — Six thousand pounds, I dare say — certainly four.

Riccabocca (suppressing a sigh, and with his wonted address). — If Mrs. Dale were still single, she would never need a friend to say what her portion might be; but Miss Jemima is so good that I am quite sure it is not Miss Jemima's fault that she is still — Miss Jemima!

The foreigner slipped away as he spoke, and sate himself down beside the whist-players.

Mrs. Dale was disappointed, but certainly not offended. — "It would be such a good thing for both," muttered she, almost audibly.

"Giacomo," said Riccabocca, as he was undressing that night in the large, comfortable, well-carpeted English bedroom, with that great English four-posted bed in the recess which seems made to shame folks out of single-blessedness — "Giacomo, I have had this evening the offer of probably six thousand pounds — certainly of four thousand."

"*Cosa meravigliosa!*" exclaimed Jackeymo—"miraculous thing!" and he crossed himself with great fervor. "Six thousand pounds English! why, that must be a hundred thousand — blockhead that I am! — more than a hundred and fifty thousand pounds Milanese!" And Jackeymo, who was considerably enlivened by the Squire's ale, commenced a series of gesticulations and capers, in the midst of which he stopped and cried, "But not for nothing?"

"Nothing! no."

"These mercenary English!—the Government wants to bribe you."

"That's not it."

"The priests want you to turn heretic."

"Worse than that," said the philosopher.

"Worse than that! O Padrone! for shame!"

"Don't be a fool, but pull off my pantaloons—they want me never to wear *these* again!"

"Never to wear what?" exclaimed Jackeymo, staring outright at his master's long legs in their linen drawers—"never to wear——"

"The breeches," said Riccabocca laconically.

"The barbarians!" faltered Jackeymo.

"My nightcap!—and never to have any comfort in this," said Riccabocca, drawing on the cotton head-gear; "and never to have any sound sleep in that," pointing to the four-posted bed. "And to be a bondsman and a slave," continued Riccabocca, waxing wroth; "and to be wheedled and purred at, and pawed, and clawed, and scolded, and fondled, and blinded, and deafened, and bridled, and saddled—bedevilled and—married!"

"Married!" said Jackeymo, more dispassionately—"that's very bad, certainly; but more than a hundred and fifty thousand *lire*, and perhaps a pretty young lady, and——"

"Pretty young lady!" growled Riccabocca, jumping into bed and drawing the clothes fiercely over him. "Put out the candle, and get along with you—do, you villanous old incendiary!"

CHAPTER IX.

It was not many days since the resurrection of those ill-omened stocks, and it was evident already, to an ordinary observer, that something wrong had got into the village. The peasants wore a sullen expression of countenance; when the Squire passed, they took off their hats with more than ordinary formality, but they did not return the same broad smile to his quick, hearty "Good day, my man." The women peered at him from the threshold of the casement, but did not, as was their wont (at least the wont of the prettiest), take occasion to come out to catch his passing compliment on their own good looks, or their tidy cottages. And the children, who used to play after work on the side of the old stocks, now shunned the place, and, indeed, seemed to cease play altogether.

On the other hand, no man likes to build, or rebuild, a great public work for nothing. Now that the Squire had resuscitated the stocks, and made them so exceedingly handsome, it was natural that he should wish to put somebody into them. Moreover, his pride and self-esteem had been wounded by the Parson's opposition; and it would be a justification to his own forethought, and a triumph over the Parson's understanding, if he could satisfactorily and practically establish a proof that the stocks had not been repaired before they were wanted.

Therefore, unconsciously to himself, there was something about the Squire more burly, and authoritative, and menacing than heretofore. Old Gaffer Solomons observed, that "they had better moind well what they were about, for that the Squire had a wicked look in the tail of his eye — just as the dun bull had afore it tossed neighbor Barnes's little boy."

For two or three days these mute signs of something brewing in the atmosphere had been rather noticeable than noticed, without any positive overt act of tyranny on the one hand, or rebellion on the other. But on the very Saturday night in which Dr. Riccabocca was installed in the four-posted bed in the chintz chamber, the threatened revolution commenced. In the dead of that night, personal outrage was committed on the stocks. And on the Sunday morning, Mr. Stirn, who was the earliest riser in the parish, perceived, in going to the farm-yard, that the knob of the column that flanked the board had been feloniously broken off; that the four holes were bunged up with mud; and that some jacobinical villain had carved on the very centre of the flourish or scroll-work, "Dam the stoks!" Mr. Stirn was much too vigilant a right-hand man, much too zealous a friend of law and order, not to regard such proceedings with horror and alarm. And when the Squire came into his dressing-room at half-past seven, his butler (who fulfilled also the duties of valet) informed him, with a mysterious air, that Mr. Stirn had something "very partikler to communicate, about a most howdacious midnight 'spiracy and 'sault."

The Squire stared, and bade Mr. Stirn be admitted.

"Well?" cried the Squire, suspending the operation of stropping his razor.

Mr. Stirn groaned.

"Well, man, what now?"

"I never knowed such a thing in this here parish 'afore," began Mr. Stirn, "and I can only 'count for it by s'posing that them foreign Papishers have been semminating ——"

"Been what?"

"Semminating ——"

"Disseminating, you blockhead—disseminating what?"

"Damn the stocks," began Mr. Stirn, plunging right *in medias res,* and by a fine use of one of the noblest figures in rhetoric.

"Mr. Stirn!" cried the Squire, reddening, "did you say, 'Damn the stocks?'—damn my new handsome pair of stocks!"

"Lord forbid, sir; that's what *they* say: that's what they have digged on it with knives and daggers, and they have stuffed mud in its four holes, and broken the capital of the elewation."

The Squire took the napkin off his shoulder, laid down strop and razor: he seated himself in his arm-chair majestically, crossed his legs, and, in a voice that affected tranquillity, said —

"Compose yourself, Stirn; you have a deposition to make, touching an assault upon — can I trust my senses? — upon my new stocks. Compose yourself — be calm. NOW! What the devil is come to the parish?"

"Ah, sir, what indeed?" replied Mr. Stirn: and then laying the fore-finger of the right hand on the palm of the left, he narrated the case.

"And whom do you suspect? Be calm now; don't speak in a passion.' You are a witness, sir — a dispassionate, unprejudiced witness. Zounds and fury! this is the most insolent, unprovoked, diabolical — but whom do you suspect, I say?"

Stirn twirled his hat, elevated his eyebrows, jerked his thumb over his shoulder, and whispered — "I hear as how the two Papishers slept at your honor's last night."

"What, dolt! do you suppose Dr. Rickeybockey got out of his warm bed to bung up the holes in my new stocks?"

"Noa; he's too cunning to do it himself, but he may have been semminating. He's mighty thick with Parson Dale, and your honor knows as how the Parson set his face ag'in the stocks. Wait a bit, sir — don't fly at me yet. There be a boy in this here parish ——"

"A boy — ah, fool, now you are nearer the mark. The Parson write 'Damn the stocks,' indeed! What boy do you mean?"

"And that boy be cockered up much by Mr. Dale; and

the Papisher went and sat with him and his mother a whole hour t'other day; and that boy is as deep as a well; and I seed him lurking about the place, and hiding hisself under the tree the day the stocks was put up — and that 'ere boy is Lenny Fairfield."

"Whew," said the Squire, whistling, "you have not your usual senses about you to-day, man. Lenny Fairfield — pattern boy of the village. Hold your tongue. I dare say it is not done by any one in the parish, after all: some good-for-nothing vagrant — that cursed tinker, who goes about with a very vicious donkey — donkey that I caught picking thistles out of the very eyes of the old stocks! Shows how the tinker brings up his donkeys! Well, keep a sharp look-out. To-day is Sunday; worst day of the week, I'm sorry and ashamed to say, for rows and depredations. Between the services, and after evening church, there are always idle fellows from all the neighboring country about, as you know too well. Depend on it, the real culprits will be found gathering round the stocks, and will betray themselves; have your eyes, ears, and wits about you, and I've no doubt we shall come to the rights of the matter before the day's out. And if we do," added the Squire, "we'll make an example of the ruffian!"

"In course," said Stirn; "and if we don't find him, we must make an example all the same. That's what it is, sir. That's why the stocks ben't respected; they has not had an example yet — we wants an example.

"On my word, I believe that's very true; and we'll

clap in the first idle fellow you catch in anything wrong, and keep him there for two hours at least."

"With the biggest pleasure, your honor — that's what it is."

And Mr. Stirn, having now got what he considered a complete and unconditional authority over all the legs and wrists of Hazeldean parish, *quoad* the stocks, took his departure.

CHAPTER X.

"RANDAL," said Mrs. Leslie, on this memorable Sunday — "Randal, do you think of going to Mr. Hazeldean's?"

"Yes, ma'am," answered Randal. "Mr. Egerton does not object to it; and as I do not return to Eton, I may have no other opportunity of seeing Frank for some time. I ought not to fail in respect to Mr. Egerton's natural heir."

"Gracious me!" cried Mrs. Leslie, who, like many women of her cast and kind, had a sort of worldliness in her notions, which she never evinced in her conduct — "gracious me!—natural heir to the old Leslie property!"

"He is Mr. Egerton's nephew, and," added Randal, ingenuously letting out his thoughts, "I am no relation to Mr. Egerton at all."

"But," said poor Mrs. Leslie, with tears in her eyes, "it would be a shame in the man, after paying your schooling ana sending you to Oxford, and having you to stay with him in the holidays, if he did not mean anything by it."

"Anything, mother—yes—but not the thing you suppose. No matter. It is enough that he has armed me for life, and I shall use the weapons as seems to me best."

Here the dialogue was suspended by the entrance of the other members of the family, dressed for church.

"It can't be time for church! No! it can't!" exclaimed Mrs. Leslie. She was never in time for anything.

"Last bell ringing," said Mr. Leslie, who, though a slow man, was methodical and punctual. Mrs. Leslie made a frantic rush at the door, the Montfydget blood being now in a blaze—dashed up the stairs—burst into her room, tore her best bonnet from the peg, snatched her newest shawl from the drawers, crushed the bonnet on her head, flung the shawl on her shoulders, thrust a desperate pin into its folds, in order to conceal a buttonless yawn in the body of her gown, and then flew back like a whirlwind. Meanwhile the family were already out of doors, in waiting; and just as the bell ceased, the procession moved from the shabby house to the dilapidated church.

The church was a large one, but the congregation was small, and so was the income of the Parson. It was a lay rectory, and the great tithes had belonged to the Leslies, but they had been long since sold. The vicarage, still in their gift, might be worth a little more than £100 a year. The present incumbent had nothing else to live upon. He was a good man, and not originally a stupid one; but penury and the anxious cares for wife and family, combined with what may be called *solitary confinement* for the cultivated mind, when, amidst the two-legged creatures round, it sees no other cultivated mind with which it can exchange one extra-parochial thought—had lulled him into a lazy mournfulness, which at times was very like imbecility. His income allowed him to do no good to the parish, whether in work, trade, or charity; and thus he had no moral weight with the parishioners beyond the example of his sinless life, and such negative effect as might be produced by his slumberous exhortations. Therefore his parishioners troubled him very little; and but for the influence which, in hours of Montfydget activity, Mrs. Leslie exercised over the most tractable—that is, the children and the aged—not half a dozen persons would have known or cared whether he shut up his church or not.

But our family were seated in state in their old seignorial pew, and Mr. Dumdrum, with a nasal twang, went lugubriously through the prayers; and the old people who could sin no more, and the children who had not yet learned to sin, croaked forth responses that might have come from the choral frogs in Aristophanes. And there was a long sermon *à propos* to nothing which could possibly interest the congregation—being, in fact, some controversial homily, which Mr. Dumdrum had composed and preached years before. And when this discourse was over, there was a loud universal grunt, as if of relief and thanksgiving, and a great clatter of shoes — and the old hobbled, and the young scrambled, to the church door.

Immediately after church, the Leslie family dined; and, as soon as dinner was over, Randal set out on his foot journey to Hazeldean Hall.

Delicate and even feeble though his frame, he had the energy and quickness of movement which belongs to nervous temperaments; and he tasked the slow stride of a peasant, whom he took to serve him as a guide for the first two or three miles. Though Randal had not the gracious, open manner with the poor which Frank inherited from his father, he was still (despite many a secret hypocritical vice at war with the character of a gentleman) gentleman enough to have no churlish pride to his inferiors. He talked little, but he suffered his guide to talk; and the boor, who was the same whom Frank had accosted, indulged in eulogistic comments on that young gentleman's pony, from which he diverged into some compliments on the young gentleman himself. Randal drew his hat over his brows. There is a wonderful tact and fine breeding in your agricultural peasant; and though Tom Stowell was but a brutish specimen of the class, he suddenly perceived that he was giving pain. He paused, scratched his head, and glancing affectionately towards his companion, exclaimed —

"But I shall live to see you on a handsomer beastis than that little pony, Master Randal; and sure I ought, for you be as good a gentleman as any in the land."

"Thank you," said Randal. "But I like walking better than riding — I am more used to it."

"Well, and you walk bra'ly — there ben't a better walker in the country. And very pleasant it is walking; and 'tis a pretty country afore you, all the way to the Hall."

Randal strode on, as if impatient of these attempts to flatter or to soothe; and, coming at length into a broader land, said — "I think I can find my way now. Many thanks to you, Tom:" and he forced a shilling into Tom's horny palm. The man took it reluctantly, and a tear started to his eye. He felt more grateful for that shilling than he had for Frank's liberal half-crown; and he thought of the poor fallen family, and forgot his own dire wrestle with the wolf at his door.

He stayed lingering in the lane till the figure of Randal was out of sight, and then returned slowly Young Leslie continued to walk on at a quick pace. With all his intellectual culture, and his restless aspirations, his breast afforded him no thought so generous, no sentiment so poetic, as those with which the unlettered clown crept slouchingly homeward.

As Randal gained a point where several lanes met on a broad piece of waste land, he began to feel tired, and his step slackened. Just then a gig emerged from one of these by-roads, and took the same direction as the pedestrian. The road was rough and hilly, and the driver proceeded at a foot's pace; so that the gig and the pedestrian went pretty well abreast.

"You seem tired, sir," said the driver, a stout young farmer of the higher class of tenants — and he looked down compassionately on the boy's pale countenance and weary stride, — "Perhaps we are going the same way, and I can gift you a lift?"

It was Randal's habitual policy to make use of every advantage proffered to him, and he accepted the proposal frankly enough to please the honest farmer.

"A nice day, sir," said the latter, as Randal sat by his side. "Have you come far?"

"From Rood Hall."

"Oh, you be young Squire Leslie," said the farmer, more respectfully, and lifting his hat.

"Yes, my name is Leslie. You know Rood, then?"

"I was brought up on your father's land, sir. You may have heard of Farmer Bruce?"

Randal. — I remember, when I was a little boy, a Mr. Bruce who rented, I believe, the best part of our land, and who used to bring us cakes when he called to see my father. He is a relation of yours?"

Farmer Bruce. — He was my uncle. He is dead now, poor man.

Randal. — Dead! I am grieved to hear it. He was very kind to us children. But it is long since he left my father's farm.

Farmer Bruce. (apologetically). — I am sure he was very sorry to go. But, you see, he had an unexpected legacy ——

Randal. — And retired from business?

Farmer Bruce. — No. But, having capital, he could afford to pay a good rent for a real good farm.

RANDAL (bitterly). — All capital seems to fly from the lands of Rood. And whose farm did he take?

FARMER BRUCE. — He took Hawleigh, under Squire Hazeldean. I rent it now. We've laid out a power o' money on it. But I don't complain. It pays well.

RANDAL. — Would the money have paid as well, sunk on my father's land?

FARMER BRUCE. — Perhaps it might, in the long run. But then, sir, we wanted new premises — barns and cattle-sheds, and a deal more — which the landlord should do; but it is not every landlord as can afford that. Squire Hazeldean's a rich man.

RANDAL. — Ay!

The road now became pretty good, and the farmer put his horse into a brisk trot.

"But which way be you going, sir? I don't care for a few miles more or less, if I can be of service."

"I am going to Hazeldean," said Randal, rousing himself from a reverie. "Don't let me take you out of your way."

"Oh, Hawleigh Farm is on the other side of the village, so it be quite my way sir."

The farmer, then, who was really a smart young fellow — one of that race which the application of capital to land has produced, and which, in point of education and refinement, are at least on a par with the sqnires of a former generation — began to talk about his handsome horse, about horses in general, about hunting and coursing: he handled all these subjects with spirit, yet with modesty. Randal pulled his hat still lower down over his brows, and did not interrupt him till they passed the casino, when, struck by the classic air of the place, and catching a scent from the orange-trees, the boy asked abruptly — "Whose house is that?"

"Oh, it belongs to Squire Hazeldean, but it is let or lent to a foreign Mounseer. They say he is quite the gentleman, but uncommonly poor."

"Poor," said Randal, turning back to gaze on the trim garden, the neat terrace, the pretty belvidere, and (the door of the house being open) catching a glimpse of the painted hall within — "poor? the place seems well kept. What do you call poor, Mr. Bruce?"

The farmer laughed. "Well, that's a home question, sir. But I believe the Mounseer is as poor as a man can be who makes no debts and does not actually starve."

"As poor as my father?" asked Randal, openly and abruptly.

"Lord, sir! your father be a very rich man compared to him."

Randal continued to gaze, and his mind's eye conjured up the contrast of his slovenly shabby home, with all its neglected appurtenances! No trim garden at Rood Hall, no scent from odorous orange-blossoms. Here poverty at least was elegant — there, how squalid! He did not comprehend at how cheap a rate the luxury of the Beautiful can be effected. They now approached the extremity of the Squire's park pales; and Randal, seeing a little gate, bade the farmer stop his gig, and descended.

The boy plunged amidst the thick oak-groves; the farmer went his way blithely, and his mellow merry whistle came to Randal's moody ear as he glided quick under the shadow of the trees.

He arrived at the Hall, to find that all the family were at church; and, according to the patriarchal custom, the church-going family embraced nearly all the servants. It was therefore an old invalid housemaid who opened the door to him. She was rather deaf, and seemed so stupid that Randal did not ask leave to enter and wait for Frank's return. He therefore said briefly that he would just stroll on the lawn, and call again when church was over.

The old woman stared, and strove to hear him; meanwhile Randal turned round abruptly, and sauntered towards the garden side of the handsome old house.

There was enough to attract any eye in the smooth greensward of the spacious lawn — in the numerous parterres of variegated flowers — in the venerable grandeur of the two mighty cedars, which threw their still shadows over the grass — and in the picturesque building, with its projecting mullions and heavy gables; yet I fear that it was with no poet's nor painter's eye that this young old man gazed on the scene before him.

He beheld the evidence of wealth — and the envy of wealth jaundiced his soul.

Folding his arms on his breast, he stood awhile, looking all around him, with closed lips and lowering brow; then he walked slowly on, his eyes fixed on the ground, and muttered to himself —

"The heir to this property is little better than a dunce; and they tell me I have talents and learning, and I have taken to my heart the maxim, 'Knowledge is power.' And yet, with all my struggles, will knowledge ever place me on the same level as that on which this dunce is born? I don't wonder that the poor should hate the rich. But of all the poor, who should hate the rich like the pauper gentleman? I suppose Audley Egerton means me to come into Parliament, and be a Tory like himself! What! keep things as they are! No; for me not even Democracy, unless there first come Revolution. I understand the cry of a Marat—'More blood!' Marat had lived as a poor man, and cultivated science—in the sight of a prince's palace."

He turned sharply round, and glared vindictively on the poor old Hall, which, though a very comfortable habitation, was certainly no palace; and, with his arm still folded on his breast, he walked backward, as if not to lose the view, nor the chain of ideas it conjured up.

"But," he continued to soliloquise—"but of revolution there is no chance. Yet the same wit and will that would thrive in revolutions should thrive in this commonplace life. Knowledge is power. Well, then, shall I have no power to oust this blockhead? Oust him—what from? His father's halls? Well, but if he were dead, who would be the heir of Hazeldean? Have I not heard my mother say that I am as near in blood to this Squire as any one, if he had no children? Oh, but the boy's life is worth ten of mine! Oust him from what?

At least from the thoughts of his Uncle Egerton — an uncle who has never even seen him! That, at least, is more feasible. 'Make my way in life,' sayest thou, Audley Egerton. Ay — and to the fortune thou hast robbed from my ancestors. Simulation — simulation. Lord Bacon allows simulation. Lord Bacon practised it — and ——"

Here the soliloquy came to a sudden end; for as, rapt in his thoughts, the boy had continued to walk backwards, he had come to the verge, where the lawn slided off into the ditch of the ha-ha; and, just as he was fortifying himself by the precept and practice of my Lord Bacon, the ground went from under him, and — slap into the ditch went Randal Leslie!

It so happened that the Squire, whose active genius was always at some repair or improvement, had been but a few days before widening and sloping off the ditch just in that part, so that the earth was fresh and damp, and not yet either turfed or flattened down. Thus when Randal, recovering his first surprise and shock, rose to his feet, he found his clothes covered with mud; while the rudeness of the fall was evinced by the fantastic and extraordinary appearance of his hat, which, hollowed here, bulging there, and crushed out of all recognition generally, was as little like the hat of a decorous, hard-reading young gentleman — *protégé* of the dignified Mr. Audley Egerton — as any hat picked out of a kennel after some drunken brawl possibly could be.

Randal was dizzy, and stunned, and bruised, and it was some moments before he took heed of his raiment.

When he did so, his spleen was greatly aggravated. He was still boy enough not to like the idea of presenting himself to the unknown Squire, and the dandy Frank, in such a trim: he resolved incontinently to regain the lane and turn home, without accomplishing the object of his journey; and seeing the footpath right before him, which led to a gate that he conceived would admit him into the highway sooner than the path by which he had come, he took it at once.

It is surprising how little we human creatures heed the warnings of our good genius. I have no doubt that some benignant power had precipitated Randal Leslie into the ditch, as a significant hint of the fate of all who choose what is, now-a-days, by no means an uncommon step in the march of intellect — viz., the walking backwards, in order to gratify a vindictive view of one's neighbor's property! I suspect that, before this century is out, many a fine fellow will thus have found his ha-ha, and scrambled out of the ditch with a much shabbier coat than he had on when he fell into it. But Randal did not thank his good genius for giving him a premonitory tumble; — and I never yet knew a man who did!

CHAPTER XI.

The Squire was greatly ruffled at breakfast that morning. He was too much of an Englishman to bear insult patiently, and he considered that he had been personally insulted in the outrage offered to his recent donation to the parish. His feelings, too, were hurt as well as his pride. There was something so ungrateful in the whole thing, just after he had taken so much pains, not only in the resuscitation, but the embellishment of the stocks. It was not, however, so rare an occurrence for the Squire to be ruffled, as to create any remark. Riccabocca, indeed, as a stranger, and Mrs. Hazeldean, as a wife, had the quick tact to perceive that the host was glum and the husband snappish; but the one was too discreet, and the other too sensible, to chafe the new sore, whatever it might be; and shortly after breakfast the Squire retired into his study, and absented himself from morning service.

In his delightful *Life of Oliver Goldsmith*, Mr. Forster takes care to touch our hearts by introducing his hero's excuse for not entering the priesthood: "He did not feel himself good enough." Thy Vicar of Wakefield, poor Goldsmith, was an excellent substitute for thee; and Dr. Primrose at least will be good enough for the world until Miss Jemima's fears are realised. Now, Squire Hazeldean had a tenderness of conscience much less reasonable than Goldsmiths's. There were occasionally days in which he did not feel good enough — I don't say for a priest, but even for one of the congregation — "days in which," said the Squire in his own blunt way, "as I have never in my life met a worse devil than a devil of a temper, I'll not carry mine into the family pew. He shan't be growling out hypocritical responses from my poor grandmother's prayer-book." So the Squire and his demon stayed at home. But the demon was generally cast out before the day was over: and, on this occasion, when the bell rang for afternoon service, it may be presumed that the Squire had reasoned or fretted himself into a proper state of mind; for he was then seen sallying forth from the porch of his hall, arm-in-arm with his wife, and at the head of his household. The second service was (as is commonly the case in rural districts) more numerously attended than the first one; and it was our Parson's wont to devote to this service his most effective discourse.

Parson Dale, though a very fair scholar, had neither the deep theology nor the archæological learning that distinguishes the rising generation of the clergy. I must doubt if he could have passed what would now be called a creditable examination in the Fathers; and as for all the nice formalities in the Rubric, he would never have been the man to divide a congregation or puzzle a bishop. Neither was Parson Dale very erudite in ecclesiastical architecture: he did not much care whether all the details in the church were purely Gothic or not: crockets and finials, round arch and pointed arch, were matters I fear, on which he had never troubled his head. But one secret Parson Dale did possess, which is perhaps of equal importance with those subtler mysteries — he knew how to fill his church! Even at morning service no pews were empty, and at evening service the church overflowed.

Parson Dale, too, may be considered, now-a-days, to hold but a mean idea of the spiritual authority of the Church. He had never been known to dispute on its exact bearing with the State — whether it was incorporated with the State, or above the State — whether it was antecedent to the Papacy, or formed from the Papacy, &c. &c. According to his favorite maxim, *Quieta non movere* (not to disturb things that are quiet), I have no doubt that he would have thought that the less discussion is provoked upon such matters the better for both Church and laity. Nor had he ever been known to regret the disuse of the ancient custom of excommunication, nor any other diminution of the powers of the priesthood, whether minatory or militant; yet, for all this, Parson Dale had a great notion of the sacred privilege of a minister of the gospel — to advise — to deter—to persuade — to reprove. And it was for the evening service that he prepared those sermons, which may be called "sermons that preach *at* you." He preferred the evening for that salutary discipline, not only because the congregation was more numerous, but also because, being a shrewd man in his own innocent way, he knew that people bear better to be preached at after dinner than before; that you arrive more insinuatingly at the heart when the stomach is at peace. There was a genial kindness in Parson Dale's way of preaching at you. It was done in so imperceptible, fatherly a manner, that you never felt offended. He did it, too, with so much art that nobody but your own guilty self knew that you were the sinner he was exhorting. Yet he did not spare rich nor poor: he preached at the Squire, and that great fat farmer, Mr. Bullock, the churchwarden, as boldly as at Hodge the ploughman and Scrub the hedger. As for Mr. Stirn, he had preached at *him* more often than at any one in the parish; but Stirn, though he had the sense to know it, never had the grace to reform. There was, too, in Parson Dale's sermons something of that boldness of illustration which would have been scholarly if he had not made it familiar, and which is found in the discourses of our elder divines. Like them, he did not scruple, now and then, to introduce an anecdote from history, or borrow an allusion from some non-scriptural author, in order to enliven the attention of his audience, or render an argument more plain. And the good man had an object in this, a little distinct from, though wholly subordinate to, the main purpose of his discourse. He was a friend to knowledge — but to knowledge accompanied by religion; and sometimes his references to sources not within the ordinary reading of his congregation would spirit up some farmer's son, with an evening's leisure on his hands, to ask the Parson for farther explanation, and so to be lured on to a little solid or graceful instruction, under a safe guide.

Now, on the present occasion, the Parson, who had always his eye and heart on his flock, and who had seen with great grief the realisation of his fears at the revival of the stocks; seen that a spirit of discontent was already at work amongst the peasants, and that magisterial and inquisitorial designs were darkening the natural benevolence of the Squire; seen, in short, the signs of a breach between classes, and the precursors of the ever-inflammable feud between the rich and the poor, meditated nothing less than a great Political Sermon — a sermon that should extract from the roots of social truths a healing virtue for the wound that lay sore, but latent, in the breast of his parish of Hazeldean.

And thus ran —

THE POLITICAL SERMON OF PARSON DALE.

CHAPTER XII.

"For every man shall bear his own burden." — GAL. vi. 5.

"BRETHREN, every man has his burden. If God designed our lives to end at the grave, may we not believe that he would have freed an existence so brief from the cares and sorrows to which, since the beginning of the world, mankind has been subjected? Suppose that I am a kind father, and have a child whom I dearly love, but I know by a Divine revelation that he will die at the age of eight years, surely I should not vex his infancy by needless preparations for the duties of life. If I am a rich man, I should not send him from the caresses of his mother to the stern discipline of school. If I am a poor man, I should not take him with me to hedge and dig, to scorch in the sun, to freeze in the winter's cold: why inflict hardships on his childhood for the purpose of fitting him for manhood, when I know that he is doomed not to grow into man? Bnt if, on the other hand, I believe my child is reserved for a more durable existence, then should I not, out of the very love I bear to him, prepare his childhood for the struggle of life, according to that station in which he is born, giving many a toil, many a pain, to the infant, in order to rear and strengthen him for his duties as man? So it is with our Father that is in heaven. Viewing this life as our infancy, and the next as our spiritual maturity, where, 'in the ages to come, he may show the exceeding riches of his grace,' it is in his tenderness, as in his wisdom, to permit the toil and the pain which, in tasking the powers and developing the virtues of the soul, prepare it for 'the earnest of our inheritance.' Hence it is that every man has his burden. Brethren, if you believe that God is good, yea, but as tender as a human father, you will know that your troubles in life are a proof that you are reared for an eternity. But each man thinks his own burden the hardest to bear; the poor man groans under his poverty, the rich man under the cares that multiply with wealth. For, so far from wealth freeing us from trouble, all the wise men who have written in all ages have repeated, with one voice, the words of the wisest: 'When goods increase, they are increased that eat them; and what good is there to the owners thereof, saving the beholding them with their eyes?' And this is literally true, my brethren; for, let a man be as rich as was the great King Solomon himself, unless he lock up all his gold in a chest, it must go abroad to be divided amongst others; yea, though, like Solomon, he make him great works — though he build houses and plant vineyards, and make him gardens and orchards, still the gold that he spends feeds but the mouths he employs; and Solomon himself could not eat with a better relish than the poorest mason who builded the house, or the humblest laborer who planted the vineyard. Therefore, 'when goods increase, they are increased that eat them.' And this, my brethren, may teach us toleration and compassion for the rich. We share their riches, whether they will or not; we do not share their cares. The profane history of our own country tells us that a princess, destined to be the greatest queen that ever sat on this throne, envied the milk-maid singing; and a profane poet, whose wisdom was only less than that of the inspired writers, represents the man who by force and wit had risen to be a king, sighing for the sleep vouchsafed to the meanest of his subjects — all bearing out the words of the son of David: 'The sleep of the laboring man is sweet, whether he eat little or much; but the abundance of the rich will not suffer him to sleep.'

"Amongst my brethren now present, there is doubtless some one who has been poor, and by honest industry has made himself comparatively rich. Let his heart answer me while I speak: are not the chief cares that now disturb him to be found in the goods he hath acquired?—has he not both vexations to his spirit and trials to his virtue, which he knew not when he went forth to his labor, and took no heed of the morrow? But it is right, my brethren, that to every station there should be its care—to every man his burden; for if the poor did not sometimes so far feel poverty to be a burden as to desire to better their condition, and (to use the language of the world) 'seek to rise in life,' their most valuable energies would never be aroused; and we should not witness that spectacle, which is so common in the land we live in—namely, the successful struggle of manly labor against adverse fortune—a struggle in which the triumph of one gives hope to thousands. It is said that necessity is the mother of invention; and the social blessings which are now as common to us as air and sunshine, have come from that law of our nature which makes us aspire towards indefinite improvement, enriches each successive generation by the labors of the last, and in free countries often lifts the child of the laborer to a place amongst the rulers of the land. Nay, if necessity is the mother of invention, poverty is the creator of the arts. If there had been no poverty, and no sense of poverty, where would have been that which we call the wealth of a country? Subtract from civilisation all that has been produced by the poor, and what remains?—the state of the savage. Where you now see laborer and prince, you would see equality indeed—the equality of wild men. No; not even equality there! for there brute force becomes lordship — and woe to the weak! Where you now see some in frieze, some in purple, you would see nakedness in all. Where stand the palace and the cot, you would behold but mud huts and caves. As far as the peasant excels the king among savages, so far does the society exalted and enriched by the struggles of labor excel the state in which Poverty feels no disparity, and Toil sighs for no ease. On the other hand, if the rich were perfectly contented with their wealth, their hearts would become hardened in the sensual enjoyments it procures. It is that feeling, by Divine Wisdom implanted in the soul, that there is vanity and vexation of spirit in the things of Mammom, which still leaves the rich man sensitive to the instincts of heaven, and teaches him to seek for happiness in those beneficent virtues which distribute his wealth to the profit of others. If you could exclude the air from the rays of the fire, the fire itself would soon languish and die in the midst of its fuel; and so a man's joy in his wealth is kept alive by the air which it warms; and if pent within itself — is extinguished.

"And this, my brethren, leads me to another view of the vast subject opened to us by the words of the apostle —'Every man shall bear his own burden.' The worldly conditions of life are unequal. Why are they unequal? O my brethren, do you not perceive? Think you that, if it had been better for our spiritual probation that there should be neither great nor lowly, rich nor poor, Providence would not so have ordered the dispensations of the world, and so, by its mysterious but merciful agencies, have influenced the framework and foundations of society? But if from the remotest period of human annals, and in all the numberless experiments of government which the wit of man has devised, still this inequality is ever found to exist, may we not suspect that there is something in the very principles of our nature to which that inequality is necessary and essential? Ask why this inequality? Why? — as well ask why life is the sphere of duty and the nursery of virtues! For if all men were equal, if there were no suffering and no ease, no poverty and no wealth, would you not sweep with one blow the half, at least, of human virtues from the world? If there were no penury and no pain, what would become of fortitude? — what of patience? — what of resignation? If there were no greatness and no wealth, what would become of benevolence, of charity, of the blessed human pity, of temperance in the midst of luxury, of justice in the exercise of power? Carry the question further; grant all conditions the same — no reverse, no rise, and no fall — nothing to hope for, nothing to fear—what a moral death you would at once inflict upon all the energies of the soul, and what a link between the Heart of man and the Providence of God would be snapped asunder! If we could annihilate evil, we should annihilate hope; and hope, my brethren, is the avenue to faith. If there be 'a time to weep and a time to laugh,' it is that he who mourns may turn to eternity for comfort, and he who rejoices may bless God for the happy hour. Ah! my brethren, were it possible to annihilate the inequalities of human life, it would be the banishment of our worthiest virtues, the torpor of our spiritual nature, the palsy of our mental faculties. The moral world, like the world without us, derives its health and its beauty from diversity and contrast.

"'Every man shall bear his own burden.' True; but now turn to an earlier verse in the same chapter,—'Bear ye one another's burdens, and so fulfil the law of Christ.' Yes; while heaven ordains to each his peculiar suffering, it connects the family of man into one household, by that feeling which, more perhaps than any other, distinguishes us from the brute creation — I mean the feeling to which we give the name of *sympathy* — the feeling for each other! The flock heedeth not the sheep that creeps into the shade to die; but man has sorrow and joy not in himself alone, but in the joy and sorrow of those around him. He who feels only for himself abjures his very nature as man; for do we not say of one who has no tenderness for mankind that he is *inhuman?* and do we not call him who sorrows with the sorrowful, *humane?*

"Now, brethren, that which especially marked the divine mission of our Lord, is the direct appeal to this sympathy which distinguishes us from the brute. He seizes, not upon some faculty of genius given but to few, but upon that ready impulse of heart which is given to us all; and in saying, 'Love one another,' 'Bear ye one another's burdens,' he elevates the most delightful of our emotions into the most sacred of His laws. The lawyer asks our Lord, 'Who is my neighbor?' Our lord replies by the parable of the good Samaritan. The priest and the Levite saw the wounded man that fell among the thieves, and passed by on the other side. That priest might have been austere in his doctrine, that Levite might have been learned in the law; but neither to the learning of the Levite, nor to the doctrine of the priest, does our Savior even deign to allude. He cites but the action of the Samaritan, and saith to the lawyer, 'Which now of these three, thinkest thou, was neighbor unto him that fell among the thieves? And he said, He that showed mercy unto him. Then said Jesus unto him, Go, and do thou likewise.'

"O shallowness of human judgments! It was enough to be born a Samaritan in order to be rejected by the priest, and despised by the Levite. Yet now, what to us the priest and the Levite — of God's chosen race though they were? They passed from the hearts of men when they passed the sufferer by the wayside; while this loathed Samaritan, half thrust from the pale of the Hebrew, becomes of our family, of our kindred; a brother amongst the brotherhood of Love, so long as Mercy and affliction shall meet in the common thoroughfare of Life!

"'Bear ye one another's burdens, and so fulfil the law of Christ.' Think not, O my brethren, that this applies only to almsgiving — to that relief of distress which is commonly called charity — to the obvious duty of devoting, from our superfluities, something that we scarcely miss, to the wants of a starving brother. No. I appeal to the poorest amongst ye, if the worst burdens are those of the body — if the kind word and the tender thought have not often lightened your hearts more than bread bestowed with a grudge, and charity that humbles you by a frown. Sympathy is a beneficence at the command of us all,—yea, of the pauper as of the king; and sympathy is Christ's wealth. Sympathy is brotherhood. The rich are told to have charity for the poor, and the poor are enjoined to respect their superiors. Good: I say not to the contrary. But I say also to the poor, *'In your turn have charity for the rich;'* and I say to the rich, *In your turn respect the poor.'*

"'Bear ye one another's burdens, and so fulfil the law of Christ.' Thou, O poor man, envy not nor grudge thy brother his larger portion of worldly goods. Believe that he hath his sorrows and crosses like thyself, and perhaps, as more delicately nurtured, he feels them more; nay, hath he not temptations so great that our Lord hath exclaimed — 'How hardly shall they that have riches enter into the kingdom of heaven!' And what are temptations but trials? — what are trials but perils and sorrows? Think not that you can bestow no charity on the rich man, even while you take your sustenance from his hands. A heathen writer, often cited by the earliest preachers of the gospel, hath truly said — 'Wherever there is room for a man, there is place for a benefit.'

"And I ask any rich brother amongst you, when he

hath gone forth to survey his barns and his granaries, his gardens and his orchards, if suddenly, in the vain pride of his heart, he sees the scowl on the brow of the laborer — if he deems himself hated in the midst of his wealth — if he feels that his least faults are treasured up against him with the hardness of malice, and his plainest benefits received with the ingratitude of envy — I ask, I say, any rich man, whether straightway all pleasure in his worldly possessions does not fade from his heart, and whether he does not feel what a wealth of gladness it is in the power of the poor man to bestow! For all these things of Mammon pass away: but there is in the smile of him whom we have served, a something that we may take with us into heaven. If, then, ye bear one another's burdens, they who are poor will have mercy on the errors, and compassion for the griefs, of the rich. To all men it was said, — yes, to Lazarus as to Dives, — 'Judge not, that ye be not judged.' But think not, O rich man, that we preach only to the poor. If it be their duty not to grudge thee thy substance, it is thine to do all that may sweeten their labor. Remember, that when our Lord said, 'How hardly shall they that have riches enter into the kingdom of heaven,' he replied also to them who asked, 'Who then shall be saved?' 'The things which are impossible with men are possible with God:' that is, man left to his own temptations would fail; but, strengthened by God, he shall be saved. If thy riches are the tests of thy trial, so may they also be the instruments of thy virtues. Prove by thy riches that thou art compassionate and tender, temperate and benign; and thy riches themselves may become the evidence at once of thy faith and of thy works.

"We have constantly on our lips the simple precept, 'Do unto others as you would be done by.' Why do we fail so often in the practice? Because we neglect to cultivate that SYMPATHY which nature implants as an instinct, and the Savior exalts as a command. If thou wouldst do unto thy neighbor as thou wouldst be done by, ponder well how thy neighbor will regard the action thou art about to do to him. Put thyself into his place. If thou art strong and he is weak, descend from thy strength and enter into his weakness; lay aside thy burden for the while, and buckle on his own; let thy sight see as through his eyes — thy heart beat as in his bosom. Do this, and thou wilt often confess that what had seemed just to thy power will seem harsh to his weakness. For 'as a zealous man hath not done his duty when he calls his brother drunkard and beast,'* even so an administrator of the law mistakes his object if he writes on the grand column of society only warnings that irritate the bold and terrify the timid: and a man will be no more in love with law than with virtue, 'if he be forced to it with rudeness and incivilities.'† If, then, ye would bear the burden of the lowly, O ye great, feel not only *for* them, but *with!* Watch that your pride does not chafe them — your power does not wantonly gall.

* JEREMY TAYLOR — *Of Christian Prudence.* Part II. † Ibid.

Your worldly inferior is of the class from which the Apostles were chosen — amidst which the Lord of Creation descended from a throne above the seraphs."

The Parson here paused a moment, and his eye glanced towards the pew near the pulpit, where sat the magnate of Hazeldean. The Squire was leaning his chin thoughtfully on his hand, his brow inclined downwards, and the natural glow of his complexion much heightened.

"But," — resumed the Parson softly, without turning to his book, and rather as if prompted by the suggestion of the moment — "but he who has cultivated sympathy commits not these errors, or, if committing them, hastens to retract. So natural is sympathy to the good man, that he obeys it mechanically when he suffers his heart to be the monitor of his conscience. In this sympathy behold the bond between rich and poor! By this sympathy, whatever our varying worldly lots, they become what they were meant to be — exercises for the virtues more peculiar to each; and thus, if in the body each man bear his own burden, yet in the fellowship of the soul all have common relief in bearing the burdens of each other.

"This is the law of Christ — fulfil it, O my flock!"

Here the Parson closed his sermon, and the congregation bowed their heads.

BOOK THIRD.

INITIAL CHAPTER.

SHOWING HOW MY NOVEL CAME TO BE CALLED "MY NOVEL."

"I AM not displeased with your novel, so far as it has gone," said my father graciously; "though as for the Sermon——"

Here I trembled! but the ladies, Heaven bless them! had taken Parson Dale under their special protection; and, observing that my father was puckering up his brows critically, they rushed boldly forward in defence of The Sermon, and Mr. Caxton was forced to beat a retreat. However, like a skilful general, he renewed the assault upon outposts less gallantly guarded. But as it is not my business to betray my weak points, I leave it to the ingenuity of cavillers to discover the places at which the author of *Human Error* directed his great guns.

"But," said the Captain, "you are a lad of too much spirit, Pisistratus, to keep us always in the obscure country quarters of Hazeldean — you will march us out into open service before you have done with us?"

PISISTRATUS (magisterially, for he has been somewhat nettled by Mr. Caxton's remarks — and he puts on an air of dignity in order to awe away minor assailants).—Yes, Captain Roland — not yet awhile, but all in good time. I have not stinted myself in canvas, and behind my foreground of the Hall and the Parsonage I propose, hereafter, to open some lengthened perspective of the varieties of English life ——"

MR. CAXTON. — Hum!

BLANCHE (putting her hand on my father's lip). — We shall know better the design, perhaps, when we know the title. Pray, Mr. Author, what is the title?

MY MOTHER (with more animation than usual). — Ay, Sisty — the title!

PISISTRATUS (startled). — The title! By the soul of Cervantes! I have never yet thought of a title!

CAPTAIN ROLAND (solemnly). — There is a great deal in a good title. As a novel-reader, I know that by experience.

MR. SQUILLS. — Certainly; there is not a catchpenny in the world but what goes down, if the title be apt and seducive. Witness "Old Parr's Life Pills." Sell by the thousand, sir, when my "Pills for Weak Stomachs," which I believe to be just the same compound, never paid for the advertising.

MR. CAXTON. — Parr's Life Pills! a fine stroke of genius! It is not every one who has a weak stomach, or time to attend to it, if he have. But who would not swallow a pill to live to a hundred and fifty-two?

PISISTRATUS (stirring the fire in great excitement). — My title! my title! — what shall be my title?

MR. CAXTON (thrusting his hand into his waistcoat, and in his most didactic of tones).—From a remote period, the choice of a title has perplexed the scribbling portion of mankind. We may guess how their invention has been racked by the strange contortions it has produced. To begin with the Hebrews, "The Lips of the Sleeping" (*Labia Dormientium*) — what book do you suppose that title to designate?—A Catalogue of Rabbinical Writers! Again, imagine some young lady of old captivated by the sentimental title of "The Pomegranate with its Flower," and opening on a Treatise on the Jewish Ceremonials! Let us turn to the Romans. Aulus Gellius commences his pleasant gossiping "Noctes" with a list of the titles in fashion in his day. For instance, "*The Muses*" and "*The Veil*," "*The Cornucopia*," "*The Beehive*," and "*The Meadow*." Some titles, indeed, were more truculent, and promised food to those who love to sup upon horrors—such as "*The Torch*," "*The Poniard*," "*The Stiletto*——"

PISISTRATUS (impatiently). — Yes, sir; but to come to My Novel.

MR. CAXTON (unheeding the interruption). — You see you have a fine choice here, and of a nature pleasing and not unfamiliar, to a classical reader; or you may borrow a hint from the early Dramatic Writers.

PISISTRATUS (more hopefully). — Ay! there is something in the Drama akin to the Novel. Now, perhaps, I may catch an idea.

Mr. Caxton.—For instance, the author of the *Curiosities of Literature* (from whom, by the way, I am plagiarising much of the information I bestow upon you) tells us of a Spanish gentleman who wrote a Comedy, by which he intended to serve what he took for Moral Philosophy.

Pisistratus (eagerly).—Well, sir?

Mr. Caxton. — And called it "The Pain of the Sleep of the World."

Pisistratus. — Very comic indeed, sir.

Mr. Caxton. — Grave things were then called Comedies, as old things are now called Novels. Then there are all the titles of early Romance itself at your disposal —"Theagines and Chariclea," or "The Ass" of Longus, or "The Golden Ass" of Apuleius; or the titles of Gothic Romance, such as "The most elegant, delicious, mellifluous, and delightful History of Perceforest, King of Great Britain." — And therewith my father ran over a list of names as long as the Directory, and about as amusing.

"Well, to my taste," said my mother, "the novels I used to read when a girl (for I have not read many since, I am ashamed to say,)——"

Mr. Caxton. — No, you need not be at all ashamed of it, Kitty.

My Mother (proceeding).—Were much more inviting than any you mention, Austin.

The Captain. — True.

Mr. Squills. — Certainly. Nothing like them now-a-days!

MY MOTHER. — "*Says she to her Neighbor, What?*"

THE CAPTAIN. — "*The Unknown, or the Northern Gallery*" ——

MR. SQUILLS. — "*There is a Secret; find it out!*"

PISISTRATUS (pushed to the verge of human endurance, and upsetting tongs, poker, and fire-shovel). — What nonsense you are talking, all of you! For heaven's sake, consider what an important matter we are called upon to decide. It is not now the titles of those very respectable works which issued from the Minerva Press that I ask you to remember — it is to invent a title for mine — My Novel!

MR. CAXTON (clapping his hands gently). — Excellent — capital! Nothing can be better; simple, natural, pertinent, concise ——

PISISTRATUS. — What is it, sir — what is it? Have you really thought of a title to My Novel?

MR. CAXTON. — You have hit it yourself — "My Novel." It is your Novel — people will know it is your Novel. Turn and twist the English language as you will — be as allegorical as Hebrew, Greek, Roman — Fabulist or Puritan — still, after all, it is your Novel, and nothing more nor less than your Novel.

PISISTRATUS (thoughtfully, and sounding the words various ways). — "My Novel" — um — um! My Novel!" rather bold — and curt, eh?

MR. CAXTON. — Add what you say you intend to depict — Varieties in English Life.

MY MOTHER. — "*My Novel; or, Varieties in English*

Life" — I don't think it sounds amiss. What say you, Roland? Would it attract you in a catalogue?

My uncle hesitates, when Mr. Caxton exclaims imperiously — "The thing is settled! Don't disturb Camarina."

SQUILLS. — If it be not too great a liberty, pray who or what is Camarina?

MR. CAXTON. — Camarina, Mr. Squills, was a lake, apt to be low, and then liable to be muddy! and "Don't disturb Camarina," was a Greek proverb derived from an Oracle of Apollo; and from that Greek proverb, no doubt, comes the origin of the injunction, "*Quieta non movere*," which became the favorite maxim of Sir Robert Walpole and Parson Dale. The Greek line, Mr. Squills (here my father's memory began to warm), is preserved by STEPHANUS BYZANTINUS, de *Urbibus*,

"Μὴ κίνει Καμάριναν, ἀκίνητος γὰρ ἀμείνων."

ZENOBIUS explains it in his proverbs; SUIDAS repeats ZENOBIUS: LUCIAN alludes to it; so does VIRGIL in the Third Book of the ÆNEID; and SILIUS ITALICUS imitates Virgil —

"Et cui non licitum fatis Camarina moveri."

Parson Dale, as a clergyman and a scholar, had, no doubt, these authorities at his fingers' end. "And I wonder he did not quote them," quoth my father; "but, to be sure, he is represented as a mild man, and so might not wish to humble the Squire overmuch in the presence of his family. Meanwhile, My Novel is My Novel; and now that that matter is settled, perhaps the tongs, poker, and shovel may be picked up, the children may go to bed, Blanche and Kitty may speculate apart upon the future dignities of the Neogilos, — taking care, nevertheless, to finish the new pinbefores he requires for the present; Roland may cast up his account-book, Mr. Squills have his brandy-and-water, and all the world be comfortable, each in his own way. Blanche, come away from the screen, get me my slippers, and leave Pisistratus to himself. Μὴ κίνει Καμάριναν — don't disturb Camarina. You see, my dear," added my father kindly, as, after settling himself into his slippers, he detained Blanche's hand in his own — "you see, my dear, every house has its Camarina. Man, who is a lazy animal, is quite content to let it alone; but woman, being the more active, bustling, curious creature, is always for giving it a sly stir."

BLANCHE (with female dignity). — I assure you, that if Pisistratus had not called me, I should not have ——

MR. CAXTON (interrupting her, without lifting his eyes from the book he has already taken). — Certainly you would not. I am now in the midst of the great Oxford Controversy. Μὴ κίνει Καμάριναν—don't disturb Camarina.

A dead silence for half an hour, at the end of which

PISISTRATUS. (from behind the screen). — Blanche, my dear, I want to consult you.

Blanche does not stir.

PISISTRATUS. — Blanche, I say.

Blanche glances in triumph towards Mr. Caxton.

Mr. Caxton (laying down his theological tract, and rubbing his spectacles mournfully).—I hear him, child; I hear him, I retract my vindication of man. Oracles warn in vain: so long as there is a woman on the other side of the screen,—it is all up with Camarina.

CHAPTER II.

It is greatly to be regretted that Mr. Stirn was not present at the Parson's Discourse—but that valuable functionary was far otherwise engaged—indeed, during the summer months he was rarely seen at the afternoon service. Not that he cared for being preached at—not he: Mr. Stirn would have snapped his fingers at the thunders of the Vatican. But the fact was, that Mr. Stirn chose to do a great deal of gratuitous business upon the day of rest. The Squire allowed all persons who chose to walk about the park on a Sunday; and many came from a distance to stroll by the lake, or recline under the elms. These visitors were objects of great suspicion, nay, of positive annoyance, to Mr. Stirn—and, indeed, not altogether without reason, for we English have a natural love of liberty, which we are even more apt to display in the grounds of other people than in those which we cultivate ourselves. Sometimes, to his inexpressible and fierce satisfaction, Mr. Stirn fell upon a lot of boys pelting the swans; sometimes he missed a young sapling, and found it in felonious hands, converted into a walking-stick; sometimes he caught a hulking fellow scrambling up the ha-ha, to gather a nosegay for his sweetheart from one of poor Mrs. Hazeldean's pet parterres; not unfrequently, indeed, when all the family were fairly at church, some curious impertinents forced or sneaked their way into the gardens, in order to peep in at the windows. For these, and various other offences of like magnitude, Mr. Stirn had long, but vainly, sought to induce the Squire to withdraw a permission so villanously abused. But though there were times when Mr. Hazeldean grunted and growled, and swore "that he would shut up the park, and fill it (illegally) with man-traps and spring-guns," his anger always evaporated in words. The park was still open to all the world on a Sunday; and that blessed day was therefore converted into a day of travail and wrath to Mr. Stirn. But it was from the last chime of the afternoon service bell until dusk, that the spirit of this vigilant functionary was most perturbed; for, amidst the flocks that gathered from the little hamlets round to the voice of the Pastor, there were always some stray sheep, or rather climbing, desultory, vagabond goats, who struck off in all perverse directions, as if for the special purpose of distracting the energetic watchfulness of Mr. Stirn. As soon as church was over, if the day were fine, the whole park became a scene animated with red cloaks, or lively shawls, Sunday waistcoats, and hats stuck full of wild flowers — which last Mr. Stirn often stoutly maintained to be Mrs. Hazeldean's newest geraniums. Now, on this Sunday, especially, there was an imperative call upon an extra exertion of vigilance on the part of the superintendent — he had not only to detect ordinary depredators and trespassers; but, first to discover the authors of the conspiracy against the stocks; and, secondly, to "make an example."

He had begun his rounds, therefore, from the early morning; and just as the afternoon bell was sounding its final peal, he emerged upon the village-green from a hedgerow, behind which he had been at watch to observe who had the most suspiciously gathered round the stocks. At that moment the place was deserted. At a distance, the superintendent saw the fast disappearing forms of some belated groups hastening towards the church; in front, the stocks stood staring at him mournfully from its four great eyes, which had been cleansed from the mud, but still looked bleared and stained with the marks of the recent outrage. Here Mr. Stirn paused, took off his hat, and wiped his brows.

"If I had sum un to watch here," thought he, "while I takes a turn by the water-side, p'r'aps summat might come out; p'r'aps them as did it ben't gone to church, but will come sneaking round to look on their villany! as they says murderers are always led back to the place where they ha' left the body. But in this here village there ben't a man, woman, nor child, as has any consarn for Squire or Parish, barring myself." It was just as he arrived at that misanthropical conclusion, that Mr. Stirn beheld Leonard Fairfield walking very fast from his own home. The superintendent clapped on his hat, and stuck his right arm akimbo. "Hallo, you sir," said he, as Lenny now came in hearing, "where be you going at that rate?"

"Please, sir, I be going to church."

"Stop, sir — stop, Master Lenny. Going to church — why, the bell's done; and you knows the Parson is very angry at them as comes in late, disturbing the congregation. You can't go to church now!"

"Please, sir —"

"I says you can't go to church now. You must learn to think a little of others, lad. You sees how I sweats to serve the Squire! and you must serve him too. Why, your mother's got the house and premishes almost rent free: you ought to have a grateful heart, Leonard Fairfield, and feel for his honor! Poor man! *his* heart is well nigh bruk, I am sure, with the goings on."

Leonard opened his innocent blue eyes, while Mr. Stirn dolorously wiped his own.

"Look at that 'ere dumb cretur," said Stirn suddenly, pointing to the stocks —"look at it. If it could speak, what would it say, Leonard Fairfield? Answer me that! —'Damn the stocks,' indeed!"

"It was very bad in them to write such naughty words," said Lenny, gravely. "Mother was quite shocked when she heard of it this morning."

Mr. Stirn.— I dare say she was, considering what she pays for the premishes: (insinuatingly) you does not know who did it — eh, Lenny?

LENNY.—No, sir; indeed I does not!

MR. STIRN.—Well, you see, you can't go to church—prayers half over by this time. You recollex that I put them stocks under your "sponsibility," and see the way you's done your duty by 'em. I've half a mind to—

Mr. Stirn cast his eyes on the eyes of the stocks.

"Please, sir," began Lenny again, rather frightened.

"No, I won't please; it ben't pleasing at all. But I forgives you this time, only keep a sharp look-out, lad, in future. Now you just stay here—no, there—under the hedge, and you watches if any person comes to loiter about, or looks at the stocks, or laughs to hisself, while I go my rounds. I shall be back either afore church is over or just arter: so you stay till I comes, and give me your report. Be sharp, boy, or it will be worse for you and your mother; I can let the premishes for four pounds a-year more to-morrow."

Concluding with that somewhat menacing and very significant remark, and not staying for an answer, Mr. Stirn waved his hand, and walked off.

Poor Lenny remained by the stocks, very much dejected, and greatly disliking the neighborhood to which he was consigned. At length he slowly crept off to the hedge, and sate himself down in the place of espionage pointed out to him. Now, philosophers tell us that what is called the point of honor is a barbarous feudal prejudice. Amongst the higher classes, wherein those feudal prejudices may be supposed to prevail, Lenny Fairfield's occupation would not have been considered peculiarly honorable; neither would it have seemed so to the more turbulent spirits among the humbler orders, who have a point of honor of their own, which consists in the adherence to each other in defiance of all lawful authority. But to Lenny Fairfield, brought up much apart from other boys, and with a profound and grateful reverence for the Squire instilled into all his habits of thought, notions of honor bounded themselves to simple honesty and straightforward truth; and as he cherished an unquestioning awe of order and constitutional authority, so it did not appear to him that there was anything derogatory and debasing in being thus set to watch for an offender. On the contrary, as he began to reconcile himself to the loss of the church service, and to enjoy the cool of the summer shade, and the occasional chirp of the birds, he got to look on the bright side of the commission to which he was deputed. In youth, at least, everything has its bright side — even the appointment of Protector to the Parish Stocks. For the stocks itself Leonard had no affection, it is true; but he had no sympathy with its aggressors, and he could well conceive that the Squire would be very much hurt at the revolutionary event of the night. "So," thought poor Leonard in his simple heart — "so, if I can serve his honor, by keeping off mischievous boys, or letting him know who did the thing, I'm sure it would be a proud day for mother." Then he began to consider that, however ungraciously Mr. Stirn had bestowed on him the appointment, still it was a compliment to him — showed trust and confidence in him, picked him out from his contemporaries as the sober moral pattern boy; and Lenny had a great deal of pride in him, especially in matters of repute and character.

All these things considered, I say, Leonard Fairfield reclined on his lurking-place, if not with positive delight and intoxicating rapture, at least with tolerable content and some complacency

Mr. Stirn might have been gone a quarter of an hour, when a boy came through a little gate in the park, just opposite to Lenny's retreat in the hedge, and, as if fatigued with walking, or oppressed by the heat of the day, paused on the green for a moment or so, and then advanced under the shade of the great tree which overhung the stocks.

Lenny pricked up his ears, and peeped out jealously.

He had never seen the boy before: it was a strange face to him.

Leonard Fairfield was not fond of strangers; moreover, he had a vague belief that strangers were at the bottom of that desecration of the stocks. The boy, then, was a stranger; but what was his rank? Was he of that grade in society in which the natural offences are or are not consonant to, or harmonious with, outrages upon stocks? On that Lenny Fairfield did not feel quite assured. According to all the experience of the villager, the boy was not dressed like a young gentleman. Leonard's notions of such aristocratic costume were naturally fashioned upon the model of Frank Hazeldean. They represented to him a dazzling vision of snow-white trowsers, and beautiful blue coats, and imcomparable cravats. Now the dress of this stranger, though not that of a peasant nor of a farmer, did not in any way correspond with Lenny's notions of the costume of a young gentleman: it looked to him highly disreputable; the coat was covered with mud, and the hat was all manner of shapes, with a gap between the side and crown.

Lenny was puzzled, till it suddenly occurred to him that the gate through which the boy had passed was in the direct path across the park from a small town, the inhabitants of which were in very bad odor at the Hall—they had immemorially furnished the most daring poachers to the preserves, the most troublesome trespassers on the park, the most unprincipled orchard robbers, and the most disputations asserters of various problematical rights of way, which, according to the Town, were public, and, according to the Hall, had been private since the Conquest. It was true that the same path led also directly from the Squire's house, but it was not probable that the wearer of attire so equivocal had been visiting there. All things considered, Lenny had no doubt in his mind but that the stranger was a shop-boy or 'prentice from the town of Thorndyke; and the notorious repute of that town, coupled with this presumption, made it probable that Lenny now saw before him one of the midnight desecrators of the stocks. As if to confirm the suspicion, which passed through Lenny's mind with a rapidity wholly disproportionate to the number of lines it costs me to convey it, the boy, now standing right before the stocks, bent down and read that pithy anathema with which it was defaced. And having read it he repeated it aloud, and Lenny actually saw him smile — such a smile! — so disagreeable and sinister! Lenny had never before seen the smile Sardonic.

But what were Lenny's pious horror and dismay when this ominous stranger fairly seated himself on the stocks, rested his heels profanely on the lids of two of the four round eyes, and, taking out a pencil and a pocket-book, began to write. Was this audacious Unknown taking an inventory of the church and the Hall for the purposes of conflagration? He looked at one, and at the other, with a strange, fixed stare as he wrote — not keeping his eyes on the paper, as Lenny had been taught to do when he sat down to his copy-book. The fact is, that Randal Leslie was tired and faint, and he felt the shock of his fall the more, after the few paces he had walked, so that he was glad to rest himself a few moments; and he took that opportunity to write a line to Frank, to excuse himself for not calling again, intending to tear the leaf on which he wrote out of his pocket-book and leave it at the first cottage he passed, with instructions to take it to the Hall.

While Randal was thus innocently engaged, Lenny came up to him, with the firm and measured pace of one who has resolved, cost what it may, to do his duty. And as Lenny, though brave, was not ferocious, so the anger he felt, and the suspicions he entertained, only exhibited themselves in the following solemn appeal to the offender's sense of propriety, —

"Ben't you ashamed of yourself? Sitting on the Squire's new stocks! Do get up, and go along with you!"

Randal turned round sharply; and though, at any other moment, he would have had sense enough to extricate himself very easily from his false position, yet, *Nemo mortalium*, &c. No one is always wise. And Randal was in an exceedingly bad humor. The affability towards his inferiors, for which I lately praised him, was entirely lost in the contempt of impertinent snobs natural to an insulted Etonian.

Therefore, eyeing Lenny with great disdain, Randal answered briefly,—

"You are an insolent young blackguard."

So curt a rejoinder made Lenny's blood fly to his face. Persuaded before that the intruder was some lawless apprentice or shop-lad, he was now more confirmed in that judgment, not only by language so uncivil, but by the truculent glance which accompanied it, and which certainly did not derive any imposing dignity from the mutilated, rakish, hang-dog, ruinous hat, under which it shot its sullen and menacing fire.

Of all the various articles of which our male attire is composed, there is perhaps not one which has so much character and expression as the top covering. A neat, well-brushed, short-napped, gentleman-like hat, put on with a certain air, gives a distinction and respectability to the whole exterior; whereas, a broken, squashed, higgledy-piggledy sort of a hat, such as Randal Leslie had on, would go far towards transforming the stateliest gentleman who ever walked down St. James's Street into the ideal of a ruffianly scamp.

Now, it is well known that there is nothing more antipathetic to your peasant-boy than a shop-boy. Even on grand political occasions, the rural working-class can rarely be coaxed into sympathy with the trading town-class. Your true English peasant is always an aristocrat. Moreover, and irrespectively of this immemorial grudge of class, there is something peculiarly hostile in the relationship between boy and boy when their backs are once up, and they are alone on a quiet bit of green. Something of the game-cock feeling — something that tends to keep alive, in the population of this island (otherwise so lamb-like and peaceful), the martial propensity to double the thumb tightly over the four fingers, and make what is called "a fist of it." Dangerous symptoms of these mingled and aggressive sentiments were visible in Lenny Fairfield at the words and the look of the unprepossessing stranger. And the stranger seemed aware of them; for his pale face grew more pale, and his sullen eye more fixed and more vigilant.

"You get off them stocks," said Lenny, disdaining to reply to the coarse expressions bestowed on him; and, suiting the action to the word, he gave the intruder what he meant for a shove, but what Randal took for a blow. The Etonian sprang up, and the quickness of his movement, aided by a slight touch of his hand, made Lenny lose his balance, and sent him neck and crop over the stocks. Burning with rage, the young villager rose alertly, and flying at Randal, struck out right and left.

CHAPTER III.

Aid me, O ye Nine! whom the incomparable Persius satirised his contemporaries for invoking, and then, all of a sudden, invoked on his own behalf—aid me to describe that famous battle by the stocks, and in defence of the stocks, which was waged by the two representatives of Saxon and Norman England. Here, sober support of law and duty and delegated trust—*pro aris et focis;* there, haughty invasion, and bellicose spirit of knighthood, and that respect for name and person, which we call "honor." Here, too, hardy physical force—there, skilful discipline. Here—The Nine are as deaf as a post, and as cold as a stone! Plague take the jades!—I can do better without them.

Randal was a year or two older than Lenny, but he was not so tall nor so strong, nor even so active; and after the first blind rush, when the two boys paused, and drew back to breathe, Lenny, eyeing the slight form and hueless cheek of his opponent, and seeing blood trickling from Randal's lip, was seized with an instantaneous and generous remorse. "It was not fair," he thought, "to fight one whom he could beat so easily." So, retreating still farther, and letting his arms fall to his side, he said, mildly — "There, let's have no more of it; but go home and be good."

Randal Leslie had no remarkable degree of that constitutional quality called physical courage; but he had some of those moral qualities which supply its place. He was proud — he was vindictive — he had high self-esteem—he had the destructive organ more than the combative; — what had once provoked his wrath it became his instinct to sweep away. Therefore, though all his nerves were quivering, and hot tears were in his eyes, he approached Lenny with the sternness of a gladiator, and said, between his teeth, which he set hard, choking back the sob of rage and pain —

"You have struck me — and you shall not stir from this ground till I have made you repent it. Put up your hands — defend yourself."

Lenny mechanically obeyed; and he had good need of the admonition; for if before he had had the advantage, now that Randal had recovered the surprise to his nerves, the battle was not to the strong.

Though Leslie had not been a fighting boy at Eton, still his temper had involved him in some conflicts when he was in the lower forms, and he had learned something of the art as well as the practice in pugilism — an excellent thing too, I am barbarous enough to believe, and which I hope will never quite die out of our public schools. Ah, many a young duke has been a better fellow for life from a fair set-to with a trader's son; and many a trader's son has learned to look a lord more manfully in the face on the hustings, from the recollection of the sound thrashing he once gave to some little Lord Leopold Dawdle.

So Randal now brought his experience and art to bear; put aside those heavy roundabout blows, and darted in his own, quick and sharp — supplying to the natural feebleness of his arm the due momentum of pugilistic mechanics. Ay, and the arm, too, was no longer so feeble: for strange is the strength that comes from passion and pluck!

Poor Lenny, who had never fought before, was bewildered; his sensations grew so entangled that he could never recall them distinctly; he had a dim reminiscence of some breathless impotent rush — of a sudden blindness followed by quick flashes of intolerable light — of a deadly faintness, from which he was roused by sharp pangs — here — there — everywhere; and then all he could remember was, that he was lying on the ground, huddled up, and panting hard, while his adversary bent over him with a countenance as dark and livid as Lara himself might have bent over the fallen Otho. For Randal Leslie was not one who, by impulse and nature, subscribed to the noble English maxim — "Never hit a foe when he is down;" and it cost him a strong if brief self-struggle, not to set his heel on that prostrate form. It was the mind, not the heart, that subdued the savage within him, as muttering something inwardly — certainly not Christian forgiveness — the victor turned gloomily away

CHAPTER IV.

Just at that precise moment, who should appear but Mr. Stirn! For, in fact, being extremely anxious to get Lenny into disgrace, he had hoped that he should have found the young villager had shirked the commission entrusted to him; and the Right-hand Man had slily come back, to see if that amiable expectation were realised. He now beheld Lenny rising with some difficulty—still panting hard—and with hysterical sounds akin to what is vulgarly called blubbering—his fine new waistcoat sprinkled with his own blood, which flowed from his nose—nose that seemed to Lenny Fairfield's feelings to be a nose no more, but a swollen, gigantic, mountainous Slawkenbergian excrescence;—in fact, he felt all nose! Turning aghast from this spectacle, Mr. Stirn surveyed, with no more respect than Lenny had manifested, the stranger boy, who had again seated himself on the stocks (whether to recover his breath, or whether to show that his victory was consummated, and that he was in his rights of possession). "Hollo," said Mr. Stirn, "what is all this?—what's the matter, Lenny, you blockhead?"

"He *will* sit there," answered Lenny, in broken gasps, "and he has beat me because I would not let him; but I doesn't mind that," added the villager, trying hard to suppress his tears, "and I'm ready again for him — that I am."

"And what do you do lollopoping there on them blessed stocks?"

"Looking at the landscape; out of my light, man!"

This tone instantly inspired Mr. Stirn with misgivings: it was a tone so disrespectful to him, that he was seized with involuntary respect; who but a gentleman could speak so to Mr. Stirn?

"And may I ask who you be?" said Stirn, falteringly, and half inclined to touch his hat. "What's your name, pray? — what's your bizness?"

"My name is Randal Leslie, and my business was to visit your master's family — that is, if you are, as I guess from your manner, Mr. Hazeldean's ploughman!"

So saying, Randal rose; and moving on a few paces, turned, and throwing half-a-crown on the road, said to Lenny, — "Let that pay you for your bruises, and remember another time how you speak to a gentleman. As for you, fellow," — and he pointed his scornful hand towards Mr. Stirn, who with his mouth open, and his hat now fairly off, stood bowing to the earth — "as for you, give my compliments to Mr. Hazeldean, and say that, when he does us the honor to visit us at Rood Hall, I trust that the manners of our villagers will make him ashamed of Hazeldean."

O my poor Squire! Rood Hall ashamed of Hazeldean! If that message had been delivered to you, you would never have looked up again!

With those bitter words, Randal swung himselr over the stile that led into the Parson's glebe, and left Lenny Fairfield still feeling his nose, and Mr. Stirn still bowing to the earth.

CHAPTER V.

Randal Leslie had a very long walk home; he was bruised and sore from head to foot, and his mind was still more sore and more bruised than his body. But if Randal Leslie had rested himself in the Squire's gardens, without walking backwards, and indulging in speculations suggested by Marat, and warranted by My Lord Bacon, he would have passed a most agreeable evening, and really availed himself of the Squire's wealth by going home in the Squire's carriage. But, because he chose to take so intellectual a view of property, he tumbled into a ditch; because he tumbled into a ditch, he spoiled his clothes; because he spoiled his clothes, he gave up his visit; because he gave up his visit, he got into the village-green, and sat on the stocks with a hat that gave him the air of a fugitive from the treadmill; because he sat on the stocks — with that hat, and a cross face under it — he had been forced into the most discreditable squabble with a clodhopper, and was now limping home, at war with gods and men; — *ergo* (this is a moral that will bear repetition) — *ergo*, when you walk in a rich man's grounds, be contented to enjoy what is yours, namely, the prospect; I dare say you will enjoy it more than he does!

CHAPTER VI.

If, in the simplicity of his heart, and the crudity of his experience, Lenny Fairfield had conceived it probable that Mr. Stirn would address to him some words in approbation of his gallantry, and in sympathy for his bruises, he soon found himself wofully mistaken. That truly great man, worthy prime-minister of Hazeldean, might, perhaps, pardon a dereliction from his orders, if such dereliction proved advantageous to the interests of the service, or redounded to the credit of the chief: but he was inexorable to that worst of diplomatic offences — an ill-timed, stupid, over-zealous obedience to orders, which, if it established the devotion of the *employé*, got the employer into what is popularly called a scrape! And though, by those unversed in the intricacies of the human heart, and unacquainted with the especial hearts of prime-ministers and right-hand men, it might have seemed natural that Mr. Stirn, as he stood still, hat in hand, in the middle of the road, stung, humbled, and exasperated by the mortification he had received from the lips of Randal Leslie, would have felt that that young gentleman was the proper object of his resentment; yet such a breach of all the etiquette of diplomatic life as resentment towards a superior power, was the last idea that would have suggested itself to the profound intellect of the Premier of Hazeldean. Still, as rage, like steam, must escape somewhere, Mr. Stirn, on feeling — as he afterwards expressed it to his wife — that his "buzzom was a burstin," turned with the natural instinct of self-preservation to the safety-valve provided for the explosion; and the vapors within him rushed into vent upon Lenny Fairfield. He clapped his hat on his head fiercely, and thus relieved his "buzzom."

"You young willain! you howdacious wiper! and so all this blessed Sabbath afternoon, when you ought to have been in church on your marrow-bones, a praying for your betters, you has been a-fitting with a young gentleman, and a wisiter to your master, on the wery place of the parridge hinstitution that you was to guard and pertect; and a-bloodying it all over, I declares, with your blackguard little nose!" Thus saying, and as if to mend the matter, Mr. Stirn aimed an additional stroke at the offending member; but, Lenny mechanically putting up both arms to defend his face, Mr. Stirn struck his knuckles against the large brass buttons that adorned the cuff of the boy's coat-sleeve — an incident which considerably aggravated his indignation. And Lenny, whose spirit was fairly roused at what the narrowness of his education conceived to be a signal injustice, placing the trunk of the tree between Mr. Stirn and himself, began that task of self-justification which it was equally impolitic to conceive and imprudent to execute, since, in such a case, to justify was to recriminate.

"I wonder at you, Master Stirn,—if mother could hear you! You know it was you who would not let me go to church; it was you who told me to ——"

"Fit a young gentleman, and break the Sabbath," said Mr. Stirn, interrupting him with a withering sneer. "O yes! I told you to disgrace his honor the Squire, and me, and the parridge, and bring us all into trouble. But the Squire told me to make an example, and I will!" With those words, quick as lightning flashed upon Mr. Stirn's mind the luminous idea of setting Lenny in the very stocks which he had too faithfully guarded. Eureka! the "example" was before him! Here, he could gratify his long grudge against the pattern boy; here by such a selection of the very best lad in the parish, he could strike terror into the worst; here he could appease the offended dignity of Randal Leslie; here was a practical apology to the Squire for the affront put upon his young visitor; here, too, there was prompt obedience to the Squire's own wish that the stocks should be provided as soon as possible with a tenant. Suiting the action to the thought, Mr. Stirn made a rapid plunge at his victim, caught him by the skirt of his jacket, and, in a few seconds more, the jaws of the stocks had opened, and Lenny Fairfield was thrust therein—a sad spectacle of the reverse of fortune. This done, and while the boy was too astounded, too stupefied by the suddenness of the calamity for the resistance he might otherwise have made—nay, for more than a few inaudible words—Mr. Stirn hurried from the spot, but not without first picking up and pocketing the half-crown designed for Lenny, and which, so great had been his first emotions, he had hitherto even almost forgotten. He then made his way towards the church, with the intention to place himself close by the door, catch the Squire as he came out, whisper to him what had passed, and lead him, with the whole congregation at his heels, to gaze upon the sacrifice offered up to the joint Powers of Nemesis and Themis.

CHAPTER VII.

Unaffectedly I say it — upon the honor of a gentleman, and the reputation of an author, unaffectedly I say it — no words of mine can do justice to the sensations experienced by Lenny Fairfield, as he sat alone in that place of penance. He felt no more the physical pain of his bruises; the anguish of his mind stifled and overbore all corporeal suffering — an anguish as great as the childish breast is capable of holding. For first and deepest of all, and earliest felt, was the burning sense of injustice. He had, it might be with erring judgment, but with all honesty, earnestness, and zeal, executed the commission intrusted to him; he had stood forth manfully in discharge of his duty; he had fought for it, suffered for it, bled for it. This was his reward! Now, in Lenny's mind there was pre-eminently that quality which distinguishes the Anglo-Saxon race — the sense of justice. It was perhaps the strongest principle in his moral constitution; and the principle had never lost its virgin bloom and freshness by any of the minor acts of oppression and iniquity which boys of higher birth often suffer from harsh parents, or in tyrannical schools. So that it was for the first time that that iron entered into his soul, and with it came its attendant feeling — the wrathful, galling sense of impotence. He had been wronged, and he had no means to right himself. Then came another sensation, if not so deep, yet more smarting and envenomed for the time — shame! He, the good boy of all good boys — he, the pattern of the school, and the pride of the Parson — he, whom the Squire, in sight of all his contemporaries, had often singled out to slap on the back, and the grand Squire's lady to pat on the head, with a smiling gratulation on his young and fair repute — he, who had already learned so dearly to prize the sweets of an honorable name — he, to be made, as it were, in the twinkling of an eye, a mark for opprobrium, a butt of scorn, a jeer, and a by-word! The streams of his life were poisoned at the fountain. And then came a tenderer thought of his mother! of the shock this would be to her — she who had already begun to look up to him as her stay and support: he bowed his head, and the tears, long suppressed, rolled down.

Then he wrestled and struggled, and strove to wrench his limbs from that hateful bondage; — for he heard steps approaching. And he began to picture to himself the arrival of all the villagers from church, the sad gaze of the Parson, the bent brow of the Squire, the idle, ill-suppressed titter of all the boys, jealous of his unspotted character — a character of which the original whiteness could never, never be restored! He would always be the boy who had sat in the stocks! And the words uttered by the Squire came back on his soul, like the voice of conscience in the ears of some doomed Macbeth. "A sad disgrace, Lenny — you'll never be in such a quandary." "Quandary," the word was unfamiliar to him; it must mean something awfully discreditable. The poor boy could have prayed for the earth to swallow him.

CHAPTER VIII.

"KETTLES and frying-pans! what has us here?" cried the Tinker.

This time Mr. Sprott was without his donkey; for it being Sunday, it is to be presumed that the donkey was enjoying his Sabbath on the Common. The Tinker was in his Sunday's best, clean and smart, about to take his lounge in the park.

Lenny Fairfield made no answer to the appeal.

"You in the wood, my baby! Well, that's the last sight I should ha' thought to see. But, we all lives to larn," added the Tinker, sententiously. "Who gave you them leggings? Can't you speak, lad?"

"Nick Stirn."

"Nick Stirn! Ay, I'd ha' ta'en my davy on that: and cos vy?"

"'Cause I did as he told me, and fought a boy as was trespassing on these very stocks; and he beat me — but I don't care for that; and that boy was a young gentleman, and going to visit the Squire; and so Nick Stirn—" Lenny stopped short, choked by rage and humiliation.

"Augh," said the Tinker, staring, "you fit with a young gentleman, did you? Sorry to hear you confess that, my lad! Sit there, and be thankful you ha' got off so cheap. 'Tis salt and battery to fit with your betters, and a Lunnon justice o' peace would have given you two months o' the treadmill. But vy should you fit cos he trespassed on the stocks? It ben't your natural side for fitting, I takes it."

Lenny murmured something not very distinguishable about serving the Squire, and doing as he was bid.

"Oh, I sees, Lenny," interrupted the Tinker, in a tone of great contempt, "you be one of those who would rayther 'unt with the 'ounds than run with the 'are! You be's the good pattern boy, and would peach agin your own horder to curry favor with the grand folks. Fie, lad! you be sarved right; stick by your horder, then you'll be 'spected when you gets into trouble, and not be 'varsally 'spised — as you'll be arter church-time! Vell, I can't be seen 'sorting with you, now you are in this drogotary fix; it might hurt my cracter, both with them as built the stocks, and them as wants to pull 'em down. Old kettles to mend! Vy, you makes me forgit the Sabbath. Sarvent, my lad, and wish you well out of it; 'specks to your mother, and say we can deal for the pan and shovel all the same for your misfortin."

The Tinker went his way. Lenny's eye followed him with the sullenness of despair. The Tinker, like all the tribe of human comforters, had only watered the brambles to invigorate the prick of the thorns. Yes, if Lenny had been caught breaking the stocks, some at least would have pitied him; but to be incarcerated for defending them, you might as well have expected that the widows and orphans of the Reign of Terror would have pitied Dr. Guillotin when he slid through the grooves of his own deadly machine. And even the Tinker, itinerant, ragamuffin vagabond as he was, felt ashamed to be found with the pattern boy! Lenny's head sank again on his breast heavily, as if it had been of lead. Some few minutes thus passed, when the unhappy prisoner became aware of the presence of another spectator to his shame: he heard no step, but he saw a shadow thrown over the sward. He held his breath, and would not look up, with some vague idea that if he refused to see him, he might escape being seen.

CHAPTER IX.

"*Per Bacco!*" said Dr. Riccabocca, putting his hand on Lenny's shoulder, and bending down to look into his face — "*Per Bacco!* my young friend; do you sit here from choice, or necessity?"

Lenny slightly shuddered, and winced under the touch of one whom he had hitherto regarded with a sort of superstitious abhorrence.

"I fear," resumed Riccabocca, after waiting in vain for an answer to his question, "that, though the situation is charming, you did not select it yourself. What is this?" — and the irony of the tone vanished — "what is this, my poor boy? You have been bleeding, and I see that those tears which you try to check come from a deep well. Tell me, *povero fanciullo mio* (the sweet Italian vowels, though Lenny did not understand them, sounded softly and soothingly) — tell me, my child, how all this happened. Perhaps I can help you — we have all erred; we should all help each other."

Lenny's heart, that just before had seemed bound in brass, found itself a way as the Italian spoke thus kindly, and the tears rushed down; but he again stopped them, and gulped out sturdily —

"I have not done no wrong; it ben't my fault — and

'tis that which kills me!" concluded Lenny, with a burst of energy.

"You have not done wrong? Then," said the philosopher, drawing out his pocket-handkerchief with great composure, and spreading it on the ground—"then I may sit beside you. I could only stoop pityingly over sin, but I can lie down on equal terms with misfortune."

Lenny Fairfield did not quite comprehend the words, but enough of their general meaning was apparent to make him cast a grateful glance on the Italian. Riccabocca resumed, as he adjusted the pocket-handkerchief, "I have a right to your confidence, my child, for I have been afflicted in my day; yet I too say with thee, 'I have not done wrong.' *Cospetto!*" and here the Doctor seated himself deliberately, resting one arm on the side-column of the stocks, in familiar contact with the captive's shoulder, while his eye wandered over the lovely scene around—"*Cospetto!* my prison, if they had caught me, would not have had so fair a look-out as this. But, to be sure, it is all one; there are no ugly loves, and no handsome prisons."

With that sententious maxim, which, indeed, he uttered in his native Italian, Riccabocca turned round, and renewed his soothing invitations to confidence. A friend in need is a friend indeed, even if he come in the guise of a Papist and wizard. All Lenny's ancient dislike to the foreigner had gone, and he told him his little tale.

Dr. Riccabocca was much too shrewd a man not to see exactly the motives which had induced Mr. Stirn to incarcerate his agent (barring only that of personal grudge, to which Lenny's account gave him no clue). That a man high in office should make a scape-goat of his own watch-dog for an unlucky snap, or even an indiscreet bark, was nothing strange to the wisdom of the student of Machiavelli. However, he set himself to the task of consolation with equal philosophy and tenderness. He began by reminding, or rather informing, Leonard Fairfield of all the instances of illustrious men afflicted by the injustice of others that occurred to his own excellent memory. He told him how the great Epictetus, when in slavery, had a master whose favorite amusement was pinching his leg, which, as the amusement ended in breaking that limb, was worse than the stocks. He also told him the anecdote of Lenny's own gallant countryman, Admiral Byng, whose execution gave rise to Voltaire's celebrated witticism, "*En Angleterre on tue un amiral pour encourager les autres*" ("In England they execute one admiral in order to encourage the others"). Many other illustrations, still more pertinent to the case in point, his erudition supplied from the stores of history. But on seeing that Lenny did not seem in the slightest degree consoled by these memorable examples, he shifted his ground, and reducing his logic to the strict *argumentum ad rem*, began to prove, 1st, that there was no disgrace at all in Lenny's present position — that every equitable person would recognise the tyranny of Stirn, and the innocence of its victim; 2dly, that if even here he were mistaken — for public opinion was not always righteous — what was public opinion, after all? — "A breath — a puff," cried Dr. Riccabocca—"a thing without matter—without length, breadth, or substance; a shadow—a goblin of our own creating. A man's own conscience is his sole tribunal, and he should care no more for that phantom 'opinion' than he should fear meeting a ghost if he cross the church-yard at dark."

Now, as Lenny did very much fear meeting a ghost if he crossed the church-yard at dark, the simile spoiled the argument, and he shook his head very mournfully. Dr. Riccabocca was about to enter into a third course of reasoning, which, had it come to an end, would doubtless have settled the matter, and reconciled Lenny to sitting in the stocks till doomsday, when the captive, with the quick ear and eye of terror and calamity, became conscious that church was over, that the congregation in a few seconds more would be flocking thitherwards. He saw visionary hats and bonnets through the trees, which Riccabocca saw not, despite all the excellence of his spectacles—heard phantasmal rustlings and murmurings which Riccabocca heard not, despite all that theoretical experience in plots, stratagems, and treasons, which should have made the Italian's ear as fine as a conspirator's or a mole's. And, with another violent but vain effort at escape, the prisoner exclaimed—

"Oh, if I could but get out before they come! Let me out—let me out. O, kind sir, have pity—let me out!"

"*Diavolo!*" said the philosopher, startled, "I wonder that I never thought of that before. After all, I believe he has hit the right nail on the head," and, looking close, he perceived that though the partition of wood had hitched firmly into a sort of spring-clasp, which defied Lenny's unaided struggles, still it was not locked (for, indeed, the padlock and key were snug in the justice-room of the Squire, who never dreamt that his orders would be executed so literally and summarily as to dispense with all formal appeal to himself). As soon as Dr. Riccabocca made that discovery, it occurred to him that all the wisdom of all the schools that ever existed can't reconcile man or boy to a bad position — the moment there is a fair opportunity of letting him out of it. Accordingly, without more ado, he lifted up the creaking board, and Lenny Fairfield darted forth like a bird from a cage — halted a moment as if for breath, or in joy; and then, taking at once to his heels, fled, as a hare to its form — fast to his mother's home.

Dr. Riccabocca dropped the yawning wood into its place, picked up his handkerchief and restored it to his pocket; and then, with some curiosity, began to examine the nature of that place of duresse which had caused so much painful emotion to its rescued victim. "Man is a very irrational animal at best," quoth the sage, soliloquising, "and is frightened by strange buggabooes! 'Tis but a piece of wood! how little it really injures! And, after all, the holes are but rests to the legs, and keep the feet out of the dirt. And this green bank to sit upon — under the shade of the elm-tree — verily the position must be more pleasant than otherwise! I've a great mind ——" Here the Doctor looked around, and seeing the coast still clear, the oddest notion imaginable took possession of him; yet not indeed a notion so odd, considered philosophically — for all philosophy is based on practical experiment — and Dr. Riccabocca felt an irresistible desire practically to experience what manner of thing that punishment of the stocks really was. "I can but try! only for a moment," said he, apologetically to his own expostulating sense of dignity. "I have time to do it before any one comes." He lifted up the partition again: but stocks are built on the true principle of English law, and don't easily allow a man to criminate himself — it was hard to get into them without the help of a friend. However, as we before noticed, obstacles only whetted Dr. Riccabocca's invention. He looked round, and saw a withered bit of stick under the tree — this he inserted in the division of the stocks, somewhat in the manner in which boys place a stick under a sieve for the purpose of ensnaring sparrows: the fatal wood thus propped, Dr. Riccabocca sat gravely down on the bank, and thrust his feet through the apertures.

"Nothing in it!" cried he triumphantly, after a moment's deliberation. "The evil is only in idea. Such is the boasted reason of mortals!" With that reflection, nevertheless, he was about to withdraw his feet from their voluntary dilemma, when the crazy stick suddenly gave way, and the partition fell back into its clasp. Dr. Riccabocca was fairly caught—"*Facilis descensus—sed revocare gradum!*" True, his hands were at liberty, but his legs were so long that, being thus fixed, they kept the hands from the rescue; and as Dr. Riccabocca's form was by no means supple, and the twin parts of the wood stuck together with that firmness of adhesion which things newly-painted possess, so, after some vain twists and contortions, in which he succeeded at length (not without a stretch of the sinews that made them crack again) in finding the clasp and breaking his nails thereon, the victim of his own rash experiment resigned himself to his fate. Dr. Riccabocca was one of those men who never do things by halves. When I say he resigned himself, I mean not only Christian but philosophical resignation. The position was not quite so pleasant as, theoretically, he had deemed it; but he resolved to make himself as comfortable as he could. At first, as is natural in all troubles to men who have grown familiar with that odoriferous comforter which Sir Walter Raleigh is said first to have bestowed upon the Caucasian races, the Doctor made use of his hand to extract from his pocket his pipe, match-box, and tobacco-pouch. After a few whiffs, he would have been quite reconciled to his situation, but for the discovery that the sun had shifted its place in the heavens, and was no longer shaded from his face by the elm-tree. The Doctor again looked round, and perceived that his red silk umbrella, which he had laid aside when he had seated himself by Lenny, was within arm's reach. Possessing himself of this treasure, he soon expanded its friendly folds. And thus, doubly fortified within and without, under shade of the umbrella, and his pipe composedly between his lips, Dr. Riccabocca gazed on his own incarcerated legs, even with complacency.

"'He who can despise all things,'" said he, in one of his native proverbs, "'possesses all things!'—if one despises freedom, one is free! This seat is as soft as a sofa! I am not sure," he resumed, soliloquising, after a pause—"I am not sure that there is not something more witty than manly and philosophical in that national proverb of mine which I quoted to the *fanciullo*, 'that there are no handsome prisons!' Did not the son of that celebrated Frenchman, surnamed *Bras de Fer*, write a book not only to prove that adversities are more necessary than prosperities, but that among all adversities a prison is the most pleasant and profitable?* But is not this condition of mine, voluntarily and experimentally incurred, a type of my life? Is it the first time that I have thrust myself into a hobble?—and if in a hobble of mine own choosing, why should I blame the gods?"

Upon this, Dr. Riccabocca fell into a train of musing so remote from time and place, that in a few minutes he no more remembered that he was in the parish stocks than a lover remembers that flesh is grass, a miser that mammon is perishable, a philosopher that wisdom is vanity. Dr. Riccabocca was in the clouds.

* "*Entre tout, l'état d'une prison est le plus doux, est le plus profitable!*"

CHAPTER X.

THE dullest dog that ever wrote a novel (and, *entre nous*, reader — but let it go no farther—we have a good many dogs among the fraternity that are not Munitos *) might have seen with half an eye that the Parson's discourse had produced a very genial and humanizing effect upon his audience. When all was over, and the congregation stood up to let Mr. Hazeldean and his family walk first down the aisle (for that was the custom at Hazeldean), moistened eyes glanced at the Squire's sun-burned manly face, with a kindness that bespoke revived memory of many a generous benefit and ready service. The head might be wrong now and then—the heart was in the right place after all. And the lady, leaning on his arm, came in for a large share of that gracious good feeling. True, she now and then gave a little offence when the cottages were not so clean as she fancied they ought to be — and poor folks don't like a liberty taken with their houses any more than the rich do; true that she was not quite so popular with the women as the Squire was, for, if the husband went too often to the ale-house, she always laid

* Munito was the name of a dog famous for his learning (a Porson of a dog) at the date of my childhood. There are no such dogs now-a-days.

the fault on the wife, and said, "No man would go out of doors for his comforts, if he had a smiling face and a clean hearth at his home;" whereas the Squire maintained the more gallant opinion, that "if Gill was a shrew, it was because Jack did not, as in duty bound, stop her mouth with a kiss!" Still, notwithstanding these more obnoxious notions on her part, and a certain awe inspired by the stiff silk gown and the handsome aquiline nose, it was impossible, especially in the softened tempers of that Sunday afternoon, not to associate the honest, comely, beaming countenance of Mrs. Hazeldean with comfortable recollections of soups, jellies, and wine in sickness, loaves and blankets in winter, cheering words and ready visits in every little distress, and pretexts afforded by improvement in the grounds and gardens (improvements which, as the Squire, who preferred productive labor, justly complained, "would never finish") for little timely jobs of work to some veteran grandsire, who still liked to earn a penny, or some ruddy urchin in a family that "came too fast." Nor was Frank, as he walked a little behind, in the whitest of trousers and the stiffest of neckcloths — with a look of suppressed roguery in his bright hazel eye, that contrasted his assumed stateliness of mien —without his portion of the silent blessing. Not that he had done anything yet to deserve it; but we all give youth so large a credit in the future. As for Miss Jemima, her trifling foibles only rose from too soft and feminine a susceptibility, too ivy-like a yearning for some masculine oak whereon to entwine her tendrils; and so little confined to self was the natural lovingness of her disposition, that she had helped many a village lass to find a husband, by the bribe of a marriage gift from her own privy purse; notwithstanding the assurances with which she accompanied the marriage gift, — viz., that "the bridegroom would turn out like the rest of his ungrateful sex; but that it was a comfort to think that it would be all one in the approaching crash." So that she had her warm partisans, especially amongst the young; while the slim Captain, on whose arm she rested her forefinger, was at least a civil-spoken gentleman, who had never done any harm, and who would, doubtless, do a deal of good if he belonged to the parish. 'Nay, even the fat footman, who came last, with the family Prayer-book, had his due share in the general association of neighborly kindness between hall and hamlet. Few were there present to whom he had not extended the right-hand of fellowship with a full horn of October in the clasp of it; and he was a Hazeldean man, too, born and bred, as two-thirds of the Squire's household (now letting themselves out from their large pew under the gallery) were.

On his part, too, you could see that the Squire was "moved withal," and a little humbled moreover. Instead of walking erect, and taking bow and curtsey as a matter of course, and of no meaning, he hung his head somewhat, and there was a slight blush on his cheek; and as he glanced upward and round him — shyly, as it were — and his eye met those friendly looks, it returned them with an earnestness that had in it something touching as well as cordial — an eye that said, as well as eye could say, "I don't quite deserve it, I fear, neighbors; but I thank you for your good-will with my whole heart." And so readily was that glance of the eye understood, that I think, if that scene had taken place out of doors instead of in the church, there would have been a hurrah as the Squire passed out of sight.

Scarcely had Mr. Hazeldean got clear of the churchyard, ere Mr. Stirn was whispering in his ear. As Stirn whispered, the Squire's face grew long, and his color rose. The congregation, now flocking out of the church, exchanged looks with each other; that ominous conjunction between Squire and man chilled back all the effects of the Parson's sermon. The Squire struck his cane violently into the ground. "I would rather you had told me Black Bess had got the glanders. A young gentleman, coming to visit my son, struck and insulted in Hazeldean; a young gentleman — 'sdeath, sir, a relation — his grandmother was a Hazeldean. I do believe Jemima's right, and the world's coming to an end! But Leonard Fairfield in the stocks! What will the Parson say, and after such a sermon! 'Rich man, respect the poor!' And the good widow too; and poor Mark, who almost died in my arms. Stirn, you have a heart of stone! You confounded, lawless, merciless miscreant, who the deuce gave you the right to imprison man or boy in my parish of Hazeldean without trial, sentence, or warrant? Run and let the boy out before any one sees him: run, or I shall ——" The Squire elevated the cane, and his eyes shot fire. Mr. Stirn did not run, but he walked off very fast. The Squire drew back a few paces, and again took his wife's arm. "Just wait a bit for the Parson, while I talk to the congregation. I want to stop 'em all, if I can, from going into the village; but how?"

Frank heard, and replied readily —

"Give 'em some beer, sir."

"Beer! on a Sunday! For shame, Frank!" cried Mrs. Hazeldean.

"Hold your tongue, Harry. Thank you, Frank," said the Squire, and his brow grew as clear as the blue sky above him. I doubt if Riccabocca could have got him out of his dilemma with the same ease as Frank had done.

"Halt there, my men—lads and lasses too—there, halt a bit. Mrs. Fairfield, do you hear? — halt. I think his reverence has given us a capital sermon. Go up to the Great House all of you, and drink a glass to his health. Frank, go with them, and tell Spruce to tap one of the casks kept for the haymakers.—Harry [this in a whisper], catch the Parson, and tell him to come to me instantly."

"My dear Hazeldean, what has happened? you are mad."

"Don't bother — do what I tell you."

"But where is the Parson to find you?"

"Where, gad zooks, Mrs. H., — at the Stocks, to be sure!"

CHAPTER XI.

Dr. Riccabocca, awakened out of his reverie by the sound of footsteps, was still so little sensible of the indignity of his position, that he enjoyed exceedingly, and with all the malice of his natural humor, the astonishment and stupor manifested by Stirn, when that functionary beheld the extraordinary substitute which fate and philosophy had found for Lenny Fairfield. Instead of the weeping, crushed, broken-hearted captive whom he had reluctantly come to deliver, he stared, speechless and aghast, upon the grotesque but tranquil figure of the Doctor, enjoying his pipe, and cooling himself under his umbrella, with a *sang-froid* that was truly appalling and diabolical. Indeed, considering that Stirn always suspected the Papisher of having had a hand in the whole of that black and midnight business, in which the stocks had been broken, bunged up, and consigned to perdition, and that the Papisher had the evil reputation of dabbling in the Black Art, the hocus-pocus way in which the Lenny he had incarcerated was transformed into the Doctor he found, conjoined with the peculiarly strange, eldritch, and Mephistophelean physiognomy and person of Riccabocca, could not but strike a thrill of superstitious dismay into the breast of the parochial tyrant.

While to his first confused and stammered exclamations and interrogatories, Riccabocca replied with so tragic an air, such ominous shakes of the head, such mysterious, equivocating, long-worded sentences, that Stirn every moment felt more and more convinced that the boy had sold himself to the Powers of Darkness; and that he himself prematurely, and in the flesh, stood face to face with the Arch-Enemy.

Mr. Stirn had not yet recovered his wonted intelligence, which, to do him justice, was usually prompt enough — when the Squire, followed hard by the Parson, arrived at the spot. Indeed, Mrs. Hazeldean's report of the Squire's urgent message, disturbed manner, and most unparalleled invitation to the parishoners, had given wings to Parson Dale's ordinarily slow and sedate movements. And while the Squire, sharing Stirn's amazement, beheld indeed a great pair of feet projecting from the stocks, and saw behind them the grave face of Doctor Riccabocca, under the majestic shade of the umbrella, but not a vestige of the only being his mind could indentify with the tenancy of the stocks, Mr. Dale catching him by the arm, and panting hard, exclaimed with a petulance he had never before known to display — except at the whist-table, —

"Mr. Hazeldean, Mr. Hazeldean, I am scandalised — I am shocked at you. I can bear a great deal from you, sir, as I ought to do; but to ask my whole congregation, the moment after divine service, to go up and guzzle ale at the Hall, and drink my health, as if a clergyman's sermon had been a speech at a cattle-fair! I am ashamed of you, and of the parish! What on earth has come to you all?"

"That's the very question I wish to Heaven I could answer," groaned the Squire, quite mildly and pathetically — "What on earth has come to us all! Ask Stirn:" (then bursting out) "Stirn, you infernal rascal, don't you hear? — what on earth has come to us all?"

"The Papisher is at the bottom of it, sir," said Stirn, provoked out of all temper. "I does my duty, but I is but a mortal man, arter all."

"A mortal fiddlestick — where's Leonard Fairfield, I say?"

"*Him* knows best," answered Stirn, retreating mechanically, for safety's sake, behind the Parson, and pointing to Dr. Riccabocca. Hitherto, though both the Squire and Parson had indeed recognised the Italian, they had merely supposed him to be seated on the bank. It never entered into their heads that so respectable and dignified a man could by any possibility be an inmate, compelled or voluntary, of the Parish Stocks. No, not even though, as I before said, the Squire had seen, just under his nose, a very long pair of soles inserted in the apertures — that sight had only confused and bewildered him, unaccompanied, as it ought to have been, with the trunk and face of Lenny Fairfield. Those soles seemed to him optical delusions, phantoms of the over-heated brain; but now, catching hold of Stirn, while the Parson in equal astonishment caught hold of him — the Squire faltered out, Well, this beats cock-fighting! The man's as mad as a

March hare, and has taken Dr. Rickeybockey for little Lenny!"

"Perhaps," said the Doctor, breaking silence with a bland smile, and attempting an inclination of the head as courteous as his position would permit — "perhaps, if it be quite the same to you, before you proceed to explanations, you will just help me out of the stocks."

The Parson, despite his perplexity and anger, could not repress a smile, as he approached his learned friend, and bent down for the purpose of extricating him.

"Lord love your reverence, you'd better not!" cried Mr. Stirn. "Don't be tempted — he only wants to get you into his claws. I would not go a-near him for all the ——"

The speech was interrupted by Dr. Riccabocca himself, who now, thanks to the parson, had risen into his full height, and half a head taller than all present — even than the tall Squire — approached Mr. Stirn, with a gracious wave of the hand. Mr. Stirn retreated rapidly towards the hedge, amidst the branches of which he plunged himself incontinently.

"I guess whom you take me for, Mr. Stirn," said the Italian, lifting his hat with his characteristic politeness. "It is certainly a great honor: but you will know better one of these days, when the gentleman in question admits you to a personal interview in another, and — a hotter world."

CHAPTER XII.

"But how on earth did you get into my new stocks?" asked the Squire, scratching his head.

"My dear sir, Pliny the elder got into the crater of Mount Etna."

"Did he, and what for?"

"To try what it was like, I suppose," answered Riccabocca.

The Squire burst out a-laughing.

"And so you got into the stocks to try what it was like. Well, I can't wonder — it is a very handsome pair of stocks," continued the Squire, with a loving look at the object of his praise. "Nobody need be ashamed of being seen in those stocks—I should not mind it myself."

"We had better move on," said the Parson, dryly, "or we shall have the whole village here presently, gazing on the lord of the manor in the same predicament as that from which we have just extricated the Doctor. Now, pray, what is the matter with Lenny Fairfield? I can't understand a word of what has passed. You don't mean to say that good Lenny Fairfield (who was absent from church, by-the-bye) can have done anything to get into disgrace?"

"Yes, he has though," cried the Squire. "Stirn, I

say Stirn" But Stirn had forced his way through the hedge and vanished. Thus left to his own powers of narrative at second-hand, Mr. Hazeldean now told all he had to communicate; the assault upon Randal Leslie, and the prompt punishment inflicted by Stirn, his own indignation at the affront to his young kinsman, and his good-natured, merciful desire to save the culprit from public humiliation.

The Parson, mollified towards the rude and hasty invention of the beer-drinking, took the Squire by the hand. "Ah, Mr. Hazeldean, forgive me," he said repentantly; "I ought to have known at once that it was only some ebullition of your heart that could stifle your sense of decorum. But this is a sad story about Lenny, brawling and fighting on the Sabbath-day. So unlike him, too — I don't know what to make of it."

"Like or unlike," said the Squire, "it has been a gross insult to young Leslie; and looks all the worse because I and Audley are not just the best friends in the world. I can't think what it is," continued Mr. Hazeldean, musingly; "but it seems that there must be always some association of fighting connected with that prim half-brother of mine. There was I, son of his own mother — who might have been shot through the lungs, only the ball lodged in the shoulder — and now his wife's kinsman — my kinsman, too — grandmother a Hazeldean — a hard-reading, sober lad, as I am given to understand, can't set his foot into the quietest parish in the three kingdoms, but what the mildest boy that ever was seen — makes a rush at him like a mad bull. It is FATALITY!" cried the Squire, solemnly.

"Ancient legends record similar instances of fatality in certain houses," observed Riccabocca. "There was the House of Pelops — and Polynices and Eteocles — the sons of Œdipus!"

"Pshaw!" said the parson; "but what's to be done?"

"Done?" said the Squire; "why, reparation must be made to young Leslie. And though I wished to spare Lenny, the young ruffian, a public disgrace — for your sake, Parson Dale, and Mrs. Fairfield's; — yet a good caning in private ——"

"Stop, sir!" said Riccabocca, mildly, "and hear me." The Italian then, with much feeling and considerable tact pleaded the cause of his poor *protégé*, and explained how Lenny's error arose only from mistaken zeal for the Squire's service, and in the execution of the orders received from Mr. Stirn.

"That alters the matter," said the Squire, softened; "and all that is necessary now will be for him to make a proper apology to my kinsman."

"Yes, that is just," rejoined the Parson; "but I still don't learn how he got out of the stocks."

Riccabocca then resumed his tale; and, after confessing his own principal share iu Lenny's escape, drew a moving picture of the boy's shame and honest mortification. "Let us march against Philip!" cried the Athenians when they heard Demosthenes ——

"Let us go at once and comfort the child!" cried the Parson, before Riccabocca could finish.

With that benevolent intention all three quickened their pace, and soon arrived at the widow's cottage. But Lenny had caught sight of their approach through the window; and not doubting that, in spite of Riccabocca's intercession, the Parson was come to upbraid, and the Squire to re-imprison, he darted out by the back way, got amongst the woods, and lay there *perdu* all the evening. Nay, it was not till after dark that his mother — who sat wringing her hands in the little kitchen, and trying in vain to listen to the Parson and Mrs. Dale, who (after sending in search of the fugitive) had kindly come to console the mother — heard a timid knock at the door and a nervous fumble at the latch. She started up, opened the door, and Lenny sprang to her bosom, and there buried his face, sobbing loud.

"No harm, my boy," said the Parson, tenderly; "you have nothing to fear — all is explained and forgiven."

Lenny looked up, and the veins on his forehead were much swollen. "Sir," said he, sturdily, "I don't want to be forgiven — I aint done no wrong. And — I've been disgraced—and I won't go to school, never no more."

"Hush, Carry!" said the Parson to his wife, who, with the usual liveliness of her littie temper, was about to expostulate. "Good night, Mrs. Fairfield. I shall come and talk to you to-morrow, Lenny; by that time you will think better of it."

The Parson then conducted his wife home, and went up to the Hall to report Lenny's safe return; for the Squire was very uneasy about him, and had even in person shared the search. As soon as he heard Lenny was safe — "Well," said the Squire, "let him go the first thing in the morning to Rood Hall, to ask Master Leslie's pardon, and all will be right and smooth again."

"A young villain!" cried Frank, with his cheeks the color of scarlet; "to strike a gentleman and an Etonian, who had just been to call on *me!* But I wonder Randal let him off so well — any other boy in the sixth form would have killed him!"

"Frank," said the Parson, sternly, "if we all had our deserts, what should be done to him who not only lets the sun go down on his own wrath, but strives with uncharitable breath to fan the dying embers of another's?"

The clergyman here turned away from Frank, who bit his lip, and seemed abashed — while even his mother said not a word in his exculpation; for when the Parson did reprove in that stern tone, the majesty of the Hall stood awed before the rebuke of the Church. Catching Riccabocca's inquisitive eye, Mr. Dale drew aside the philosopher, and whispered to him his fears that it would be a very hard matter to induce Lenny to beg Randal Leslie's pardon, and that the proud stomach of the pattern boy would not digest the stocks with as much ease as a long regimen of philosophy had enabled the sage to do. This conference Miss Jemima soon interrupted by a direct appeal to the Doctor respecting the number of years (even without any previous and more violent incident) that the world could possibly withstand its own wear and tear.

"Ma'am," said the Doctor, reluctantly summoned away,

to look at a passage in some prophetic periodical upon that interesting subject — "ma'am, it is very hard that you should make one remember the end of the world, since, in conversing with you, one's natural temptation is to forget its existence."

Miss Jemima's cheeks were suffused with a deeper scarlet than Frank's had been a few minutes before. Certainly that deceitful, heartless compliment justified all her contempt for the male sex; and yet — such is human blindness — it went far to redeem all mankind in her credulous and too confiding soul.

"He is about to propose," sighed Miss Jemima.

"Giacomo," said Riccabocca, as he drew on his night-cap, and stepped majestically into the four-posted bed, "I think we shall get that boy for the garden now!"

Thus each spurred his hobby, or drove her car, round the Hazeldean whirligig

---

CHAPTER XIII.

Whatever may be the ultimate success of Miss Jemima Hazeldean's designs upon Dr. Riccabocca, the Machiavellian sagacity with which the Italian had counted upon securing the services of Lenny Fairfield was speedily and triumphantly established by the result. No voice of the Parson's, charmed he ever so wisely, could persuade the peasant-boy to go and ask pardon of the young gentleman, to whom, because he had done as he was bid, he owed an agonising defeat, and a shameful incarceration. And, to Mrs. Dale's vexation, the widow took the boy's part. She was deeply offended at the unjust disgrace Lenny had undergone in being put in the stocks; she shared his pride, and openly approved his spirit. Nor was it without great difficulty that Lenny could be induced to resume his lessons at school; nay, even to set foot beyond the precincts of his mother's holding. The point of the school at last he yielded, though sullenly; and the Parson thought it better to temporise as to the more unpalatable demand. Unluckily, Lenny's apprehensions of the mockery that awaited him in the merciless world of his village were realised. Though Stirn at first kept his own counsel, the Tinker blabbed the whole affair. And after the search instituted for Lenny on the fatal night, all attempts to hush up what had passed would have been impossible. So then Stirn told his story, as the Tinker had told his own; both tales were very unfavorable to Leonard Fairfield. The pattern-boy had broken the Sabbath, fought with his betters, and been well mauled into the bargain; the village lad had sided with Stirn and the authorities in spying out the misdemeanors of his equals: therefore Leonard Fairfield, in both capacities of degraded pattern-boy and baffled spy, could expect no mercy; he was ridiculed in the one, and hated in the other.

It is true that, in the presence of the schoolmaster, and under the eye of Mr. Dale, no one openly gave vent to malignant feelings; but the moment those checks were removed, popular persecution began.

Some pointed and mowed at him; some cursed him for a sneak, and all shunned his society; voices were heard in the hedgerows, as he passed through the village at dusk, "Who was put in the stocks?—baa!" "Who got a bloody nob for playing spy to Nick Stirn?—baa!" To resist this species of aggression would have been a vain attempt for a wiser head and a colder temper than our poor pattern-boy's. He took his resolution at once, and his mother approved it; and the second or third day after Dr. Riccabocca's return to the Casino, Lenny Fairfield presented himself on the terrace with a little bundle in his hand. "Please, sir," said he to the Doctor, who was sitting cross-legged on the balustrade, with his red silk umbrella over his head—"please, sir, if you'll be good enough to take me now, and give me any hole to sleep in, I'll work for your honor night and day; and as for the wages, mother says, 'just suit yourself, sir.'"

"My child," said the Doctor, taking Lenny by the hand, and looking at him with the sagacious eye of a wizard, "I knew you would come! and Giacomo is already prepared for you! As to wages, we'll talk of them by-and-bye."

Lenny being thus settled, his mother looked for some evenings on the vacant chair, where he had so long sate in the place of her beloved Mark; and the chair seemed so comfortless and desolate, thus left all to itself, that she could bear it no longer.

Indeed the village had grown as distasteful to her as to Lenny — perhaps more so; and one morning she hailed the Steward as he was trotting his hog-maned cob beside the door, and bade him tell the Squire that "she would take it very kind if he would let her off the six months' notice for the land and premises she held — there were plenty to step into the place at a much better rent."

"You're a fool," said the good-natured Steward; "and I'm very glad you did not speak to that fellow Stirn instead of to me. You've been doing extremely well here, and have the place, I may say, for nothing."

"Nothin' as to rent, sir, but a great deal as to feelin'," said the widow; "and now Lenny has gone to work with the foreign gentleman, I should like to go and live near him."

"Ah, yes — I heard Lenny had taken himself off to the Casino — more fool he; but, bless your heart, 'tis no distance — two miles or so. Can't he come home every night after work?"

"No, sir," exclaimed the widow, almost fiercely; "he shan't come home here, to be called bad names and jeered at! — he whom my dead good-man was so fond and proud of. No, sir; we poor folks have our feelings, as I said to Mrs. Dale, and as I will say to the Squire hisself. Not that I don't thank him for all favors — he be a good gentleman if let alone; but he says he won't come near us till Lenny goes and axes pardin. Pardin for what, I should like to know? Poor lamb! I wish you could ha' seen his nose, sir — as big as your two fists. Ax pardin! if the Squire had had such a nose as that, I don't think it's pardin he'd been ha' axing. But I let the passion get the better of me — I humbly beg you'll excuse it, sir. I'm no scholard as poor Mark was, and Lenny would have been, if the Lord had not visited us otherways. Therefore just get the Squire to let me go as soon as may be; and as for the bit o' hay and what's on the grounds and orchard, the new comer will no doubt settle that."

The Steward, finding no eloquence of his could induce the widow to relinquish her resolution, took her message to the Squire. Mr. Hazeldean, who was indeed really offended at the boy's obstinate refusal to make the *amende honorable* to Randal Leslie, at first only bestowed a hearty curse or two on the pride and ingratitude both of mother and son. It may be supposed, however, that his second thoughts were more gentle, since that evening, though he did not go himself to the widow, he sent his "Harry." Now, though Harry was sometimes austere and *brusque* enough on her own account, and in such business as might especially be transacted between herself and the cottagers, yet she never appeared as the delegate of her lord except in the capacity of a herald of peace and mediating angel. It was with good heart, too, that she undertook this mission, since, as we have seen, both mother and son were great favorites of hers. She entered the cottage with the friendliest beam in her bright blue eye, and it was with the softest tone of her frank, cordial voice that she accosted the widow. But she was no more successful than the Steward had been. The truth is, that I don't believe the haughtiest duke in the three kingdoms is really so proud as your plain English rural peasant, nor half so hard to propitiate and deal with when his sense of dignity is ruffled. Nor are there many of my own literary brethren (thin-skinned creatures though we are) so sensitively alive to the Public Opinion, wisely despised by Dr. Riccabocca, as that same peasant. He can endure a good deal of contumely sometimes, it is true, from his superiors (though, thank Heaven! *that* he rarely meets with unjustly); but to be looked down upon, and mocked, and pointed at by his own equals — his own little world — cuts him to the soul. And if you can succeed in breaking this pride, and destroying this sensitiveness, then he is a lost being. He can never recover his self-esteem, and you have chucked him halfway — a stolid, inert, sullen victim — to the perdition of the prison or the convict-ship.

Of this stuff was the nature both of the widow and her son. Had the honey of Plato flowed from the tongue of Mrs. Hazeldean, it could not have turned into sweetness the bitter spirit upon which it descended. But Mrs. Hazeldean, though an excellent woman, was rather a bluff, plain-spoken one — and, after all, she had some little feeling for the son of a gentleman, and a decayed, fallen gentleman, who, even by Lenny's account, had been assailed without any intelligible provocation; nor could she, with her strong common sense, attach all the importance which Mrs. Fairfield did to the unmannerly impertinence of a few young cubs, which she said truly, "would soon die away if no notice was taken of it." The widow's mind was made up, and Mrs. Hazeldean departed — with much chagrin and some displeasure.

Mrs. Fairfield, however, tacitly understood that the request she had made was granted, and early one morning her door was found locked — the key left at a neighbor's to be given to the Steward: and, on further inquiry, it was ascertained that her furniture and effects had been removed by the errand-cart, in the dead of the night. Lenny had succeeded in finding a cottage on the roadside, not far from the Casino; and there, with a joyous face, he waited to welcome his mother to breakfast, and show how he had spent the night in arranging her furniture.

Parson!" cried the Squire when all this news came upon him, as he was walking arm-in-arm with Mr. Dale, to inspect some proposed improvement in the Alms-house, "this is all your fault. Why did not you go and talk to that brute of a boy, and that dolt of a woman? You've got 'soft sawder enough,' as Frank calls it in his new-fashioned slang."

"As if I had not talked myself hoarse to both!" said the Parson, in a tone of reproachful surprise at the accusation. "But it was in vain! O Squire, if you had taken my advice about the stocks — *quieta non movere!*"

"Bother!" said the Squire. "I suppose I am to be held up as a tyrant, a Nero, a Richard the Third, or a Grand Inquisitor, merely for having things smart and tidy! Stocks indeed! — your friend Rickeybockey said he was never more comfortable in his life — quite enjoyed sitting there. And what did not hurt Rickeybockey's dignity (a very gentleman-like man he is, when he pleases) ought to be no such great matter to Master Leonard Fairfield. But 'tis no use talking! What's to be done now? The woman must not starve; and I'm sure she can't live out of Rickeybockey's wages to Lenny — (by the way, I hope he don't board the boy upon his and Jackeymo's leavings: I hear they dine upon newts and sticklebacks — faugh!) — I'll tell you what, Parson, now I think of it — at the back of the cottage which she has taken there are some fields of capital land just vacant. Rickeybockey wants to have 'em, and sounded me as to the rent when he was at the Hall. I only half-promised him the refusal. And he must give up four or five acres of the best land round the cottage to the widow — just enough for her to manage — and she can keep a dairy. If she want capital, I'll lend her some in your name — only don't tell Stirn; and as for the rent — we'll talk of that when we see how she gets on, thankless, obstinate jade that she is! You see," added the Squire, as if he felt there was some apology due for this generosity to an object whom he professed to consider so ungrateful, "her husband was a faithful servant, and so — I wish you would not stand there staring me out of countenance, but go down to the woman at once, or Stirn will have let the land to Rickeybockey, as sure as a gun. And harkye, Dale, perhaps you can contrive, if the woman is so cursedly stiff-backed, not to say the land is mine, or that it is any favor I want to do her — or, in short, manage it as you can for the best." Still even this charitable message failed. The widow knew that the land was the Squire's, and worth a good £3 an acre. "She thanked him humbly for that and all favors; but she could not afford to buy cows, and she did not wish to be beholden to any one for her living. And Lenny was well off at Mr. Rickeybockey's, and coming on wonderfully in the garden way — and she did not doubt she could get some washing; at all events, her haystack would bring in a good bit of money, and she should do nicely, thank their honors."

Nothing farther could be done in the direct way, but the remark about the washing suggested some mode of indirectly benefiting the widow. And a little time afterwards, the sole laundress in that immediate neighborhood happening to die, a hint from the Squire obtained from the landlady of the inn opposite the Casino such custom as she had to bestow, which at times was not inconsiderable. And what with Lenny's wages (whatever that mysterious item might be,) the mother and son contrived to live without exhibiting any of those physical signs of fast and abstinence which Riccabocca and his valet gratuitously afforded to the student in animal anatomy.

CHAPTER XIV.

Of all the wares and commodities in exchange and barter, wherein so mainly consists the civilisation of our modern world, there is not one which is so carefully weighed—so accurately measured—so plumbed and gauged — so doled and scraped — so poured out in *minima* and balanced with scruples — as that necessary of social commerce called "an apology!" If the chemists were half so careful in vending their poisons, there would be a notable diminution in the yearly average of victims to arsenic and oxalic acid. But, alas, in the matter of apology, it is not from the excess of the dose, but the timid, niggardly, miserly manner in which it is dispensed, that poor Humanity is hurried off to the Styx! How many times does a life depend on the exact proportions of an apology! Is it a hair-breadth too short to cover the scratch for which you want it? Make your will — you are a dead man! A life, do I say? — a hecatomb of lives! How many wars would have been prevented, how many thrones would be standing, dynasties flourishing — commonwealths brawling round a *bema,* or fitting out galleys for corn and cotton — if an inch or two more of apology had been added to the proffered ell! But then that plaguy, jealous, suspicious, old vinegar-faced Honor, and her partner Pride — as penny-wise and pound-foolish a she-skinflint as herself — have the monopoly of the article. And what with the time they lose in adjusting their spectacles, hunting in the precise shelf for the precise quality demanded, then (quality found) the haggling as to quantum — considering whether it should be Apothecary's weight or Avoirdupois, or English measure or Flemish — and, finally, the hullabuloo they make if the customer is not perfectly satisfied with the monstrous little he gets for his money — I don't wonder, for my part, how one loses temper and patience, and sends Pride, Honor, and Apology, all to the devil. Aristophanes, in his "Comedy of *Peace*," insinuates a beautiful allegory by only suffering that goddess, though in fact she is his heroine, to appear as a mnte. She takes care never to open her lips. The shrewd Greek knew very well that she would cease to be Peace, if she once began to chatter. Wherefore, O reader, if ever you find your pump under the iron heel of another man's boot, heaven grant that you may hold your tongue, and not make things past all endurance and forgiveness by bawling out for an apology!

CHAPTER XV.

But the Squire and his son, Frank, were large-hearted, generous creatures in the article of apology, as in all things less skimpingly dealt out. And seeing that Leonard Fairfield would offer no plaster to Randal Leslie, they made amends for his stinginess by their own prodigality. The Squire accompanied his son to Rood Hall, and none of the family choosing to be at home, the Squire in his own hand, and from his own head, indited and composed an epistle which might have satisfied all the wounds which the dignity of the Leslies had ever received.

This letter of apology ended with a hearty request that Randal would come and spend a few days with his son. Frank's epistle was to the same purport, only more Etonian and less legible.

It was some days before Randal's replies to these epistles were received. The replies bore the address of a village near London, and stated that the writer was now reading with a tutor preparatory to entrance at Oxford, and could not, therefore, accept the invitation extended to him.

For the rest, Randal expressed himself with good sense, though not with much generosity. He excused his participation in the vulgarity of such a conflict by a bitter but short allusion to the obstinacy and ignorance of the village boor; and did not do what you, my kind reader, certainly would have done under similar circumstances — viz.: intercede in behalf of a brave and unfortunate antagonist. Most of us like a foe better after we have fought him — that is, if we are the conquering party; this was not the case with Randal Leslie. There, so far as the Etonian was concerned, the matter rested. And the Squire, irritated that he could not repair whatever wrong that young gentleman had sustained, no longer felt a pang of regret as he passed by Mrs. Fairfield's deserted cottage.

CHAPTER XVI.

Lenny Fairfield continued to give great satisfaction to his new employers, and to profit in many respects by the familiar kindness with which he was treated. Riccabocca, who valued himself on penetrating into character, had, from the first, seen that much stuff of no common quality and texture was to be found in the disposition and mind of the English village boy. On farther acquaintance, he perceived that, under a child's innocent simplicity, there were the workings of an acuteness that required but development and direction. He ascertained that the pattern-boy's progress at the village school proceeded from something more than mechanical docility and readiness of comprehension. Lenny had a keen thirst for knowledge, and through all the disadvantages of birth and circumstance, there were the indications of that natural genius which converts disadvantages themselves into stimulants. Still, with the germs of good qualities lay the embryos of those which, difficult to separate, and hard to destroy, often mar the produce of the soil. With a remarkable and generous pride in self-repute, there was some stubbornness; with great sensibility to kindness, there was also strong reluctance to forgive affront.

This mixed nature in an uncultivated peasant's breast interested Riccabocca, who, though long secluded from the commerce of mankind, still looked upon man as the most various and entertaining volume which philosophical research can explore. He soon accustomed the boy to the tone of a conversation generally subtle and suggestive; and Lenny's language and ideas became insensibly less rustic and more refined. Then Riccabocca selected from his library, small as it was, books that, though elementary, were of a higher class than Lenny could have found within his reach at Hazeldean. Riccabocca knew the English language well — better in grammar, construction, and genius than many a not ill-educated Englishman; for he had studied it with the minuteness with which a scholar studies a dead language, and amidst his collection he had many of the books which had formerly served him for that purpose. These were the first works he lent to Lenny. Meanwhile Jackeymo imparted to the boy many secrets in practical gardening and minute husbandry, for at that day farming in England (some favored counties and estates excepted) was far below the nicety to which the art has been immemorially carried in the north of Italy—where, indeed, you may travel for miles and miles as through a series of market-gardens — so that, all these things considered, Leonard Fairfield might be said to have made a change for the better. Yet, in truth, and looking below the surface, that might be fair matter of doubt. For the same reason which had induced the boy to fly his native village, he no longer repaired to the church of Hazeldean. The old, intimate intercourse between him and the Parson became necessarily suspended, or bounded to an occasional kindly visit from the latter — visits which grew more rare, and less familiar, as he found his former pupil in no want of his services, and wholly deaf to his mild entreaties to forget and forgive the past, and come at least to his old seat in the parish church. Lenny still went to church — a church a long way off in another parish — but the sermons did not do him the same good as Parson Dale's had done; and the clergyman, who had his own flock to attend to, did not condescend, as Parson Dale would have done, to explain what seemed obscure, and enforce what was profitable, in private talk, with that stray lamb from another's fold.

Now I question much if all Dr. Riccabocca's maxims, though they were often very moral, and generally very wise, served to expand the peasant boy's native good qualities, and correct his bad, half so well as the few simple words, not at all indebted to Machiavelli, which Leonard had once reverently listened to when he stood by Mark's elbow-chair, yielded up for the moment to the good Parson, worthy to sit in it; for Mr. Dale had a heart in which all the fatherless of the parish found their place. Nor was this loss of tender, intimate, spiritual lore so counterbalanced by the greater facilities for purely intellectual instruction, as modern enlightenment might presume. For, without disputing the advantage of knowledge in a general way, knowledge, in itself, is not friendly to content. Its tendency, of course, is to increase the desires, to dissatisfy us with what is, in order to urge progress to what may be; and, in that progress, what unnoticed martyrs among the many must fall, baffled and crushed by the way! To how large a number will be given desires they will never realise, dissatisfaction of the lot from which they will never rise! *Allons!* one is viewing the dark side of the question. It is all the fault of that confounded Riccabocca, who has already caused Lenny Fairfield to lean gloomily on his spade, and, after looking round and seeing no one near him, groan out querulously—

"And am I born to dig a potato-ground?"

Pardieu, my friend Lenny, if you live to be seventy, and ride in your crrriage, and by the help of a dinner-pill digest a spoonful of curry, you may sigh to think what a relish there was in potatoes roasted in ashes after you had digged them out of that ground with your own stout young hands. Dig on, Lenny Fairfield, dig on! Dr. Riccabocca will tell you that there was once an illustrious personage* who made experience of two very different occupations — one was ruling men, the other was planting cabbages; he thought planting cabbages much the pleasanter of the two!

CHAPTER XVII.

Dr. Riccabocca had secured Lenny Fairfield, and might therefore be considered to have ridden his hobby in the great whirligig with adroitness and success. But Miss Jemima was still driving round in her car, handling the reins, and flourishing the whip, without apparently having got an inch nearer to the flying form of Dr. Riccabocca.

Indeed, that excellent and only too susceptible spinster, with all her experience of the villany of man, had never conceived the wretch to be so thoroughly beyond the reach of redemption as when Dr. Riccabocca took his leave, and once more interred himself amidst the solitudes of the Casino, without having made any formal renunciation of his criminal celibacy. For some days she shut herself up in her own chamber, and brooded with more than her usual gloomy satisfaction on the certainty of the approaching crash. Indeed, many signs of that universal calamity, which, while the visit of Riccabocca lasted, she had permitted herself to consider ambiguous, now became

---

* The Emperor Diocletian.

luminously apparent. Even the newspaper, which during that credulous and happy period had given half a column to Births and Marriages, now bore an ominously long catalogue of Deaths; so that it seemed as if the whole population had lost heart, and had no chance of repairing its daily losses. The leading articles spoke, with the obscurity of a Pythian, of an impending CRISIS. Monstrous turnips sprouted out from the paragraphs devoted to General News. Cows bore calves with two heads, whales were stranded in the Humber, showers of frogs descended in the High-street of Cheltenham.

All these symptoms of the world's decrepitude and consummation, which by the side of the fascinating Riccabocca might admit of some doubt as to their origin and cause, now conjoined with the worst of all, viz., the frightfully progressive wickedness of man — left to Miss Jemima no ray of hope save that afforded by the reflection that she could contemplate the wreck of matter without a single sentiment of regret.

Mrs. Dale, however, by no means shared the despondency of her fair friend, and, having gained access to Miss Jemima's chamber, succeeded, though not without difficulty, in her kindly attempts to cheer the drooping spirits of that female misanthropist. Nor, in her benevolent desire to speed the car of Miss Jemima to its hymeneal goal, was Mrs. Dale so cruel towards her male friend, Dr. Riccabocca, as she seemed to her husband. For Mrs. Dale was a woman of shrewdness and penetration, as most quick-tempered women are; and she knew that Miss

Jemima was one of those excellent young ladies who are likely to value a husband in proportion to the difficulty of obtaining him. In fact, my readers of both sexes must often have met, in the course of their experience, with that peculiar sort of feminine disposition, which requires the warmth of the conjugal hearth to develop all its native good qualities; nor is it to be blamed overmuch if, innocently aware of this tendency in its nature, it turns towards what is best fitted for its growth and improvement, by laws akin to those which make the sun-flower turn to the sun, or the willow to the stream. Ladies of this disposition, permanently thwarted in their affectionate bias, gradually languish away into intellectual inanition, or sprout out into those abnormal eccentricities which are classed under the general name of "oddity" or "character." But, once admitted to their proper soil, it is astonishing what healthful improvement takes place — how the poor heart, before starved and stinted of nourishment, throws out its suckers, and bursts into bloom and fruit. And thus many a belle from whom the beaux have stood aloof, only because the puppies think she could be had for the asking, they see sfterwards settled down into true wife and fond mother, with amaze at their former disparagement, and a sigh at their blind hardness of heart.

In all probability, Mrs. Dale took this view of the subject; and certainly, in addition to all the hitherto dormant virtues which would be awakened in Miss Jemima when fairly Mrs. Riccabocca, she counted somewhat upon the mere worldly advantage which such a match would bestow upon the exile. So respectable a connection with one of the oldest, wealthiest, and most popular families in the shire, would in itself give him a position not to be despised by a poor stranger in the land; and though the interest in Miss Jemima's dowry might not be much, regarded in the light of English pounds (not Milanese *lire*), still it would suffice to prevent that gradual process of dematerialisation which the lengthened diet upon minnows and sticklebacks had already made apparent in the fine and slow-evanishing form of the philosopher.

Like all persons convinced of the expediency of a thing, Mrs. Dale saw nothing wanting but opportunities to insure its success. And that these might be forthcoming, she not only renewed with greater frequency, and more urgent instance than ever, her friendly invitations to Riccabocca to drink tea and spend the evening, but she so artfully chafed the Squire on his sore point of hospitality, that the Doctor received weekly a pressing solicitation to dine and sleep at the Hall.

At first the Italian pished and grunted, and said *Cospetto*, and *Per Bacco*, and *Diavolo*, and tried to creep out of so much proffered courtesy. But, like all single gentlemen, he was a little under the tyrannical influence of his faithful servant; and Jackeymo, though he could bear starving as well as his master, when necessary, still, when he had the option, preferred roast-beef and plum-pudding. Moreover, that vain and incautious confidence of Riccabocca, touching the vast sum at his command, and with no heavier drawback than that of so amiable a lady as

Miss Jemima — who had already shown him (Jackeymo) many little delicate attentions — had greatly whetted the cupidity which was in the servant's Italian nature; a cupidity the more keen because, long debarred its legitimate exercise on his own mercenary interests, he carried it all to the account of his master's!

Thus tempted by his enemy, and betrayed by his servant, the unfortunate Riccabocca fell, though with eyes not blinded, into the hospitable snares extended for the destruction of his — celibacy! He went often to the Parsonage, often to the Hall, and by degrees the sweets of the social domestic life, long denied him, began to exercise their enervating charm upon the stoicism of our poor exile. Frank had now returned to Eton. An unexpected invitation had carried off Captain Higginbotham to pass a few weeks at Bath with a distant relation, who had lately returned from India, and who, as rich as Crœsus, felt so estranged and solitary in his native isle, that, when the Captain "claimed kindred there," to his own amaze, "he had his claims allowed;" while a very protracted sitting of Parliament still delayed in London the Squire's habitual visitors during the later summer; so that — a chasm thus made in his society — Mr. Hazeldean welcomed with no hollow cordiality the diversion or distraction he found in the foreigner's companionship. Thus, with pleasure to all parties, and strong hopes to the two female conspirators, the intimacy between the Casino and Hall rapidly thickened; but still not a word resembling a distinct proposal did Dr. Riccabocca breathe. And still, if such an idea obtruded itself on his mind, it was chased therefrom with so determined a *Diavolo*, that perhaps, if not the end of the world, at least the end of Miss Jemima's tenure in it, might have approached, and seen her still Miss Jemima, but for a certain letter with a foreign post-mark that reached the Doctor one Tuesday morning.

CHAPTER XVIII.

The servant saw that something had gone wrong, and, under pretence of syringing the orange-trees, he lingered near his master, and peered through the sunny leaves upon Riccabocca's melancholy brows.

The Doctor sighed heavily. Nor did he, as was his wont, after some such sigh, mechanically take up that dear comforter the pipe. But though the tobacco-pouch lay by his side on the balustrade, and the pipe stood against the wall between his knees, childlike lifting up its lips to the customary caress — he heeded neither the one nor the other, but laid the letter silently on his lap, and fixed his eyes upon the ground.

"It must be bad news, indeed!" thought Jackeymo, and desisted from his work. Approaching his master, he took up the pipe and the tobacco-pouch, and filled the bowl slowly, glancing all the while towards that dark musing face, on which, when abandoned by the expression of intellectual vivacity or the exquisite smile of Italian courtesy, the deep downward lines revealed the characters of sorrow. Jackeymo did not venture to speak; but the continued silence of his master disturbed him much. He laid that peculiar tinder which your smokers use upon the steel, and struck the spark—still not a word, nor did Riccabocca stretch forth his hand.

"I never knew him in this taking before," thought Jackeymo; and delicately he insinuated the neck of the pipe into the nerveless fingers of the hand that lay supine on those quiet knees. The pipe fell to the ground.

Jackeymo crossed himself, and began praying to his sainted namesake with great fervor.

The Doctor rose slowly, and as if with an effort; he walked once or twice to and fro the terrace; and then he halted abruptly, and said —

"Friend!"

"Blessed *Monsignore San Giacomo,* I knew thou wouldst hear me!" cried the servant; and he raised his master's hand to his lips, then abruptly turned away and wiped his eyes.

"Friend," repeated Riccabocca, and this time with a tremulous emphasis, and in the softest tone of a voice never wholly without the music of the sweet South, "I would talk to thee of my child."

CHAPTER XIX.

"THE letter, then, relates to the Signorina. She is well?"

"Yes, she is well now. She is in our native Italy."

Jackeymo raised his eyes involuntarily towards the orange-trees, and the morning breeze swept by and bore to him the odor of their blossoms.

"Those are sweet even here, with care," said he, pointing to the trees. "I think I have said that before to the Padrone."

But Riccabocca was now looking again at the letter, and did not notice either the gesture or the remark of his servant.

"My aunt is no more!" said he, after a pause.

"We will pray for her soul!" answered Jackeymo solemnly. "But she was very old, and had been a long time ailing. Let it not grieve the Padrone too keenly: at that age, and with those infirmities, death comes as a friend."

"Peace be to her dust!" returned the Italian. "If she had her faults, be they now forgotten for ever; and in the hour of my danger and distress she sheltered my infant! That shelter is destroyed. This letter is from the priest, her confessor. And the home of which my child is bereaved falls to the inheritance of my enemy."

"Traitor!" muttered Jackeymo; and his right hand seemed to feel for the weapon which the Italians of the lower rank often openly wear in their girdles.

"The priest," resumed Riccabocca, calmly, "has rightly judged in removing my child as a guest from the house in which that traitor enters as lord."

"And where is the Signorina?"

"With the poor priest. See, Giacomo—here, here—this is her handwriting at the end of the letter—the first lines she ever yet traced to me."

Jackeymo took off his hat, and looked reverently on the large characters of a child's writing. But large as they were, they seemed indistinct, for the paper was blistered with the child's tears; and on the place where they had *not* fallen, there was a round, fresh, moist stain of the tear that had dropped from the lids of the father. Riccabocca renewed,—"The priest recommends a convent."

"To the devil with the priest!" cried the servant; then crossing himself rapidly, he added, "I did not mean that, Monsignore San Giacomo—forgive me! But your Excellency * does not think of making a nun of his only child!"

"And yet why not?" said Riccabocca mournfully; "what can I give her in the world? Is the land of the

* The title of Excellency does not, in Italian, necessarily express any exalted rank; but is often given by servants to their masters.

stranger a better refuge than the home of peace in her native clime?"

"In the land of the stranger beats her father's heart!"

"And if that beat were stilled, what then? Ill fares the life that a single death can bereave of all. In a convent at least (and the priest's influence can obtain her that asylum amongst her equals and amidst her sex) she is safe from trial and from penury — to her grave."

"Penury! Just see how rich we shall be when we take those fields at Michaelmas."

"*Pazzie!*" (follies) said Riccabocca listlessly. "Are these suns more serene than ours, or the soil more fertile? Yet in our own Italy, saith the proverb, 'he who sows land reaps more care than corn.' It were different," continued the father, after a pause, and in a more resolute tone, "if I had some independence, however small, to count on—nay, if among all my tribe of dainty relatives there were but one female who would accompany Violante to the exile's hearth—Ishmael had his Hagar. But how can we two rough-bearded men provide for all the nameless wants and cares of a frail female child? And she has been so delicately reared—the woman child needs the fostering hand and tender eye of a woman."

"And with a word," said Jackeymo resolutely, "the Padrone might secure to his child all that he needs to save her from the sepulchre of a convent; and ere the autumn leaves fall, she might be sitting on his knee. Padrone, do not think that you can conceal from me the truth, that you love your child better than all things in the world — now the Patria is as dead to you as the dust of your fathers — and your heart-strings would crack with the effort to tear her from them, and consign her to a convent. Padrone, never again to hear her voice — never again to see her face! Those little arms that twined round your neck that dark night, when we fled fast for life and freedom, and you said, as you felt their clasp, 'Friend, all is not yet lost.'"

"Giacomo!" exclaimed the father reproachfully, and his voice seemed to choke him. Riccabocca turned away, and walked restlessly to and fro the terrace; then, lifting his arms with a wild gesture, as he still continued his long irregular strides, he muttered, "Yes, heaven is my witness that I could have borne reverse and banishment without a murmur, had I permitted myself that young partner in exile and privation. Heaven is my witness that, if I hesitate now, it is because I would not listen to my own selfish heart. Yet never, never to see her again — my child! And it was but as the infant that I beheld her! O friend, friend — " (and, stopping short with a burst of uncontrollable emotion, he bowed his head upon his servant's shoulder) — "thou knowest what I have endured and suffered at my hearth, as in my country; the wrong, the perfidy, the — the —" His voice again failed him; he clung to his servant's breast, and his whole frame shook.

"But your child, the innocent one — think now only of her!" faltered Giacomo, struggling with his own sobs.

"True, only of her," replied the exile, raising his face

—"only of her. Put aside thy thoughts for thyself, friend—counsel me. If I were to send for Violante, and if, transplanted to these keen airs, she drooped and died—look, look—the priest says that she needs such tender care; or if I myself were summoned from the world, to leave her in it alone, friendless, homeless, breadless perhaps, at the age of woman's sharpest trial against temptation, would she not live to mourn the cruel egotism that closed on her infant innocence the gates of the House of God?"

Jackeymo was appalled by this appeal; and indeed Riccabocca had never before thus revererently spoken of the cloister. In his hours of philosophy, he was wont to sneer at monks and nuns, priesthood and superstition. But now, in that hour of emotion, the Old Religion reclaimed her empire; and the sceptical world-wise man, thinking only of his child, spoke and felt with a child's simple faith.

CHAPTER XX.

"But again I say," murmured Jackeymo scarce audibly, and after a long silence, "if the Padrone would make up his mind—to marry!"

He expected that his master would start up in his customary indignation at such a suggestion—nay, he might not have been sorry so to have changed the current of feeling; but the poor Italian only winced slightly, and mildly withdrawing himself from his servant's supporting arm, again paced the terrace, but this time quietly and in silence. A quarter of an hour thus passed. "Give me the pipe," said Dr. Riccabocca, passing into the Belvidere.

Jackeymo again struck the spark, and, wonderfully relieved at the Padrone's return to the habitual adviser, mentally besought his sainted namesake to bestow a double portion of soothing wisdom on the benignant influences of the weed.

CHAPTER XXI.

Dr. Riccabocca had been some time in the solitude of the Belvidere, when Lenny Fairfield, not knowing that his employer was therein, entered to lay down a book which the Doctor had lent him, with injunctions to leave it on a certain table when done with. Riccabocca looked up at the sound of the young peasant's step.

"I beg your honor's pardon — I did not know——"

"Never mind: lay the book there. I wish to speak with you. You look well, my child: this air agrees with you as well as that of Hazeldean?"

"Oh, yes, sir!"

"Yet it is higher ground — more exposed?"

"That can hardly be, sir," said Lenny; "there are many plants grow here which don't flourish at the Squire's.

The hill yonder keeps off the east wind, and the place lays to the south."

"Lies, not *lays*, Lenny. What are the principal complaints in these parts?"

"Eh, sir?"

"I mean what maladies, what diseases?"

"I never heard tell of any, sir, except the rheumatism."

"No low fevers? — no consumption?"

"Never heard of them, sir."

Riccabocca drew a long breath, as if relieved.

"That seems a very kind family at the Hall."

"I have nothing to say against it," answered Lenny, bluntly. "I have not been treated justly. But as that book says, sir, 'It is not every one who comes into the world with a silver spoon in his mouth.'"

Little thought the Doctor that those wise maxims may leave sore thoughts behind them. He was too occupied with the subject most at his own heart to think then of what was in Lenny Fairfield's.

"Yes; a kind, English domestic family. Did you see much of Miss Hazeldean?"

"Not so much as of the Lady."

"Is she liked in the village, think you?"

"Miss Jemima? Yes. She never did harm. Her little dog bit me once — she did not ask me to beg its pardon, she asked mine! She's a very nice young lady; the girls say she is very affable; and," added Lenny with a smile, "there are always more weddings going on when she is down at the Hall

"Oh!" said Riccabocca. Then, after a long whiff,

"Did you ever see her play with the little children? Is she fond of children, do you think?"

"Lord, sir, you guess everything! She's never so pleased as when she's playing with the babies."

"Humph!" grunted Riccabocca. "Babies — well, that's woman-like. I don't mean exactly babies, but when they're older — little girls?"

"Indeed, sir, I dare say; but," said Lenny primly, "I never as yet kept company with the little girls."

"Quite right, Lenny; be equally discreet all your life. Mrs. Dale is very intimate with Miss Hazeldean — more than with the Squire's lady. Why is that, think you?"

"Well, sir," said Leonard shrewdly, "Mrs. Dale has her little tempers, though she's a very good lady; and Madam Hazeldean is rather high, and has a spirit. But Miss Jemima is so soft: any one could live with Miss Jemima, as Joe and the servants say at the Hall!"

"Indeed! Get my hat out of the parlor, and — just bring a clothes-brush, Lenny. A fine sunny day for a walk."

After this most mean and dishonorable inquisition into the character and popular repute of Miss Hazeldean, Signior Riccabocca seemed as much cheered up and elated as if he had committed some very noble action; and he walked forth in the direction of the Hall with a far lighter and livelier step than that with which he had paced the terrace.

"*Monsignore San Giacomo*, by thy help and the pipe's, the Padrone shall have his child!" muttered the servant, looking up from the garden.

CHAPTER XXII.

YET Dr. Riccabocca was not rash. The man who wants his wedding-garment to fit him must allow plenty of time for the measure. But, from that day, the Italian notably changed his manner towards Miss Hazeldean. He ceased that profusion of compliment in which he had hitherto carried off in safety all serious meaning. For indeed the Doctor considered that compliments to a single gentleman were what the inky liquid it dispenses is to the cuttle-fish, that by obscuring the water sails away from its enemy. Neither did he, as before, avoid prolonged conversations with the young lady, and contrive to escape from all solitary rambles by her side. On the contrary, he now sought every occasion to be in her society; and, entirely dropping the language of gallantry, he assumed something of the earnest tone of friendship. He bent down his intellect to examine and plumb her own. To use a very homely simile, he blew away that froth which there is on the surface of mere acquaintanceships, especially with the opposite sex; and which, while it lasts, scarce allows you to distinguish between small beer and double X. Apparently Dr. Riccabocca was satisfied with his scrutiny — at all events, under that froth there was no taste of bitter. The Italian might not find any great strength of intellect in Miss Jemima, but he found that, disentangled from many little whims and foibles — which he had himself the sense to perceive were harmless enough if they lasted, and not so absolutely constitutional but what they might be removed by a tender hand—Miss Hazeldean had quite enough sense to comprehend the plain duties of married life ; and if the sense could fail, it found a substitute in good old homely English principles, and the instincts of amiable, kindly feelings.

I know not how it is, but your very clever man never seems to care as much as your less gifted mortals for cleverness in his helpmate. Your scholars, and poets, and ministers of state, are more often than not found assorted with exceedingly humdrum, good sort of women, and apparently like them all the better for their deficiencies. Just see how happily Racine lived with his wife, and what an angel he thought her, and yet she had never read his plays. Certainly Goethe never troubled the lady who called him "Mr. Privy Councillor" with whims about "monads," and speculations on color, nor those stiff metaphysical problems on which one breaks one's shins in the Second Part of the Faust. Probably it may be that such great geniuses — knowing that, as compared with themselves, there is little difference between your clever woman and your humdrum woman — merge at once all minor distinctions, relinquish all attempts at sympathy in hard intellectual pursuits, and are quite satisfied to establish that tie which, after all, best resists wear and tear — viz., the tough household bond between one human heart and another.

At all events, this, I suspect, was the reasoning of Dr. Riccabocca, when one morning, after a long walk with Miss Hazeldean, he muttered to himself—

"Duro con duro
Non fece mai buon muro.'

Which may bear the paraphrase, "Bricks without mortar would make a very bad wall." There was quite enough in Miss Jemima's disposition to make excellent mortar: the Doctor took the bricks to himself.

When his examination was concluded, our philosopher symbolically evinced the result he had arrived at by a very simple proceeding on his part, which would have puzzled you greatly if you had not paused, and meditated thereon, till you saw all that it implied. *Dr. Riccabocca took off his spectacles!* He wiped them carefully, put them into their shagreen case, and locked them in his bureau:—that is to say, he left off wearing his spectacles.

You will observe that there was a wonderful depth of meaning in that critical symptom, whether it be regarded as a sign outward, positive, and explicit; or a sign metaphysical, mystical, and esoteric. For, as to the last, it denoted that the task of the spectacles was over; that, when a philosopher has made up his mind to marry, it is better henceforth to be short-sighted—nay, even somewhat purblind—than to be always scrutinising the domestic felicity, to which he is about to resign himself, through a pair of cold, unillusory barnacles. And for the things beyond the hearth, if he cannot see without spectacles, is he not about to ally to his own defective vision a good, sharp pair of eyes, never at fault where his interests are concerned? On the other hand, regarded positively, categorically, and explicitly, Dr. Riccabocca, by laying aside those spectacles, signified that he was about to commence that happy imitation of courtship when every man, be he ever so much a philosopher, wishes to look as young and as handsome as time and nature will allow. Vain task to speed the soft language of the eyes through the medium of those glassy interpreters! I remember, for my own part, that once, on a visit to the town of Adelaide, I — Pisistratus Caxton — was in great danger of falling in love — with a young lady, too, who would have brought me a very good fortune, when she suddenly produced from her reticule a very neat pair of No. 4, set in tortoise-shell, and fixing upon me their Gorgon gaze, froze the astonished Cupid into stone! And I hold it a great proof of the wisdom of Riccabocca, and of his vast experience in mankind, that he was not above the consideration of what your pseudo sages would have regarded as foppish and ridiculous trifles. It argued all the better for that happiness which is our being's end and aim, that in condescending to play the lover, he put those unbecoming petrifiers under lock and key.

And certainly, now the spectacles were abandoned, it was impossible to deny that the Italian had remarkably handsome eyes. Even through the spectacles, or lifted a little above them, they were always bright and expressive; but without those adjuncts, the blaze was softer and more tempered: they had that look which the French call *veloute*, or velvety; and he appeared altogether ten years younger. If our Ulysses, thus rejuvenated by his Minerva, has not fully made up his mind to make a Penelope of Miss Jemima, all I can say is, that he is worse than Polyphemus, who was only an Anthropophagos; —

He preys upon the weaker sex, and is a Gynophagite!

CHAPTER XXIII.

"And you commission me, then, to speak to our dear Jemima?" said Mrs. Dale, joyfully, and without any bitterness whatever in that "dear."

Dr. Riccabocca. — Nay, before speaking to Miss Hazeldean, it would surely be proper to know how far my addresses would be acceptable to the family.

Mrs. Dale. — Ah!

Dr. Riccabocca. — The Squire is, of course, the head of the family.

Mrs. Dale (absent and *distraite*). — The Squire — yes, very true — quite proper (then looking up, and with *naïveté*), can you believe me, I never thought of the Squire? And he is such an odd man, and has so many English prejudices, that really — dear me, how vexatious that it should never once have occurred to me that Mr. Hazeldean had a voice in the matter! Indeed, the relationship is so distant, — it is not like being her father; and Jemima is of age, and can do as she pleases; and —

but, as you say, it is quite proper that he should be consulted, as the head of the family.

Dr. Riccabocca. — And you think that the Squire of Hazeldean might reject my alliance? — Pshaw! that's a grand word, indeed; — I mean, that he might object very reasonably to his cousin's marriage with a foreigner, of whom he can know nothing, except that which in all countries is disreputable, and is said in this to be criminal — poverty?

Mrs. Dale (kindly). — You misjudge us poor English people, and you wrong the Squire, Heaven bless him! for we were poor enough when he singled out my husband from a hundred for the minister of his parish, for his neighbor and his friend. I will speak to him fearlessly——

Dr. Riccabocca. — And frankly. And now I have used that word, let me go on with the confession which your kindly readiness, my fair friend, somewhat interrupted. I said that if I might presume to think my addresses would be acceptable to Miss Hazeldean and her family, I was too sensible of her amiable qualities not to — not to ——

Mrs. Dale (with demure archness). — Not to be the happiest of men: that's the customary English phrase, Doctor.

Riccabocca (gallantly). — There cannot be a better. But, continued he, seriously, I wish it first to be understood that I have — been married before.

Mrs. Dale (astonished). — Married before!

Riccabocca. — And that I have an only child, dear to

me — inexpressibly dear. That child, a daughter, has hitherto lived abroad; circumstances now render it desirable that she should make her home with me. And I own fairly that nothing has so attached me to Miss Hazeldean, nor so induced my desire for our matrimonial connection, as my belief that she has the heart and the temper to become a kind mother to my little one.

Mrs. Dale (with feeling and warmth).—You judge her rightly there.

Riccabocca. — Now in pecuniary matters, as you may conjecture from my mode of life, I have nothing to offer to Miss Hazeldean corresponding with her own fortune, whatever that may be!

Mrs. Dale. — That difficulty is obviated by settling Miss Hazeldean's fortune on herself, which is customary in such cases.

Dr. Riccabocca's face lengthened. "And my child, then?" said he, feelingly. There was something in that appeal so alien from all sordid and merely personal mercenary motives, that Mrs. Dale could not have had the heart to make the very rational suggestion, — "But that child is not Jemima's, and you may have children by her."

She was touched, and replied, hesitatingly, — "But, from what you and Jemima may jointly possess, you can save something annually, — you can insure your life for your child. We did so when our poor child whom we lost was born (the tears rushed into Mrs. Dale's eyes;) and I fear that Charles still insures his life for my sake, though Heaven knows that — that ——"

The tears burst out. That little heart, quick and petulant though it was, had not a fibre of the elastic muscular tissues which are mercifully bestowed on the hearts of predestined widows. Dr. Riccabocca could not pursue the subject of life insurances further. But the idea — which had never occurred to the foreigner before, though so familiar to us English people when only possessed of a life income — pleased him greatly. I will do him the justice to say that he preferred it to the thought of actually appropriating to himself and to his child a portion of Miss Hazeldean's dower.

Shortly afterwards he took his leave, and Mrs. Dale hastened to seek her husband in his study, inform him of the success of her matrimonial scheme, and consult him as to the chance of the Squire's acquiescence therein. "You see," said she, hesitatingly, "though the Squire might be glad to see Jemima married to some Englishman, yet if he asks who and what is this Dr. Riccabocca, how am I to answer him?"

"You should have thought of that before," said Mr. Dale, with unwonted asperity; "and, indeed, if I had ever believed anything serious could come out of what seemed to me so absurd, I should long since have requested you not to interfere in such matters. Good heavens!" continued the Parson, changing color, "if we should have assisted, underhand as it were, to introduce into the family of a man to whom we owe so much, a connection that he would dislike! how base we should be! — how ungrateful!"

Poor Mrs. Dale was frightened by this speech, and still more by her husband's consternation and displeasure. To do Mrs. Dale justice, whenever her mild partner was really either grieved or offended, her little temper vanished — she became as meek as a lamb. As soon as she recovered the first shock she experienced, she hastened to dissipate the Parson's apprehensions. She assured him that she was convinced that, if the Squire disapproved of Riccabocca's pretensions, the Italian would withdraw them at once, and Miss Hazeldean would never know of his proposals. Therefore, in that case, no harm would be done.

This assurance, coinciding with Mr. Dale's convictions as to Riccabocca's scruples on the point of honor, tended much to compose the good man; and if he did not, as my reader of the gentler sex would expect from him, feel alarm lest Miss Jemima's affections should have been irretrievably engaged, and her happiness thus put in jeopardy by the Squire's refusal, it was not that the Parson wanted tenderness of heart, but experience in womankind; and he believed, very erroneously, that Miss Jemima Hazeldean was not one upon whom a disappointment of that kind would produce a lasting impression. Therefore Mr. Dale, after a pause of consideration, said kindly —

"Well, don't vex yourself — and I was to blame quite as much as you. But, indeed, I should have thought it easier for the Squire to have transplanted one of his tall cedars into his kitchen-garden, than for you to inveigle

Dr. Riccabocca into matrimonial intentions. But a man who could voluntarily put himself into the Parish Stocks for the sake of experiment, must be capable of anything! However, I think it better that I, rather than yourself, should speak to the Squire, and I will go at once."

CHAPTER XXIV.

THE Parson put on the shovel-hat, which — conjoined with other details in his dress peculiarly clerical, and already, even then, beginning to be out of fashion with churchmen — had served to fix upon him, emphatically, the dignified but antiquated style and cognomen of "Parson," and took his way towards the Home Farm, at which he expected to find the Squire. But he had scarcely entered upon the village-green when he beheld Mr. Hazeldean, leaning both hands on his stick, and gazing intently upon the Parish Stocks. Now, sorry am I to say that, ever since the Hegira of Lenny and his mother, the Anti-Stockian and Revolutionary spirit in Hazeldean, which the memorable homily of our Parson had awhile averted or suspended, had broken forth afresh. For though, while Lenny was present to be mowed and jeered at, there had been no pity for him, yet no sooner was he removed from the scene of trial, than a universal compassion for the barbarous usage he had received produced what is called "the reaction of public opinion."

Not that those who had mowed and jeered repented them of their mockery, or considered themselves in the slightest degree the cause of his expatriation. No; they, with the rest of the villagers, laid all the blame upon the stocks. It was not to be expected that a lad of such exemplary character could be thrust into that place of ignominy, and not be sensible of the affront. And who, in the whole village, was safe, if such goings-on and puttings-in were to be tolerated in silence, and at the expense of the very best and quietest lad the village had ever known? Thus, a few days after the widow's departure, the stocks was again the object of midnight desecration: it was bedaubed and bescratched — it was hacked and hewed — it was scrawled over with pithy lamentations for Lenny, and laconic execrations on tyrants. Night after night new inscriptions appeared, testifying the sarcastic wit and the vindictive sentiment of the parish. And perhaps the stocks was only spared from axe and bonfire by the convenience it afforded to the malice of the disaffected: it became the Pasquin of Hazeldean.

As disaffection naturally produces a correspondent vigor in authority, so affairs had been lately administered with greater severity than had been hitherto wont in the easy rule of the Squire and his predecessors. Suspected persons were naturally marked out by Mr. Stirn, and reported to his employer, who, too proud or too pained to charge them openly with ingratitude, at first only passed them by in his walks with a silent and stiff inclination of his head; and afterwards gradually yielding to the baleful influence of Stirn, the Squire grumbled forth "that he did not see why he should be always putting himself out of his way to show kindness to those who made such a return. There ought to be a difference between the good and the bad." Encouraged by this admission, Stirn had conducted himself towards the suspected parties, and their whole kith and kin, with the iron-handed justice that belonged to his character. For some, habitual donations of milk from the dairy, and vegetables from the gardens, were surlily suspended; others were informed that their pigs were always trespassing on the woods in search of acorns; or that they were violating the Game Laws in keeping lurchers. A beer-house, popular in the neighborhood, but of late resorted to overmuch by the grievance-mongers (and no wonder, since they had become the popular party), was threatened with an application to the magistrates for the withdrawal of its license. Sundry old women, whose grandsons were notoriously ill-disposed towards the stocks, were interdicted from gathering dead sticks under the avenues, on pretence that they broke down the live boughs; and, what was more obnoxious to the younger members of the parish than most other retaliatory measures, three chestnut trees, one walnut, and two cherry trees, standing at the bottom of the Park, and which had, from time immemorial, been given up to the youth of Hazeldean, were now solemnly placed under the general defence of "private property." And the crier had announced that, henceforth, all depredators on the fruit trees of Copse Hollow would be punished with the utmost rigor of the law.

Stirn, indeed, recommended much more stringent proceedings than all these indications of a change of policy, which, he averred, would soon bring the parish to its senses — such as discontinuing many little jobs of unprofitable work that employed the surplus labor of the village. But there the Squire, falling into the department, and under the benigner influence of his Harry, was as yet not properly hardened. When it came to a question that affected the absolute quantity of loaves to be consumed by the graceless mouths that fed upon him, the milk of human kindness — with which Providence has so bountifully snpplied that class of the mammalia called the "Bucolic," and of which our Squire had an extra "yield" — burst forth, and washed away all the indignation of the harsher Adam.

Still your policy of half measures, which irritates without crushing its victims, which flaps an exasperated wasp-nest with a silk pocket-handkerchief, instead of blowing it up with a match and train, is rarely successful; and, after three or four other and much guiltier victims than Lenny had been incarcerated in the stocks, the parish of Hazeldean was ripe for any enormity. Pestilent Jacobinical tracts, conceived and composed in the sinks of manufacturing towns — found their way into the popular beer-house — heaven knows how, though the Tinker was suspected of being the disseminator by all but Stirn, who still, in a whisper, accused the Papishers. And, finally, there appeared amongst the other graphic embellishments which the poor stocks had received, the rude *gravure* of a gentleman in a broad-brimmed hat and top-boots, suspended from a gibbet, with the inscription beneath — "A warnin to hall tirans — mind your hi! — sighnde Captin sTraw."

It was upon this significant and emblematic portraiture that the Squire was gazing when the Parson joined him.

"Well, Parson," said Mr. Hazeldean, with a smile which he meant to be pleasant and easy, but which was exceedingly bitter and grim, "I wish you joy of your flock — you see they have just hanged me in effigy!"

The Parson stared, and though greatly shocked, smothered his emotions; and attempted, with the wisdom of the serpent and the mildness of the dove, to find another original for the effigy.

"It is very bad, but not so bad as all that, Squire; that's not the shape of your hat. It is evidently meant for Mr. Stirn."

"Do you think so?" said the Squire, softened. "Yet the top-boots — Stirn never wears top-boots."

"No more do you, except in the hunting-field. If you look again, those are not tops — they are leggings — Stirn wears leggings. Besides, that flourish, which is meant for a nose, is a kind of a hook, like Stirn's; whereas your nose — though by no means a snub — rather turns up than not, as the Apollo's does, according to the plaster cast in Riccabocca's parlor."

"Poor Stirn!" said the Squire, in a tone that evinced complacency, not unmingled with compassion, "that's what a man gets in this world by being a faithful servant, and doing his duty with zeal for his employer. But you see that things have come to a strange pass, and the question now is, what course to pursue. The miscreants hitherto have defied all vigilance, and Stirn recommends the employment of a regular night-watch, with a lanthorn and bludgeon."

"That may protect the stocks, certainly; but will it keep those detestable tracts out of the beer-house?"

"We shall shut the beer-house up the next sessions."

"The tracts will break out elsewhere—the humor's in the blood!"

"I've half a mind to run off to Brighton or Leamington—good hunting at Leamington—for a year, just to let the rogues see how they can get on without me!"

The Squire's lip trembled.

"My dear Mr. Hazeldean," said the Parson, taking his friend's hand, "I don't want to parade my superior wisdom; but, if you had taken my advice, *quieta non movere!* Was there ever a parish so peaceable as this, or a country-gentleman so beloved as you were, before you undertook the task which has dethroned kings and ruined states—that of wantonly meddling with antiquity, whether for the purpose of uncalled-for repairs, or the revival of obsolete uses?"

At this rebuke, the Squire did not manifest his constitutional tendencies to choler; but he replied almost meekly, "If it were to do again, faith, I would leave the parish to the enjoyment of the shabbiest pair of stocks that ever disgraced a village. Certainly I meant it for the best — an ornament to the green ; however, now the stocks is rebuilt, the stocks must be supported. Will Hazeldean is not the man to give way to a set of thankless rapscallions."

"I think," said the Parson, "that you will allow that the House of Tudor, whatever its faults, was a determined, resolute dynasty enough—high-hearted and strong-headed. A Tudor would never have fallen into the same calamities as the poor Stuart did!"

"What the plague has the House of Tudor got to do with my stocks?"

"A great deal. Henry VIII. found a subsidy so unpopular that he gave it up; and the people, in return, allowed him to cut off as many heads as he pleased, besides those in his own family. Good Queen Bess, who, I know, is your idol in history ——"

"To be sure! — she knighted my ancestor at Tilbury Fort."

"Good Queen Bess struggled hard to maintain a certain monopoly; she saw it would not do, and she surrendered it with that frank heartiness which becomes a sovereign, and makes surrender a grace."

"Ha! and you would have me give up the stocks?"

"I would much rather the stocks had remained as it was before you touched it; but, as it is, if you could find a good plausible pretext — and there is an excellent one at hand:—the sternest kings open prisons, and grant favors, upon joyful occasions — now a marriage in the royal family is of course a joyful occasion! — and so it should be in that of the King of Hazeldean." Admire that artful turn in the Parson's eloquence!—it was worthy of Riccabocca himself. Indeed, Mr. Dale had profited much by his companionship with that Machiavellian intellect.

"A marriage — yes; but Frank has only just got into coat-tails!"

"I did not allude to Frank, but to your cousin Jemima!"

CHAPTER XXV.

The Squire staggered as if the breath had been knocked out of him, and, for want of a better seat, sat down on the stocks.

All the female heads in the neighboring cottages peered, themselves unseen, through the casements. What could the Squire be about? — what new mischief did he meditate? Did he mean to fortify the stocks? Old Gaffer Solomons, who had an indefinite idea of the lawful power of squires, and who had been for the last ten minutes at watch on his threshold, shook his head and said — "Them as a cut out the mon a-hanging, as a put it in the Squire's head!"

"Put what?" asked his grand-daughter.

"The gallus!" answered Solomons — "he be a-going to have it hung from the great elm-tree. And the Parson, good mon, is a-quoting Scripture agin it — you see he's a-taking off his gloves, and a-putting his two han's together, as he do when he pray for the sick, Jeany."

That description of the Parson's mien and manner, which, with his usual niceness of observation, Gaffer Solomons thus sketched off, will convey to you some idea of the earnestness with which the Parson pleaded the cause he had undertaken to advocate. He dwelt much upon the sense of propriety which the foreigner had evinced in requesting that the Squire might be consulted before any formal communication to his cousin; and he repeated Mrs. Dale's assurance, that such were Riccabocca's high standard of honor and belief in the sacred rights of hospitality, that, if the Squire withheld his consent to his proposals, the Parson was convinced that the Italian would instantly retract them. Now, considering that Miss Hazeldean was, to say the least, come to years of discretion, and the Squire had long since placed her property entirely at her own disposal, Mr. Hazeldean was forced to acquiesce in the Parson's corollary remark, "That this was a delicacy which could not be expected from every English pretender to the lady's hand." Seeing that he had so far cleared ground, the Parson went on to intimate, though with great tact, that since Miss Jemima would probably marry sooner or later (and, indeed, that the Squire could not wish to prevent her), it might be better for all parties concerned that it should be with some one who, though a foreigner, was settled in the neighborhood, and of whose character what was known was certainly favorable, rather than run the hazard of her being married for her money by some adventurer, or Irish fortune-hunter, at the watering-places she yearly visited. Then he touched lightly on Riccabocca's agreeable and companionable qualities; and concluded with a skilful peroration upon the excellent occasion the wedding would afford to reconcile Hall and Parish, by making a voluntary holocaust of the stocks.

As he concluded, the Squire's brow, before thoughtful, though not sullen, cleared up benignly. To say truth, the Squire was dying to get rid of the stocks, if he could but do so handsomely and with dignity; and had all the stars in the astrological horoscope conjoined together to give Miss Jemima "assurance of a husband," they could not so have served her with the Squire, as that conjunction between the altar and the stocks which the Parson had effected!

Accordingly, when Mr. Dale had come to an end, the Squire replied, with great placidity and good sense, "That Mr. Rickeybockey had behaved very much like a gentleman, and that he was very much obliged to him; that he (the Squire) had no right to interfere in the matter, farther than with his advice; that Jemima was old enough to choose for herself, and that, as the Parson had implied, after all, she might go farther and fare worse —indeed, the farther she went (that is, the longer she waited), the worse she was likely to fare. I own, for my part," continued the Squire, "that though I like Rickeybockey very much, I never suspected that Jemima was caught with his long face; but there's no accounting for tastes. My Harry, indeed, was more shrewd, and gave me many a hint, for which I only laughed at her. Still I ought to have thought it looked queer when Mounseer took to disguising himself by leaving off his glasses, ha — ha! I wonder what Harry will say; let's go and talk to her."

The Parson, rejoiced at this easy way of taking the matter, hooked his arm into the Squire's, and they walked amicably towards the Hall. But on coming first into the gardens they found Mrs. Hazeldean herself, clipping dead leaves or fading flowers from her rose-trees. The Squire stole slily behind her, and startled her in her turn by putting his arm round her waist, and saluting her smooth cheek with one of his hearty kisses; which, by the way, from some association of ideas, was a conjugal freedom that he usually indulged whenever a wedding was going on in the village.

"Fie, William!" said Mrs. Hazeldean, coyly, and blushing as she saw the Parson. "Well, who's going to be married now?"

"Lord, was there ever such a woman? — she's guessed it!" cried the Squlre, in great admiration. "Tell her all about it, Parson."

The Parson obeyed.

Mrs. Hazeldean, as the reader may suppose, showed much less surprise than her husband had done; but she took the news graciously, and made much the same answer as that whlch had occurred to the Squire, only with somewhat more qualification and reserve. "Signor Riccabocca had behaved very handsomely; and though a daughter of the Hazeldeans of Hazeldean might expect a much better marriage in a worldly point of view, yet as the lady in question had deferred finding one so long, it would be equally idle and impertinent now to quarrel with her choice — if indeed she should decide on accepting Signor Riccabocca. As for fortune, that was a consideration for the two contracting parties. Still, it ought to be pointed out to Miss Jemima that the interest of her fortune would afford but a very small income. That Dr. Riccabocca was a widower was another matter for deliberation; and it seemed rather suspicious that he should have been hitherto so close upon all matters connected with his former life. Certainly his manners were in his favor, and as long as he was merely an acquaintance, and at most a tenant, no one had a right to institute inquiries of a strictly private nature; but that, when he was about to marry a Hazeldean of Hazeldean, it became the Squire at least to know a little more about him — who and what he was. Why did he leave his own country? English people went abroad to save: no foreigner would choose England as a country in which to save money! She supposed that a foreign Doctor was no very great things; probably he had been a professor in some Italian university. At all events, if the Squire interfered at all, it was on such points that he should request information."

"My dear madam," said the Parson, "what you say

is extremely just. As to the causes which have induced our friend to expatriate himself, I think we need not look far for them. He is evidently one of the many Italian refugees whom political disturbances have driven to a land of which it is the boast to receive all exiles of whatever party. For his respectability of birth and family, he certainly ought to obtain some vouchers. And if that be the only objection, I trust we may soon congratulate Miss Hazeldean on a marriage with a man who, though certainly very poor, has borne privations without a murmur; has preferred all hardship to debt; has scorned to attempt betraying the young lady into any clandestine connection; who, in short, has shown himself so upright and honest, that I hope my dear Mr. Hazeldean will forgive him if he is only a doctor — probably of Laws — and not, as most foreigners pretend to be, a marquis or a baron at least."

"As to that," cried the Squire, "'tis the best thing I know about Rickeybockey, that he don't attempt to humbug us by any such foreign trumpery. Thank heaven, the Hazeldeans of Hazeldean were never tuft-hunters and title-mongers; and if I never ran after an English lord, I should certainly be devilishly ashamed of a brother-in-law whom I was forced to call markee or count! I should feel sure he was a courier, or runaway valley-de-sham. Turn up your nose at a doctor, indeed, Harry; — pshaw, good English style that! Doctor! my aunt married a Doctor of Divinity — excellent man — wore a wig, and was made a dean! So long as Rickeybockey is not a doctor of physic, I don't care a button. If he's *that*, indeed, it would be suspicious; because, you see, those foreign doctors of physic are quacks, and tell fortunes, and go about on a stage with a Merry-Andrew."

"Lord, Hazeldean! where on earth did you pick up that idea?" said Harry, laughing.

"Pick it up! — why I saw a fellow myself at the cattle-fair last year — when I was buying short-horns — with a red waistcoat and a cocked-hat, a little like the Parson's shovel. He called himself Doctor Phoscophornio — and sold pills! The Merry-Andrew was the funniest creature — in salmon-colored tights — turned head over heels, and said he came from Timbuctoo. No, no; if Rickeybockey's a physic Doctor, we shall have Jemima in a pink tinsel dress, tramping about the country in a caravan!"

At this notion both the Squire and his wife laughed so heartily, that the Parson felt the thing was settled, and slipped away, with the intention of making his report to Riccabocca.

CHAPTER XXVI.

It was with a slight disturbance of his ordinary suave and well-bred equanimity that the Italian received the information, that he need apprehend no obstacle to his suit from the insular prejudices or the worldly views of the lady's family. Not that he was mean and cowardly enough to recoil from the near and unclouded prospect of that felicity which he had left off his glasses to behold with unblinking naked eyes: — no, there his mind was made up; but he had met in life with much that inclines a man towards misanthropy, and he was touched not only by the interest in his welfare testified by an heretical priest, but by the generosity with which he was admitted into a well-born and wealthy family, despite his notorious poverty and his foreign descent. He conceded the propriety of the only stipulation, which was conveyed to him by the Parson with all the delicacy that became one long professionally habituated to deal with the subtler susceptibilities of mankind — viz., that, amongst Riccabocca's friends or kindred, some person should be found whose report would confirm the persuasion of his respectability entertained by his neighbors; he assented, I say, to the propriety of this condition; but it was not with alacrity and eagerness. His brow became clouded. The Parson hastened to assure him that the Squire was not a man *qui stupet in titulis* (who was besotted with titles), that he neither expected nor desired to find an origin and rank for his brother-in-law above that decent mediocrity of condition to which it was evident, from Riccabocca's breeding and accomplishments, he could easily establish his claim. "And though," said he, smiling, "the Squire is a warm politician in his own country, and would never see his sister again, I fear, if she married some convicted enemy of our happy constitution, yet, for foreign politics he does not care a straw; so that if, as I suspect, your exile arises from some quarrel with your Government — which, being foreign, he takes for granted must be insupportable — he would but consider you as he would a Saxon who fled from the iron hand of William the Conqueror, or a Lancastrian expelled by the Yorkists in our Wars of the Roses."

The Italian smiled. "Mr. Hazeldean shall be satisfied," said he simply. "I see, by the Squire's newspaper, that an English gentleman who knew me in my own country has just arrrived in London. I will write to him for a testimonial, at least to my probity and character. Probably he may be known to you by name — nay, he must be, for he was a distinguished officer in the late war. I allude to Lord L'Estrange."

The Parson started.

"You know Lord L'Estrange? — a profligate, bad man, I fear."

"Profligate! — bad!" exclaimed Riccabocca. "Well, calumnious as the world is, I should never have thought that such expressions would be applied to one who, though I knew him but little — knew him chiefly by the service he once rendered to me — first taught me to love and revere the English name!"

"He may be changed since——" The Parson paused.

"Since when?" asked Riccabocca, with evident curiosity.

Mr. Dale seemed embarrassed. "Excuse me," said he, "it is many years ago; and, in short, the opinion I then formed of the nobleman you named was based upon circumstances which I cannot communicate."

The punctilious Italian bowed in silence, but he still looked as if he should have liked to prosecute inquiry.

After a pause, he said, "Whatever your impression respecting Lord L'Estrange, there is nothing, I suppose, which would lead you to doubt his honor, or reject his testimonial in my favor?"

"According to fashionable morality," said Mr. Dale, rather precisely, "I know of nothing that could induce me to suppose that Lord L'Estrange would not, in this instance, speak the truth. And he has unquestionably a high reputation as a soldier, and a considerable position in the world." Therewith the Parson took his leave. A few days afterwards, Dr. Riccabocca enclosed to the Squire, in a blank envelope, a letter he had received from Harley L'Estrange. It was evidently intended for the Squire's eye, and to serve as a voucher for the Italian's respectability; but this object was fulfilled, not in the coarse form of a direct testimonial, but with a tact and delicacy which seemed to show more than the fine breeding to be expected from one in Lord L'Estrange's station. It evinced that most exquisite of all politeness which comes from the heart: a certain tone of affectionate respect (which even the homely sense of the Squire felt, intuitively, proved far more in favor of Riccabocca than the most elaborate certificate of his qualities and antecedents) pervaded the whole, and would have sufficed in itself to remove all scruples from a mind much more suspicious and exacting than that of the Squire of Hazeldean. But, lo and behold! an obstacle now occurred to the Parson, of which he ought to have thought long before — viz., the Papistical religion of the Italian. Dr. Riccabocca was professedly a Roman Catholic. He so little obtruded that fact — and, indeed, had assented so readily to any animadversions upon the superstition and priestcraft which, according to Protestants, are the essential characteristics of Papistical communities — that it was not till the hymeneal torch, which brings all faults to light, was fairly illumined for the altar, that the remembrance of a faith so cast into a shade burst upon the conscience of the Parson. The first idea that then occurred to him was the proper and professional one — viz., the conversion of Dr. Riccabocca. He hastened to his study, took down from his shelves long-neglected volumes of controversial divinity, armed himself with an arsenal of authorities, arguments, and texts; then, seizing the shovel-hat, posted off to the Casino.

CHAPTER XXVII.

THE Parson burst upon the philosopher like an avalanche! He was so full of his subject that he could not let it out in prudent driblets. No, he went souse upon the astounded Riccabocca —

> "Tremendo
> Jupiter ipse ruens tumultu."

The sage — shrinking deeper into his arm-chair, and

drawing his dressing-robe more closely round him — suffered the Parson to talk for three-quarters of an hour, till, indeed, he had thoroughly proved his case; and, like Brutus, "paused for a reply."

Then said Riccabocca, mildly, "In much of what you have urged so ably, and so suddenly, I am inclined to agree. But base is the man who formally forswears the creed he has inherited from his fathers, and professed since the cradle up to years of maturity, when the change presents itself in the guise of a bribe; when, for such is human nature, he can hardly distinguish or disentangle the appeal to his reason from the lure to his interest — here a text, and there a dowry! — here Protestantism, there Jemima! Own, my friend, that the soberest casuist would see double under the inebriating effects produced by so mixing his polemical liquors. Appeal, my good Mr. Dale, from Philip drunken to Philip sober! — from Riccabocca intoxicated with the assurance of your excellent lady, that he is about to be 'the happiest of men,' to Riccabocca accustomed to his happiness, and carrying it off with the seasoned equability of one grown familiar with stimulants — in a word, appeal from Riccabocca the wooer to Riccabocca the spouse. I may be convertible, but conversion is a slow process; courtship should be a quick one — ask Miss Jemima. *Finalmente*, marry me first, and convert me afterwards!"

"You take this too jestingly," began the Parson: "and I don't see why with your excellent understanding, truths so plain and obvious should not strike you at once."

"Truths," interrupted Riccabocca, profoundly, "are the slowest-growing things in the world! It took fifteen hundred years from the date of the Christian era to produce your own Luther, and then he flung his Bible at Satan (I have seen the mark made by the book on the wall of his prison in Germany), besides running off with a nun, which no Protestant clergyman would think it proper and right to do now-a-days." Then he added, with seriousness, "Look you, my dear sir, — I should lose my own esteem if I were even to listen to you now with becoming attention, — now, I say, when you hint that the creed I have professed may be in the way of my advantage. If so, I must keep the creed and resign the advantage. But if, as I trust — not only as a Christian, but a man of honor — you will defer this discussion, I will promise to listen to you hereafter; and though, to say the truth, I believe that you will not convert me, I will promise you faithfully never to interfere with my wife's religion."

"And any children you may have?"

"Children!" said Dr. Riccabocca, recoiling — "you are not contented with firing your pocket-pistol right in my face; you must also pepper me all over with small-shot. Children! well, if they are girls, let them follow the faith of their mother; and if boys, while in childhood, let them be contented with learning to be Christians; and when they grow into men, let them choose for themselves which is the best form for the practice of the great principles which all sects have in common."

"But," began Mr. Dale again, pulling a large book from his pocket.

Dr. Riccabocca flung open the window, and jumped out of it.

It was the rapidest and most dastardly flight you could possibly conceive; but it was a great compliment to the argumentative powers of the Parson, and he felt it as such. Nevertheless, Mr. Dale thought it right to have a long conversation, both with the Squire and Miss Jemima herself, upon the subject which his intended convert had so ignominiously escaped.

The Squire, though a great foe to Popery, politically considered, had also quite as great a hatred to renegades and apostates. And in his heart he would have despised Riccabocca if he could have thrown off his religion as easily as he had done his spectacles. Therefore he said simply — "Well, it is certainly a great pity that Rickeybockey is not of the Church of England, though, I take it, that would be unreasonable to expect in a man born and bred under the nose of the Inquisition" (the Squire firmly believed that the Inquisition was in full force in all the Italian states, with whips, racks, and thumbscrews; and, indeed, his chief information of Italy was gathered from a perusal he had given in early youth to *The One-Handed Monk*); "but I think he speaks very fairly, on the whole, as to his wife and children. And the thing's gone too far now to retract. It's all your fault for not thinking of it before; and I've now just made up my mind as to the course to pursue respecting the — d——d stocks!"

As for Miss Jemima, the Parson left her with a pious thanksgiving that Riccabocca at least was a Christian, and not a Pagan, Mahometan, or Jew!

CHAPTER XXVIII.

There is that in a wedding which appeals to a universal sympathy. No other event in the lives of their superiors in rank creates an equal sensation amongst the humbler classes.

From the moment the news that Miss Jemima was to be married had spread throughout the village, all the old affection for the Squire and his House burst forth the stronger for its temporary suspension. Who could think of the stocks in such a season? The stocks was swept out of fashion — hunted from remembrance as completely as the question of Repeal or the thought of Rebellion from the warm Irish heart, when the fair young face of the Royal Wife beamed on the sister isle.

Again cordial curtseys were dropped at the thresholds by which the Squire passed to his own farm; again the sun-burnt brows uncovered — no more with sullen ceremony — were smoothed into cheerful gladness at his nod. Nay, the little ones began again to assemble at their ancient rendezvous by the stocks, as if either familiarised with the Phenomenon, or convinced that, in the general sentiment of good-will, its powers of evil were annulled.

The Squire tasted once more the sweets of the only popularity which is much worth having, and the loss of which a wise man would reasonably deplore — viz., the popularity which arises from a persuasion of our goodness, and a reluctance to recall our faults. Like all blessings, the more sensibly felt from previous interruption, the Squire enjoyed this restored popularity with an exhilarated sense of existence; his stout heart beat more vigorously; his stalwart step trod more lightly; his comely English face looked comelier and more English than ever; — you would have been a merrier man for a week, to have come within hearing of his jovial laugh.

He felt grateful to Jemima and to Riccabocca as the special agents of Providence in this general *integratio amoris.* To have looked at him, you would suppose that it was the Squire who was going to be married a second time to his Harry!

One may well conceive that such would have been an inauspicious moment for Parson Dale's theological scruples. To have stopped that marriage — chilled all the sunshine it diffused over the village — seen himself surrounded again by long sulky visages,—I verily believe, though a better friend of Church and State never stood on a hustings, that, rather than court such a revulsion, the Squire would have found jesuitical excuses for the marriage if Riccabocca had been discovered to be the Pope in disguise! As for the stocks, its fate was now irrevocably sealed. In short, the marriage was concluded —first privately, according to the bridegroom's creed, by a Roman Catholic clergyman, who lived in a town some miles off, and next publicly in the village church of Hazeldean.

It was the heartiest rural wedding! Village girls strewed flowers on the way;—a booth was placed amidst the prettiest scenery of the Park on the margin of the lake—for there was to be a dance later in the day; — an ox was roasted whole. Even Mr. Stirn — no, Mr. Stirn was *not* present, so much happiness would have been the death of him! And the Papisher too, who had conjured Lenny out of the stocks; nay, who had himself sat in the stocks for the very purpose of bringing them into contempt — the Papisher! he had as lief Miss Jemima had married the devil! Indeed he was persuaded that, in point of fact, it was all one and the same. Therefore Mr. Stirn had asked leave to go and attend his uncle the pawnbroker, about to undergo a torturing operation for the stone! Frank was there, summoned from Eton for the occasion — having grown two inches taller since he left—for the one inch of which nature was to be thanked, for the other a new pair of resplendent Wellingtons. But the boy's joy was less apparent than that of others. For Jemima was a special favorite with him, as she would have been with all boys — for she was always kind and gentle, and made him many pretty presents whenever she came from the watering-places. And Frank knew that he should miss her sadly, and thought she had made a very queer choice.

Captain Higginbotham had been invited; but, to the astonishment of Jemima, he had replied to the invitation by a letter to herself, marked "*private and confidential.*" "She must have long known," said the latter, "of his devoted attachment to her! motives of delicacy, arising from the narrowness of his income, and the magnanimity of his sentiments, had alone prevented his formal proposals; but now that he was informed (he could scarcely believe his senses or command his passions) that her relations wished to force her into a BARBAROUS marriage with a foreigner of MOST FORBIDDING APPEARANCE, and most *abject circumstances*, he lost not a moment in laying at her feet his own hand and fortune. And he did this the more confidently, inasmuch as he could not but be aware of Miss Jemima's SECRET feelings towards him, while he was *proud* and *happy* to say, that his dear and distinguished cousin, Mr. Sharpe Currie, had honored him with a warmth of regard, which justified the most *brilliant* EXPECTATIONS — likely to be *soon* realised — as his eminent relative had contracted a *very bad liver complaint* in the service of his country, and could not last long!"

In all the years they had known each other, Miss Jemima, strange as it may appear, had never once suspected the Captain of any other feelings to her than those of a brother. To say that she was not gratified by learning her mistake, would be to say that she was more than woman. Indeed, it must have been a source of no ignoble triumph to think that she could prove her disinterested affection to her dear Riccabocca, by a prompt rejection of this more brilliant offer. She couched the rejection, it is true, in the most soothing terms. But the Captain evidently considered himself ill used; he did not reply to the letter, and did not come to the wedding.

To let the reader into a secret, never known to Miss Jemima, Captain Higginbotham was much less influenced by Cupid than by Plutus in the offer he had made. The Captain was one of that class of gentlemen who read their accounts by those corpse-lights, or will-o'-the-wisps, called *expectations*. Ever since the Squire's grandfather had left him — then in short clothes — a legacy of £500, the Captain had peopled the future with expectations! He talked of his expectations as a man talks of shares in a Tontine; they might fluctuate a little — be now up and now down—but it was morally impossible, if he lived on, but that he should be a *millionaire* one of these days. Now, though Miss Jemima was a good fifteen years younger than himself, yet she always stood for a good round sum in the ghostly books of the Captain. She was an *expectation* to the full amount of her £4,000, seeing that Frank was an only child, and it would be carrying coals to Newcastle to leave *him* anything.

Rather than see so considerable a cipher suddenly spunged out of his visionary ledger—rather than so much money should vanish clean out of the family, Captain Higginbotham had taken what he conceived, if a desperate, at least a certain, step for the preservation of his property. If the golden horn could not be had without the heifer, why, he must take the heifer into the bargain. He had never formed to himself an idea that a heifer so gentle would toss and fling him over. The blow was stunning. But no one compassionates the misfortunes of the covetous, though few perhaps are in greater need of compassion. And leaving poor Captain Higginbotham to retrieve his illusory fortunes as he best may among "the expectations" which gathered round the form of Mr. Sharpe Currie, who was the crossest old tyrant imaginable, and never allowed at his table any dishes not compounded with rice, which played Old Nick with the Captain's constitutional functions,—I return to the wedding at Hazeldean, just in time to see the bridegroom — who looked singularly well on the occasion — hand the bride (who, between sunshiny tears and affectionate smiles, was really a very interesting and even a pretty bride, as brides go) into a carriage which the Squire had presented to them, and depart on the orthodox nuptial excursion amidst the blessings of the assembled crowd.

It may be thought strange by the unreflective that these rural spectators should so have approved and blessed the marriage of a Hazeldean of Hazeldean with a poor, outlandish, long-haired foreigner; but, besides that Riccabocca, after all, had become one of the neighborhood, and was proverbially "a civil-spoken gentleman," it is generally noticeable that on wedding occasions the bride so monopolises interest, curiosity, and admiration, that the bridegroom himself goes for little or nothing. He is merely the passive agent in the affair — the unregarded cause of the general satisfaction. It was not Riccabocca himself that they approved and blessed—it was the gentleman in the white waistcoat who had made Miss Jemima — Madam Rickeybockey!

Leaning on his wife's arm (for it was a habit of the Squire to lean on his wife's arm rather than she on his, when he was specially pleased; and there was something touching in the sight of that strong, sturdy frame thus insensibly, in hours of happiness, seeking dependence on the frail arm of woman) — leaning, I say, on his wife's arm, the Squire, about the hour of sunset, walked down to the booth by the lake.

All the parish — young and old, woman, and child — were assembled there, and their faces seemed to bear one family likeness, in the common emotion which animated all, as they turned to his frank, fatherly smile. Squire Hazeldean stood at the head of the long table: he filled a horn with ale from the brimming tankard beside him. Then he looked round, and lifted his hand to request silence; and, ascending the chair, rose in full view of all. Every one felt that the Squire was about to make a speech, and the earnestness of the attention was proportioned to the rarity of the event; for (though he was not unpractised in the oratory of the hustings) only thrice before had the Squire made what could fairly be called "a speech" to the villagers of Hazeldean — once on a kindred festive occasion, when he had presented to them his bride — once in a contested election for the shire, in which he took more than ordinary interest, and was not quite so sober as he ought to have been — once in a time of great agricultural distress, when, in spite of reduction of rents, the farmers had been compelled to discard a large number of their customary laborers; and when the Squire had said — "I have given up keeping the hounds, because I want to make a fine piece of water" — that was the origin of the lake, — "and to drain all the low lands round the Park. Let every man who wants work come to me!" and that sad year the parish rates of Hazeldean were not a penny the heavier.

Now, for the fourth time, the Squire rose, and thus he spoke. At his right hand, Harry; at his left, Frank. At the bottom of the table, as vice-president, Parson Dale, his little wife behind him, only obscurely seen. She cried readily, and her handkerchief was already before her eyes.

CHAPTER XXIX.

THE SQUIRE'S SPEECH.

"Friends and neighbors, — I thank you kindly for coming round me this day, and for showing so much interest in me and mine. My cousin was not born amongst you as I was, but you have known her from a child. It is a familiar face, and one that never frowned, which you will miss at your cottage doors, as I and mine will miss it long in the old Hall ——"

Here there was a sob from some of the women, and nothing was seen of Mrs. Dale but the white handkerchief. The squire himself paused, and brushed away a tear with the back of his hand. Then he resumed, with a sudden change of voice that was electrical, —

"For we none of us prize a blessing till we have lost it! Now, friends and neighbors; a little time ago, it seemed as if some ill-will had crept in the village — ill-will between you and me, neighbors! — why, that is not like Hazeldean!"

The audience hung their heads! You never saw people look so thoroughly ashamed of themselves. The Squire proceeded, —

"I don't say it was all your fault; perhaps it was mine."

"Noa — noa — noa," burst forth in a general chorus.

"Nay, friends, continued the Squire, humbly, and in one of those illustrative aphorisms which, if less subtle than Riccabocca's, were more within reach of the popular comprehension, — "nay, we are all human, and every man has his hobby; sometimes he breaks in the hobby, and sometimes the hobby, if it is very hard in the mouth, breaks in him. One man's hobby has an ill habit of always stopping at the public-house! (Laughter.) Another man's hobby refuses to stir a peg beyond the door where some buxom lass patted its neck the week before — a hobby I rode pretty often when I went courting my good wife here! (Much laughter and applause.) Others have a lazy hobby, that there's no getting on; others, a runaway hobby that there's no stopping: but, to cut the matter short, my favorite hobby as you well know, is always trotted out to any place on my property which seems to want the eye and hand of the master. I hate," cried the Squire, warming, "to see things neglected and decayed, and going to the dogs! This land we live in is a good mother to us, and we can't do too much for her. It is very true, neighbors, that I owe her a good many acres, and ought to speak well of her; but what then? I live amongst you, and what I take from the rent with one hand, I divide amongst you with the other. (Low but assenting murmurs.) Now, the more I improve my property, the more mouths it feeds. My great-grandfather kept a Field-Book, in which were entered, not only the names of all the farmers, and the quantity of land they held, but the average number of the laborers each employed. My grandfather and father followed his example: I have done the same. I find, neighbors, that our rents have doubled since my great-grandfather began to make the book. Ay, but there are more than four times the number of laborers employed on the estate, and at much better wages, too! Well, my men, that says a great deal in favor of improving property, and not letting it go to the dogs. (Applause.) And therefore, neighbors, you will kindly excuse my hobby: it carries grist to your mill. (Reiterated applause.) Well, but you will say, 'What's the Squire driving at?' Why this, my friends: There was only one worn-out, dilapidated, tumble-down thing in the parish of Hazeldean, and it became an eyesore to me; so I saddled my hobby, and rode at it. O ho! you know what I mean now! Yes, but neighbors, you need not have taken it so to heart. That was a scurvy trick of some of you to hang me in effigy, as they call it."

"It war'nt you," cried a voice in the crowd; "it war Nick Stirn."

The Squire recognised the voice of the Tinker; but though he now guessed at the ringleader, on that day of general amnesty he had the prudence and magnanimity not to say, "Stand forth, Sprott: thou art the man." Yet his gallant English spirit would not suffer him to come off at the expense of his servant.

"If it was Nick Stirn you meant," said he, gravely, "more shame for you. It showed some pluck to hang the master; but to hang the poor servant, who only thought to do his duty, careless of what ill-will it brought upon him, was a shabby trick,—so little like the lads of Hazeldean, that I suspect the man who taught it to them was never born in the parish. But let bygones be bygones. One thing is clear, you don't take kindly to my new pair of stocks! The stocks has been a stumbling-block and a grievance, and there's no denying that we went on very pleasantly without it. I may also say that, in spite of it, we have been coming together again lately. And I can't tell you what good it did me to see your children playing again on the green, and your honest faces, in spite of the stocks, and those diabolical tracts you've been reading lately, lighted up at the thought that something pleasant was going on at the Hall. Do you know, neighbors, you put me in mind of an old story which, besides applying to the parish, all who are married, and all who intend to marry, will do well to recollect. A worthy couple, named John and Joan, had lived happily together many a long year, till one unlucky day they bought a new bolster. Joan said the bolster was too hard, and John that it was too soft; so, of course, they quarrelled. After sulking all day, they agreed to put the bolster between them at night." (Roars of laughter amongst the men; the women did not know which way to look, except, indeed, Mrs. Hazeldean, who, though she was more than usually rosy, maintained her innocent, genial smile, as much as to say, "There is no harm in the Squire's jests.") The orator resumed:—"After they had thus lain apart for a little time, very silent and sullen, John sneezed. 'God bless you!' says Joan, over the bolster. 'Did you say God bless me?' cries John;—'then here goes the bolster!'" (Prolonged laughter and tumultuous applause.)

"Friends and neighbors," said the Squire, when silence was restored, and lifting the horn of ale, "I have the pleasure to inform you that I have ordered the stocks to be taken down, and made into a bench for the chimney-nook of our old friend Gaffer Solomons yonder. But mind me, lads, if ever you make the parish regret the loss of the stocks, and the overseers come to me with long faces, and say, 'the stocks must be rebuilded,' why——" Here from all the youth of the village rose so deprecating a clamor, that the Squire would have been the most bungling orator in the world, if he had said a word further on the subject. He elevated the horn over his head,— "Why, that's my old Hazeldean again! Health and long life to you all!"

The Tinker had sneaked out of the assembly, and did not show his face in the village for the next six months. And as to those poisonous tracts, in spite of their salubrious labels, "The Poor Man's Friend," or "The Rights of Labor," you could no more have found one of them lurking in the drawers of the kitchen-dressers in Hazeldean, than you would have found the deadly nightshade on the flower-stands in the drawing-room of the Hall. As for the revolutionary beer-house, there was no need to apply to the magistrates to shut it up—it shut itself up before the week was out.

O young head of the great House of Hapsburg, what a Hazeldean you might have made of Hungary!—What a "*Moriamur pro rege nostro*" would have rung in your infant reign,—if you had made such a speech as the Squire's!

BOOK FOURTH.

INITIAL CHAPTER.

COMPRISING MR. CAXTON'S OPINIONS ON THE MATRIMONIAL STATE, SUPPORTED BY LEARNED AUTHORITIES.

"It was no bad idea of yours, Pisistratus," said my father, graciously, "to depict the heightened affections and the serious intention of Signor Riccabocca by a single stroke — *He left off his spectacles!* Good."

"Yet," quoth my uncle, "I think Shakspeare represents a lover as falling into slovenly habits, neglecting his person, and suffering his hose to be ungartered, rather than paying that attention to his outer man which induces Signor Riccabocca to leave off his spectacles, and look as handsome as nature will permit him."

"There are different degrees and many phases of this passion," replied my father. "Shakspeare is speaking of an ill-treated, pining, woe-begone lover, much aggrieved by the cruelty of his mistress — a lover who has found it of no avail to smarten himself up, and has fallen despondently into the opposite extreme. Whereas Signor

Riccabocca has nothing to complain of in the barbarity of Miss Jemima."

"Indeed he has not!" cried Blanche, tossing her head — "forward creature!"

"Yes, my dear," said my mother, trying her best to look stately, "I am decidedly of opinion that, in that respect, Pisistratus has lowered the dignity of the sex. Not intentionally," added my mother, mildly, and afraid she had said something too bitter; "but it is very hard for a man to describe us women."

The Captain nodded approvingly; Mr. Squills smiled; my father quietly resumed the thread of his discourse.

"To continue," quoth he. "Riccabocca has no reason to despair of success in his suit, nor any object in moving his mistress to compassion. He may, therefore, very properly tie up his garters and leave off his spectacles. What do you say, Mr. Squills? — for, after all, since love-making cannot fail to be a great constitutional derangement, the experience of a medical man must be the best to consult."

"Mr. Caxton," replied Squills, obviously flattered, "you are quite right: when a man makes love, the organs of self-esteem and desire of applause are greatly stimulated, and therefore, of course, he sets himself off to the best advantage. It is only, as you observe, when, like Shakspeare's lover, he has given up making love as a bad job, and has received that severe hit on the ganglions which the cruelty of a mistress inflicts, that he neglects his personal appearance: he neglects it, not because he is in love, but because his nervous system is depressed. That was the cause, if you remember, with poor Major Prim. He wore his wig all awry when Susan Smart jilted him; but I set it right for him."

"By shaming Miss Smart into repentance, or getting him a new sweetheart?" asked my uncle.

"Pooh!" answered Squills, "by quinine and cold bathing."

"We may therefore grant," renewed my father, "that, as a general rule, the process of courtship tends to the spruceness, and even foppery, of the individual engaged in the experiment, as Voltaire has very prettily proved somewhere. Nay, the Mexicans, indeed, were of opinion, that the lady at least ought to continue those cares of her person even after marriage. There is extant, in Sahagun's *History of New Spain*, the advice of an Aztec or Mexican mother to her daughter, in which she says — 'That your husband may not take you in dislike, adorn yourself, wash yourself, and let your garments be clean.' It is true that the good lady adds — 'Do it in moderation; since, if every day you are washing yourself and your clothes, the world will say that you are over-delicate; and particular people will call you — TAPETZON TINEMAXOCH!' What those words precisely mean," added my father, modestly, "I cannot say, since I never had the opportunity to acquire the ancient Aztec language — but something very opprobrious and horrible, no doubt."

"I dare say a philosopher like Signor Riccabocca," said my uncle, "was not himself very *Tapetzon tine*—

what d'ye call it?—and a good healthy English wife, that poor affectionate Jemima, was thrown away upon him."

"Roland," said my father, "you don't like foreigners: a respectable prejudice, and quite natural in a man who has been trying his best to hew them in pieces and blow them up into splinters. But you don't like philosophers either—and for that dislike you have no equally good reason."

"I only implied that they are not much addicted to soap and water," said my uncle.

"A notable mistake. Many great philosophers have been very great beaux. Aristotle was a notorious fop. Buffon put on his best laced ruffles when he sat down to write, which implies that he washed his hands first. Pythagoras insists greatly on the holiness of frequent ablutions; and Horace—who, in his own way, was as good a philosopher as any the Romans produced—takes care to let us know what a neat, well-dressed, dapper little gentleman he was. But I don't think you ever read the 'Apology of Apuleius?"

"Not I—what is it about?" asked the Captain.

"About a great many things. It is that Sage's vindication from several malignant charges—amongst others, and principally, indeed, that of being much too refined and effeminate for a philosopher. Nothing can exceed the rhetorical skill with which he excuses himself for using—tooth-powder. 'Ought a philosopher,' he exclaims, 'to allow anything unclean about him, especially in the mouth—the mouth, which is the vestibule of the soul, the gate of discourse, the portico of thought! Ah, but Æmilianus [the accuser of Apuleius] never opens *his* mouth but for slander and calumny—tooth-powder would indeed be unbecoming to *him!* Or, if he use any, it will not be my good Arabian tooth-powder, but charcoal and cinders. Ay, his teeth should be as foul as his language! And yet even the crocodile likes to have his teeth cleaned; insects get into them, and horrible reptile though he be, he opens his jaws inoffensively to a faithful dentistical bird, who volunteers his beak for a tooth-pick.' "

My father was now warm in the subject he had started, and soared miles away from Riccabocca and "My Novel." "And observe," he exclaimed—"observe with what gravity this eminent Platonist pleads guilty to the charge of having a mirror. 'Why, what,' he exclaims, 'more worthy of the regards of a human creature than his own image,' (*nihil respectabilius homini quam formam suam!*) Is not that one of our children the most dear to us who is called 'the picture of his father?' But take what pains you will with a picture, it can never be so like you as the face in your mirror! Think it discreditable to look with proper attention on one's-self in the glass! Did not Socrates recommend such attention to his disciples—did he not make a great moral agent of the speculum? The handsome, in admiring their beauty therein, were admonished that handsome is who handsome does; and the more the ugly stared at themselves, the more they became naturally anxious to hide the disgrace of their features in the loveliness of their merits. Was not Demosthenes always at his speculum? Did he not rehearse his causes before it as before a master in the art? He learned his eloquence from Plato, his dialectics from Eubulides; but as for his delivery — there, he came to the mirror!

"Therefore," concluded Mr. Caxton, returning unexpectedly to the subject — "therefore, it is no reason to suppose that Dr. Riccabocca is averse to cleanliness and decent care of the person because he is a philosopher; and, all things considered, he never showed himself more a philosopher than when he left off his spectacles and looked his best."

"Well," said my mother kindly, "I only hope it may turn out happily. But I should have been better pleased if Pisistratus had not made Dr. Riccabocca so reluctant a wooer."

"Very true," said the Captain; "the Italian does not shine as a lover. Throw a little more fire into him, Pisistratus — something gallant and chivalrous."

"Fire — gallantry — chivalry!" cried my father, who had taken Riccabocca under his special protection — "why, don't you see that the man is described as a philosopher? — and I should like to know when a philosopher ever plunged into matrimony without considerable misgiving and cold shivers. Indeed, it seems that — perhaps before he was a philosopher — Riccabocca *had* tried the experiment, and knew what it was. Why, even that plain-speaking, sensible, practical man, Metellus Numidicus, who was not even a philosopher, but only a

Roman Censor, thus expressed himself in an exhortation to the people to perpetrate matrimony—'If, O Quirites, we could do without wives, we should all dispense with that subject of care (*eâ molestiâ careremus;*) but since nature has so managed it that we cannot live with women comfortably, nor without them at all, let us rather provide for the human race than our own temporary felicity.'"

Here the ladies set up a cry of such indignation, that both Roland and myself endeavored to appease their wrath by hasty assurances that we utterly repudiated the damnable doctrine of Metellus Numidicus.

My father, wholly unmoved, as soon as a sullen silence was established, recommenced — "Do not think, ladies," said he, "that you were without advocates at that day: there were many Romans gallant enough to blame the Censor for a mode of expressing himself which they held to be equally impolite and injudicious. 'Surely,' said they, with some plausibility, 'if Numidicus wished men to marry, he need not have referred so peremptorily to the disquietudes of the connection, and thus have made them more inclined to turn away from matrimony than given them a relish for it.' But against these critics one honest man (whose name of Titus Castricius should not be forgotten by posterity) maintained that Metellus Numidicus could not have spoken more properly: 'For remark,' said he, 'that Metellus was a censor, not a rhetorician. It becomes rhetoricians to adorn and disguise, and make the best of things; but Metellus, *sanctus vir* — a holy and blameless man, grave and sincere to wit, and addressing the Roman people in the solemn capacity of Censor — was bound to speak the plain truth, especially as he was treating of a subject on which the observation of every day, and the experience of every life, could not leave the least doubt upon the mind of his audience.' Still, Riccabocca, having decided to marry, has no doubt prepared himself to bear all the concomitant evils — as becomes a professed sage; and I own I admire the art with which Pisistratus has drawn the kind of woman most likely to suit a philosopher ——"

Pisistratus bows and looks round complacently; but recoils from two very peevish and discontented faces feminine.

Mr. Caxton (completing his sentence.) — Not only as regards mildness of temper and other household qualifications, but as regards the very *person* of the object of his choice. For you evidently remember, Pisistratus, the reply of Bias, when asked his opinion on marriage: '"Ητοι καλὴν ἕξεις ἢ αἰσχράν· καὶ εἰ καλὴν, ἕξεις κοινήν· εἰ δὴ αἰσχρὰν ἕξεις ποινήν.'

Pisistratus tries to look as if he had the opinion of Bias by heart, and nods acquiescingly.

Mr. Caxton. — That is, my dears, "the woman you would marry is either handsome or ugly; if handsome, she is koiné, viz.: you don't have her to yourself; if ugly, she is poiné — that is, a fury." But, as it is observed in Aulus Gellius (whence I borrow this citation), there is a wide interval between handsome and ugly. And thus Ennius, in his tragedy of *Menalippus*, uses an admirable expression to designate women of the proper degree of matrimonial comeliness, such as a philosopher would select. He calls this degree *stata forma* — a rational, mediocre sort of beauty, which is not liable to be either koiné or poiné. And Favorinus, who was a remarkably sensible man, and came from Provence — the male inhabitants of which district have always valued themselves on their knowledge of love and ladies — calls this said *stata forma* the beauty of wives — the uxorial beauty. Ennius says, that women of a *stata forma* are almost always safe and modest. Now, Jemima, you observe, is described as possessing this *stata forma*; and it is the nicety of your observation in this respect, which I like the most in the whole of your description of a philosopher's matrimonial courtship, Pisistratus (excepting only the stroke of the spectacles,) for it shows that you had properly considered the opinion of Bias, and mastered all the counter-logic suggested in Book V., chapter xi., of Aulus Gellius.

"For all that," said Blanche, half archly, half demurely, with a smile in the eye and a pout of the lip, "I don't remember that Pisistratus, in the days when he wished to be most complimentary, ever assured me that I had a *stata forma* — a rational, mediocre sort of beauty."

"And I think," observed my uncle, "that when he comes to his real heroine, whoever she may be, he will not trouble his head much about either Bias or Aulus Gellius."

CHAPTER II.

MATRIMONY is certainly a great change in life. One is astonished not to find a notable alteration in one's friend, even if he or she have been only wedded a week. In the instance of Dr. and Mrs. Riccabocca the change was peculiarly visible. To speak first of the lady, as in chivalry bound, Mrs. Riccabocca had entirely renounced that melancholy which had characterised Miss Jemima: she became even sprightly and gay, and looked all the better and prettier for the alteration. She did not scruple to confess honestly to Mrs. Dale, that she was now of opinion that the world was very far from approaching its end. But, in the meanwhile, she did not neglect the duty which the belief she had abandoned serves to inculcate — "She set her house in order." The cold and penurious elegance that had characterised the Casino disappeared like enchantment — that is, the elegance remained, but the cold and penury fled before the smile of woman. Like Puss-in-Boots, after the nuptials of his master, Jackeymo only now caught minnows and sticklebacks for his own amusement. Jackeymo looked much plumper, and so did Riccabocca. In a word, the fair Jemima became an excellent wife. Riccabocca secretly thought her extravagant, but like a wise man, declined to look at the house-bills, and ate his joint in unreproachful silence.

Indeed, there was so much unaffected kindness in the nature of Mrs. Riccabocca — beneath the quiet of her manner, there beat so genially the heart of the Hazeldeans — that she fairly justified the favorable anticipations of Mrs. Dale. And though the Doctor did not noisily boast of his felicity, nor, as some new-married folks do, thrust it insultingly under the *nimis unctis naribus* — the turned-up noses of your surly old married folks — nor force it gaudily and glaringly on the envious eyes of the single, you might still see that he was a more cheerful and light-hearted man than before. His smile was less ironical, his politeness less distinct. He did not study Machiavelli so intensely — and he did not return to the spectacles; which last was an excellent sign. Moreover, the humanising influence of the tidy English wife might be seen in the improvement of his outward or artificial man. His clothes seemed to fit him better; indeed the clothes were new. Mrs. Dale no longer remarked that the buttons were off the wristbands, which was a great satisfaction to her. But the sage still remained faithful to the pipe, the cloak, and the red silk umbrella. Mrs. Riccabocca had (to her credit be it spoken) used all becoming and wife-like arts against these three remnants of the old bachelor Adam, but in vain. "*Anima mia*" (soul of mine), said the Doctor, tenderly; "I hold the cloak, the umbrella, and the pipe, as the sole relics that remain to me of my native country. Respect and spare them."

Mrs. Riccabocca was touched, and had the good sense to perceive that man, let him be ever so much married, retains certain signs of his ancient independence — certain tokens of his old identity, which a wife, the most despotic, will do well to concede. She conceded the cloak, she submitted to the umbrella, she overcame her abhorrence of the pipe. After all, considering the natural villany of our sex, she confessed to herself that she might have been worse off. But, through all the calm and cheerfulness of Riccabocca, a nervous perturbation was sufficiently perceptible; — it commenced after the second week of marriage — it went on increasing, till one bright sunny afternoon, as he was standing on his terrace, gazing down upon the road, at which Jackeymo was placed — lo, a stage-coach stopped! The Dotor made a bound, and put both hands to his heart as if he had been shot; he then leaped over the balustrade, and his wife from her window beheld him flying down the hill, with his long hair streaming in the wind, till the trees hid him from her sight.

"Ah," thought she, with a natural pang of conjugal jealousy, "henceforth I am only second in his home. He has gone to welcome his child!" And at that reflection Mrs. Riccabocca shed tears.

But so naturally amiable was she, that she hastened to curb her emotion, and efface as well as she could the trace of a step-mother's grief. When this was done, and a silent, self-rebuking prayer murmured over, the good woman descended the stairs with alacrity, and summoning up her best smiles, emerged on the terrace.

She was repaid; for scarcely had she come into the open air, when two little arms were thrown around her, and the sweetest voice that ever came from a child's lips, sighed out in broken English, "Good mamma, love me a little."

"Love you? with my whole heart!" cried the step-mother, with all a mother's honest passion. And she clasped the child to her breast.

"God bless you, my wife!" said Riccabocca, in a husky tone.

"Please take this too," added Jackeymo, in Italian, as well as his sobs would let him — and he broke off a great bough full of blossoms from his favorite orange-tree, and thrust it into his mistress's hand. She had not the slightest notion what he meant by it!

CHAPTER III.

VIOLANTE was indeed a bewitching child — a child to whom I defy Mrs. Caudle herself (immortal Mrs. Caudle!) to have been a harsh step-mother.

Look at her now, as, released from those kindly arms, she stands, still clinging with one hand to her new mamma, and holding out the other to Riccabocca,—with those large dark eyes swimming in happy tears. What a lovely smile! — what an ingenuous, candid brow! She looks delicate — she evidently requires care — she wants the mother. And rare is the woman who would not love her the better for that! Still, what an innocent, infantine bloom in those clear, smooth cheeks! — and in that slight frame, what exquisite natural grace!

"And this, I suppose, is your nurse, darling?" said Mrs. Riccabocca, observing a dark, foreign-looking woman, dressed very strangely, without cap or bonnet, but a great silver arrow stuck in her hair, and a filagree chain or necklace resting upon her kerchief.

"Ah, good Anetta," said Violante in Italian. "Papa, she says she is to go back; but she is not to go back — is she?"

Riccabocca, who had scarcely before noticed the woman, started at that question — exchanged a rapid glance with Jackeymo — and then, muttering some inaudible excuse, approached the nurse, and, beckoning her to follow him, went away into the grounds. He did not return for more than an hour, nor did the woman then accompany him home. He said briefly to his wife that the nurse was obliged to return at once to Italy, and that she would stay in the village to catch the mail; that indeed she would be of no use in their establishment, as she could not speak a word of English; but that he was sadly afraid Violante would pine for her. And Violante did pine at first. But still, to a child it is so great a thing to find a parent — to be at home — that, tender and grateful as Violante was, she could not be inconsolable while her father was there to comfort.

For the first few days, Riccabocca scarcely permitted any one to be with his daughter but himself. He would not even leave her alone with his Jemima. They walked out together — sat together for hours in the Belvidere. Then by degrees he began to resign her more and more to Jemima's care and tuition, especially in English, of which language at present she spoke only a few sentences (previously, perhaps, learned by heart), so as to be clearly intelligible.

CHAPTER IV.

There was one person in the establishment of Dr. Riccabocca, who was satisfied neither with the marriage of his master nor the arrival of Violante — and that was our friend Lenny Fairfield. Previous to the all-absorbing duties of courtship, the young peasant had secured a very large share of Riccabocca's attention. The sage had felt an interest in the growth of this rude intelligence struggling up to light. But what with the wooing, and what with the wedding, Lenny Fairfield had sunk very much out of his artificial position as pupil, into his natural station of under-gardener. And on the arrival of Violante, he saw, with natural bitterness, that he was clean forgotten, not only by Riccabocca, but almost by Jackeymo.

It was true that the master still lent him books, and the servant still gave him lectures on horticulture. But Riccabocca had no time nor inclination now to amuse himself with enlightening that tumult of conjecture which the books created. And if Jackeymo had been covetous of those mines of gold buried beneath the acres now fairly taken from the Squire (and good-naturedly added rent-free, as an aid to Jemima's dower), before the advent of the young lady whose future dowry the produce was to swell — now that she was actually under the eyes of the faithful servant, such a stimulus was given to his industry that he could think of nothing else but the land, and the revolution he designed to effect in its natural English crops. The garden, save only the orange-trees, was abandoned entirely to Lenny, and additional laborers were called in for the field-work. Jackeymo had discovered that one part of the soil was suited to lavender, that another would grow camomile. He had in his heart apportioned a beautiful field of rich loam to flax; but against the growth of flax the Squire set his face obstinately. That most lucrative, perhaps, of all crops, when soil and skill suit, was formerly attempted in England much more commonly than it is now, since you will find few old leases which do not contain a clause prohibitory of flax, as an impoverishment of the land. And though Jackeymo learnedly endeavored to prove to the Squire that the flax itself contained particles which, if returned to the soil, repaid all that the crop took away, Mr. Hazeldean had his old-fashioned prejudices on the matter, which were insuperable. "My forefathers," quoth he, "did not put that clause in their leases without good cause; and as the Casino lands are entailed on Frank, I have no right to gratify your foreign whims at his expense."

To make up for the loss of the flax, Jackeymo resolved to convert a very nice bit of pasture into orchard ground, which he calculated would bring in £10 net per acre by the time Miss Violante was marriageable. At this the Squire pished a little; but as it was quite clear that the land would be all the more valuable hereafter for the fruit-trees, he consented to permit the "grass-land" to be thus partially broken up.

All these changes left poor Lenny Fairfield very much to himself—at a time when the new and strange devices which the initiation into book knowledge creates made it most desirable that he should have the constant guidance of a superior mind.

One evening after his work, as Lenny was returning to his mother's cottage, very sullen and very moody, he suddenly came in contact with Sprott the Tinker.

CHAPTER V.

THE Tinker was seated under a hedge, hammering away at an old kettle—with a little fire burning in front of him —and the donkey hard by, indulging in a placid doze. Mr. Sprott looked up as Lenny passed—nodded kindly, and said—

"Good evenin', Lenny: glad to hear you be so 'spectably sitivated with Mounseer."

"Ay," answered Lenny, with a leaven of rancor in his recollections, "you're not ashamed to speak to me now that I am not in disgrace. But it was in disgrace, when it wasn't my fault, that the real gentleman was most kind to me."

"Ar——r, Lenny," said the Tinker, with a prolonged rattle in that said Ar——r, which was not without great significance. "But you sees the real gentleman, who han't got his bread to get, can hafford to 'spise his cracter in the world. A poor Tinker must be timbersome and nice in his 'sociations. But sit down here a bit, Lenny; I've summut to say to ye!"

"To me—"

"To ye. Give the neddy a shove out i' the vay, and sit down, I say."

Lenny rather reluctantly, and somewhat superciliously, accepted this invitation.

"I hears," said the tinker in a voice made rather ndistinct by a couple of nails which he had inserted between his teeth — "I hears as how you be unkimmon fond of reading. I ha' sum nice cheap books in my bag yonder — sum as low as a penny."

"I should like to see them," said Lenny, his eyes sparkling.

The Tinker rose, opened one of the panniers on the ass's back, took out a bag, which he placed before Lenny, and told him to suit himself. The young peasant desired no better. He spread all the contents of the bag on the sward, and a motley collection of food for the mind was there — food and poison — *serpentes avibus* — good and evil. Here Milton's Paradise Lost, there The Age of Reason — here Methodist Tracts, there True Principles of Socialism — Treatises on Useful Knowledge by sound learning actuated by pure benevolence — Appeals to Operatives by the shallowest reasoners, instigated by the same ambition that had moved Eratosthenes to the conflagration of a temple; works of fiction admirable as Robinson Crusoe, or innocent as the Old English Baron; besides coarse translations of such garbage as had rotted away the youth of France under Louis Quinze. This miscellany was an epitome, in short, of the mixed World of Books, of that vast City of the Press, with its palaces and hovels, its aqueducts and sewers — which opens all alike to the naked eye and the curious mind of him to whom you say, in the Tinker's careless phrase, "Suit yourself."

But it is not the first impulse of a nature, healthful and

still pure, to settle in the hovel and lose itself amidst the sewers; and Lenny Fairfield turned innocently over the bad books, and selecting two or three of the best, brought them to the Tinker, and asked the price.

"Why," said Mr. Sprott, putting on his spectacles, "you has taken the werry dearest: them 'ere be much cheaper, and more hinterestin'."

"But I don't fancy them," answered Lenny; "I don't understand what they are about, and this seems to tell one how the steam-engine is made, and has nice plates; and this is Robinson Crusoe, which Parson Dale once said he would give me — I'd rather buy it out of my own money."

"Well, please yourself," quoth the Tinker; "you shall have the books for four bob, and yon can pay me next month."

"Four bobs — four shillings? it is a great sum," said Lenny; "but I will lay by, as you are kind enough to trust me: good evening, Mr. Sprott."

"Stay a bit," said the Tinker; "I'll just throw you these two little tracts into the bargain; they be only a shilling a dozen, so 'tis but tuppence — and when you has read *those*, vy, you'll be a reglar customer."

The Tinker tossed to Lenny Nos. 1 and 2 of Appeals to Operatives, and the peasant took them up gratefully.

The young knowledge-seeker went his way across the green fields, and under the still autumn foliage of the hedge-rows. He looked first at one book, then at another; he did not know on which to settle.

The Tinker rose and made a fire with leaves, and furze, and sticks, some dry and some green.

Lenny has now opened No. 1 of the tracts: they are the shortest to read, and don't require so much effort of the mind as the explanation of the steam-engine.

The Tinker has set on his grimy glue-pot, and the glue simmers.

CHAPTER VI.

As Violante became more familiar with her new home, and those around her became more familiar with Violante, she was remarked for a certain stateliness of manner and bearing, which, had it been less evidently natural and inborn, would have seemed misplaced in the daughter of a forlorn exile, and would have been rare at so early an age among children of the loftiest pretensions. It was with the air of a little princess that she presented her tiny hand to a friendly pressure, or submitted her calm clear cheek to a presuming kiss. Yet withal she was so graceful, and her very stateliness was so pretty and captivating, that she was not the less loved for all her grand airs. And, indeed, she deserved to be loved; for though she was certainly prouder than Mr. Dale could approve of, her pride was devoid of egotism; and that is a pride by no means common. She had an intuitive forethought for others: you could see that she was capable of that grand woman-heroism, abnegation of self; and though she was an original child, and often grave and musing, with a tinge of melancholy, sweet, but deep in her character, still she was not above the happy, genial merriment of childhood—only her silver laugh was more attuned, and her gestures more composed, than those of children habituated to many playfellows usually are. Mrs. Hazeldean liked her best when she was grave, and said "she would become a very sensible woman." Mrs. Dale liked her best when she was gay, and said "she was born to make many a heart ache;" for which Mrs. Dale was properly reproved by the Parson. Mrs. Hazeldean gave her a little set of garden tools; Mrs. Dale a picture-book and a beautiful doll. For a long time the book and the doll had the preference. But Mrs. Hazeldean having observed to Riccabocca that the poor child looked pale, and ought to be a good deal in the open air, the wise father ingeniously pretended to Violante that Mrs. Riccabocca had taken a great fancy to the picture-book, and that he should be very glad to have the doll, upon which Violante hastened to give them both away, and was never so happy as when mamma (as she called Mrs. Riccabocca) was admiring the picture-book, and Riccabocca with austere gravity dandled the doll. Then Riccabocca assured her that she could be of great use to him in the garden; and Violante instantly put into movement her spade, hoe, and wheel-barrow.

This last occupation brought her into immediate contact with Mr. Leonard Fairfield; and that personage one morning, to his great horror, found Miss Violante had nearly exterminated a whole celery-bed, which she had ignorantly conceived to be a crop of weeds.

Lenny was extremely angry. He snatched away the hoe, and said angrily, "You must not do that, Miss; I'll tell your papa if you—"

Violante drew herself up, and never having been so spoken to before, at least since her arrival in England, there was something comic in the surprise of her large eyes, as well as something tragic in the dignity of her offended mien. "It is very naughty of you, Miss," continued Leonard in a milder tone, for he was both softened by the eyes and awed by the mien, "and I trust you will not do it again."

"*Non capisco*," (I don't understand), murmured Violante, and the dark eyes filled with tears. At that moment, up came Jackeymo: and Violante, pointing to Leonard, said, with an effort not to betray her emotion, "*Il fanciullo è molto grossolano*," (he is a very rude boy).

Jackeymo turned to Leonard with the look of an enraged tiger. "How you dare, scum of de earth that you are," cried he,* "how you dare mako cry the signorina?" And his English not supplying familiar vituperatives sufficiently, he poured out upon Lenny such a profusion of Italian abuse, that the boy turned red and white, in a breath, with rage and perplexity.

Violante took instant compassion upon the victim she

* It need scarcely be observed, that Jackeymo, in his conversations with his master or Violante, or his conferences with himself, employs his native language, which is therefore translated without the blunders that he is driven to commit when compelled to trust himself to the tongue of the country in which he is a sojourner.

had made, and, with true feminine caprice, now began to scold Jackeymo for his anger, and, finally approaching Leonard, laid her hand on his arm, and said with a kindness at once child-like and queenly, and in the prettiest imaginable mixture of imperfect English and soft Italian, to which I cannot pretend to do justice, and shall therefore translate: "Don't mind him. I dare say it was all my fault, only I did not understand you; are not these things weeds?"

"No, my darling signorina," said Jackeymo in Italian, looking ruefully at the celery-bed, "they are not weeds, and they sell very well at this time of the year. But still if it amuses you to pluck them up, I should like to see who's to prevent it."

Lenny walked away. He had been called "the scum of the earth," by a foreigner too! He had again been ill-treated for doing what he conceived his duty. He was again feeling the distinction between rich and poor, and he now fancied that that distinction involved deadly warfare, for he had read from beginning to end those two damnable tracts which the Tinker had presented to him. But in the midst of all the angry disturbance of his mind, he felt the soft touch of the infant's hand, the soothing influence of her conciliating words, and he was half ashamed that he had spoken so roughly to a child.

Still, not trusting himself to speak, he walked away, and sat down at a distance. "I don't see," thought he, "why there should be rich and poor, master and servant." Lenny, be it remembered, had not heard the Parson's Political Sermon.

An hour after, having composed himself, Lenny returned to his work. Jackeymo was no longer in the garden: he had gone to the fields; but Riccabocca was standing by the celery-bed, and holding the red silk umbrella over Violante as she sat on the ground looking up at her father with those eyes already so full of intelligence, and love, and soul.

"Lenny," said Riccabocca, "my young lady has been telling me that she has been very naughty, and Giacomo very unjust to you. Forgive them both."

Lenny's sullenness melted in an instant: the reminiscences of tracts Nos. 1 and 2,

"Like the baseless fabric of a vision,
Left not a wreck behind."

He raised eyes, swimming with all his native goodness, towards the wise man, and dropped them gratefully on the infant peace-maker. Then he turned away his head and fairly wept. The Parson was right: "O ye poor, have charity for the rich; O ye rich, respect the poor."

CHAPTER VII.

Now from that day the humble Lenny and regal Violante became great friends. With what pride he taught her to distinguish between celery and weeds — and how proud too was she when she learned that she was *useful!* There is not a greater pleasure you can give children, especially female children, than to make them feel they are already of value in the world, and serviceable as well as protected. Weeks and months rolled away, and Lenny still read, not only the books lent him by the Doctor, but those he bought of Mr. Sprott. As for the bombs and shells against religion which the Tinker carried in his bag, Lenny was not induced to blow himself up with them. He had been reared from his cradle in simple love and reverence for the Divine Father, and the tender Savior, whose life beyond all epics of mortal heroism, no being whose infancy has been taught to supplicate the Merciful and adore the Holy, yea, even though his later life may be entangled amidst the thorns of some desolate pyrrhonism, can ever hear reviled and scoffed without a shock to the conscience and a revolt to the heart. As the deer recoils by instinct from the tiger, as the very look of the scorpion deters you from handling it, though you never saw a scorpion before, so the very first line in some ribald profanity on which the Tinker put his black finger, made Lenny's blood run cold. Safe, too, was the peasant boy from any temptation in works of a gross and licentious nature, not only because of the happy ignorance of his rural life, but because of a more enduring safeguard — genius! Genius, that, manly, robust, healthful as it be, is long before it lose its instinctive Dorian modesty; shamefaced, because so susceptible to glory — genius, that loves indeed to dream, but on the violet bank, not the dunghill. Wherefore, even in the error of the senses, it seeks to escape from the sensual into worlds of fancy, subtle and refined. But apart from the passions, true genius is the most practical of all human gifts. Like the Apollo whom the Greek worshipped as its type, even Arcady is its exile, not its home. Soon weary of the dalliance of Tempé, it ascends to its mission — the Archer of the silver bow, the guide of the car of light. Speaking more plainly, genius is the enthusiasm for self-improvement; it ceases or sleeps the moment it desist from seeking some object which it believes of value, and by that object it insensibly connects its self-improvement with the positive advance of the world. At present Lenny's genius had no bias that was not to the Positive and Useful. It took the direction natural to its sphere, and the wants therein — viz., to the arts which we call mechanical. He wanted to know about steam-engines and Artesian wells; and to know about them it was necessary to know something of mechanics and hydrostatics; so he bought popular elementary works on those mystic sciences, and set all the powers of his mind at work on experiments.

Noble and generous spirits are ye, who, with small care for fame, and little reward from pelf, have opened to the intellects of the poor the portals of wisdom! I honor and revere ye; only do not think ye have done all that is needful. Consider, I pray ye, whether so good a choice from the Tinker's bag would have been made by a boy whom religion had not scared from the Pestilent, and genius had not led to the self-improving. And Lenny did not wholly escape from the mephitic portions of the motley elements from which his awakening mind drew its nurture. Think not it was all pure oxygen that the panting lip drew in. No; there were still those inflammatory tracts. Political I do not like to call them, for politics means the art of government, and the tracts I speak of assailed all government which mankind has hitherto recognised. Sad rubbish, perhaps, were such tracts to you, O sound thinker, in your easy-chair! Or to you practised statesman, at your post on the Treasury Bench — to you, calm dignitary of a learned Church — or to you, my lord judge, who may often have sent from your bar to the dire Orcus of Norfolk's Isle the ghosts of men whom that rubbish, falling simultaneously on the bumps of acquisitiveness and combativeness, hath untimely slain! Sad rubbish to you! But seems it such rubbish to the poor man, to whom it promises a paradise on the easy terms of upsetting a world? For ye see, those "Appeals to Operatives" represent that same world-upsetting as the simplest thing imaginable — a sort of two-and-two-make-four proposition. The poor have only got to set their strong hands to the axle, and heave-a-hoy! and hurrah for the topsy-turvy! Then, just to put a little wholesome rage into the heave-a-hoy! it is so facile to accompany the eloquence of "Appeals" with a kind of stir-the-bile-up statistics — "Abuses of the Aristocracy" — "Jobs of the Priesthood" — "Expenses of the Army kept up for Peers' younger sons" — "Wars contracted for the villanous purpose of raising the rents of the land-owners" — all arithmetically dished up, and seasoned with tales of every gentleman who has committed a misdeed, every clergyman who has dishonored his cloth; as if such instances were fair specimens of average gentlemen and ministers of religion! All this passionately advanced (and observe, never answered, for that literature admits no controversialists, and the writer has it all his own way,) may be rubbish; but it is out of such rubbish that operatives build barricades for attack, and legislators prisons for defence.

Our poor friend Lenny drew plenty of this stuff from the Tinker's bag. He thought it very clever and very eloquent; and he supposed the statistics were as true as mathematical demonstrations.

A famous knowledge-diffuser is looking over my shoulder, and tells me, "Increase education, and cheapen good books, and all this rubbish will disappear!" Sir, I don't believe a word of it. If you printed Ricardo and Adam Smith at a farthing a volume, I still believe that they would be as little read by the operatives as they are now-a-days by a very large proportion of highly-cultivated men. I still believe that, while the press works, attacks on the rich, and propositions for heave-a-hoys, will always form a popular portion of the Literature of Labor. There's Lenny Fairfield reading a treatise on hydraulics, and constructing a model for a fountain into the bargain; but that does not prevent his acquiescence in any proposition for getting rid of a National Debt, which he certainly never agreed to pay, and which he is told makes sugar and tea so shamefully dear. No, I tell you what does a little counteract these eloquent incentives to break his own head against the strong walls of the Social System — it is, that he has two eyes in that head, which are not always employed in reading. And, having been told in print that masters are tyrants, parsons hypocrites or drones in the hive, and land-owners vampires and blood-suckers, he looks out into the little world around him, and, first, he is compelled to acknowledge that his master is not a tyrant (perhaps because he is a foreigner and a philosopher, and, for what I and Lenny know, a republican.) But then Parson Dale, though High Church to the marrow, is neither hypocrite nor drone. He has a very good living, it is true — much better than he ought to have, according to the "political" opinions of those tracts! but Lenny is obliged to confess that, if Parson Dale were a penny the poorer, he would do a penny-worth's less good; and, comparing one parish with another, such as Rood Hall and Hazeldean, he is dimly aware that there is no greater CIVILISER than a person tolerably well off. Then, too, Squire Hazeldean, though as arrant a Tory as ever stood upon shoe-leather, is certainly not a vampire nor blood-sucker. He does not feed on the public; a great many of the public feed upon him: and, therefore, his practical experience a little staggers and perplexes Lenny Fairfield as to the gospel accuracy of his theoretical dogmas. Masters, parsons, and land-owners! having, at the risk of all popularity, just given a *coup de patte* to certain sages extremely the fashion at present, I am not going to let you off without an admonitory flea in the ear. Don't suppose that any mere scribbling and typework will suffice to answer the scribbling and typework set at work to demolish you — *write* down that rubbish you can't — *live* it down you may. If you are rich, like Squire Hazeldean, do good with your money; if you are poor, like Signor Riccabocca, do good with your kindness.

See! there is Lenny now receiving his week's wages; and though Lenny knows that he can get higher wages in the very next parish, his blue eyes are sparkling with gratitude, not at the chink of the money, but at the poor exile's friendly talk on things apart from all service; while Violante is descending the steps from the terrace, charged by her mother-in-law with a little basket of sago, and such like delicacies, for Mrs. Fairfield, who has been ailing the last few days.

Lenny will see the Tinker as he goes home, and he will buy a most Demosthenean "Appeal"—a tract of tracts, upon the Propriety of Strikes, and the Avarice of Masters. But, somehow or other, I think a few words from Signor Riccabocca, that did not cost the Signor a farthing, and the sight of his mother's smile at the contents of the basket, which cost very little, will serve to neutralize the effects of that "Appeal," much more efficaciously than the best article a Brougham or a Mill could write on the subject.

CHAPTER VIII.

SPRING had come again; and one beautiful May-day, Leonard Fairfield sat beside the little fountain which he had now actually constructed in the garden. The butterflies were hovering over the belt of flowers which he had placed around his fountain, and the birds were singing overhead. Leonard Fairfield was resting from his day's work, to enjoy his abstemious dinner, beside the cool play of the sparkling waters, and, with the yet keener appetite of knowledge, he devoured his book as he munched his crusts.

A penny tract is the shoeing-horn of literature! it draws on a great many books, and some too tight to be very useful in walking. The penny tract quotes a celebrated writer — you long to read him; it props a startling assertion by a grave authority—you long to refer to it. During the nights of the past winter, Leonard's intelligence had made vast progress! he had taught himself more than the elements of mechanics, and put to practice the principles he had acquired, not only in the hydraulical achievement of the fountain, and in the still more notable application of science, commenced on the stream in which Jackeymo had fished for minnows, and which Lenny had diverted to the purpose of irrigating two fields, but in various ingenious contrivances for the facilitation or abridgment of labor, which had excited great wonder and praise in the neighborhood. On the other hand, those rabid little tracts, which dealt so summarily with the destinies of the human race, even when his growing reason, and the perusal of works more classical or more logical, had led him to perceive that they were illiterate, and to suspect that they jumped from premises to conclusions with a celerity very different from the careful ratiocination of mechanical science, had still, in the citations and references wherewith they abounded, lured him on to philosophers more specious and more perilous. Out of the Tinker's bag he had drawn a translation of Condorcet's *Progress of Man*, and another of Rousseau's *Social Contract.* Works so eloquent had induced him to select from the tracts in the Tinker's miscellany those which abounded most in professions of philanthropy, and predictions of some coming Golden Age, to which old Saturn's was a joke—tracts so mild and mother-like in their language, that it required a much more practical experience than Lenny's to perceive that you would have to pass a river of blood before you had the slightest chance of setting foot on the flowery banks on which they invited you to repose—tracts which rouged poor Christianity on the cheeks, clapped a crown of innocent daffodillies on her head, and set her to dancing a *pas de zephyr* in the pastoral ballet in which St. Simon pipes to the flock he shears; or having first laid it down as a preliminary axiom that

"The cloud-capt towers, the gorgeous palaces,
The solemn temples, the great globe itself—
Yea, all which it inherit, shall dissolve,"

substituted in place thereof Monsieur Fourier's symmetrical phalanstere, or Mr. Owen's architectural parallelogram. It was with some such tract that Lenny was seasoning his crusts and his radishes, when Riccabocca, bending his long dark face over the student's shoulder, said abruptly—

"*Diavolo,* my friend! what on earth have you got there! Just let me look at it, will you?"

Leonard rose respectfully, and colored deeply as he surrendered the tract to Riccabocca.

The wise man read the first page attentively, the second more cursorily, and only ran his eye over the rest. He had gone through too vast a range of problems political, not to have passed over that venerable *Pons Asinorum* of Socialism, on which Fouriers and St. Simons sit straddling, and cry aloud that they have arrived at the last boundary of knowledge!

"All this is as old as the hills," quoth Riccabocca irreverently; "but the hills stand still, and this—there it goes!" and the sage pointed to a cloud emitted from his pipe. "Did you ever read Sir David Brewster on Optical Delusions? No! Well, I'll lend it to you. You will find therein a story of a lady who always saw a black cat on her hearth-rug. The black cat existed only in her fancy, but the hallucination was natural and reasonable—eh—what do you think?"

"Why, sir," said Leonard, not catching the Italian's meaning, "I don't exactly see that it was natural and reasonable."

"Foolish boy, yes! because black cats are things possible and known. But who ever saw upon earth a community of men such as sit on the hearth-rugs of Messrs. Owen and Fourier? If the lady's hallucination was not reasonable, what is his who believes in such visions as these?"

Leonard bit his lip.

"My dear boy," cried Riccabocca kindly, "the only thing sure and tangible to which these writers would lead you, lies at the first step, and that is what is commonly called a Revolution. Now, I know what that is. I have gone, not indeed through a revolution, but an attempt at one."

Leonard raised his eyes towards his master with a look of profound respect, and great curiosity.

"Yes," added Riccabocca, and the face on which the boy gazed exchanged its usual grotesque and sardonic expression for one animated, noble, and heroic. "Yes, not a revolution for chimeras, but for that cause which the coldest allow to be good, and which, when successful, all time approves as divine — the redemption of our native soil from the rule of the foreigner! I have shared in such an attempt. And," continued the Italian mournfully, "recalling now all the evil passions it arouses, all the ties it dissolves, all the blood that it commands to flow, all the healthful industry it arrests, all the madmen that it arms, all the victims that it dupes, I question whether one man really honest, pure, and humane, who has once gone through such an ordeal, would ever hazard it again, unless he was assured that the victory was certain — ay, and the object for which he fights not to be wrested from his hands amidst the uproar of the elements that the battle had released."

The Italian paused, shaded his brow with his hand, and remained long silent. Then gradually sesuming his ordinary tone, he continued —

"Revolutions that have no definite objects made clear by the positive experience of history; revolutions, in a word, that aim less at substituting one law or one dynasty for another, than at changing the whole scheme of society, have been little attempted by real statesmen. Even Lycurgus is proved to be a myth who never existed. Such organic changes are but in the day-dreams of philosophers who lived apart from the actual world, and whose opinions (though generally they were very benevolent, good sort of men, and wrote in an elegant poetical style) one would no more take on a plain matter of life, than one would look upon Virgil's *Eclogues* as a faithful picture of the ordinary pains and pleasures of the peasants who tend our sheep. Read them as you would read poets, and they are delightful. But attempt to shape the world according to the poetry, and fit yourself for a madhouse. The farther off the age is from the realisation of such projects, the more these poor philosophers have indulged them. Thus, it was amidst the saddest corruption of court manners that it became the fashion in Paris to sit for one's picture, with a crook in one's hand, as Alexis or Daphne. Just as liberty was fast dying out of Greece, and the successors of Alexander were founding their monarchies, and Rome was growing up to crush in its iron grasp all states save its own, Plato withdraws his eyes from the world, to open them in his dreamy Atlantis. Just in the grimmest period of English history, with the axe hanging over his head, Sir Thomas More gives you his *Utopia.* Just when the world is to be the theatre of a new Sesostris, the sages of France tell you that the age is too enlightened for war, that man is henceforth to be governed by pure reason, and live in a paradise. Very pretty reading all this to a man like me, Lenny, who can admire and smile at it. But to you, to the man who has to work for his living, to the man who thinks it would be so much more pleasant to live at his ease in a phalanstere than to work eight or ten hours a-day; to the man of talent, and action, and industry, whose future is invested in that tranquillity and order of a state in which talent, and action, and industry are a certain capital; — why, Messrs. Coutts, the great bankers, had better encourage a theory to upset the system of banking! Whatever disturbs society, yea, even by a causeless panic, much more by an actual struggle, falls first upon the market of labor, and thence affects prejudicially every department of intelligence. In such times the arts are arrested; literature is neglected; people are too busy to read anything save appeals to their passions. And capital, shaken in its sense of security, no longer ventures boldly through the land, calling forth all the energies of toil and enterprise, and extending to every workman his reward. Now, Lenny, take this piece of advice. You are young, clever, and aspiring: men rarely succeed in changing the world; but a man seldom fails of success, if he lets the world alone, and resolves to make the best of it. You are in the midst of the great crisis of your life; it is the struggle between the new desires knowledge excites, and that sense of poverty, which those desires convert either into hope and emulation, or into envy and despair. I grant that it is an up-hill work that lies before you; but don't you think it is always easier to climb a mountain than it is to level it? These books call on you to level the mountain; and that mountain is the property of other people, subdivided amongst a great many proprietors, and protected by law. At the first stroke of the pickaxe, it is ten to one but what you are taken up for a trespass. But the path up the mountain is a right of way uncontested. You may be safe at the summit, before (even if the owners are fools enough to let you) you could have levelled a yard. *Cospetto!*" quoth the doctor, "it is more than two thousand years ago since poor Plato began to level it, and the mountain is as high as ever!"

Thus saying, Riccabocca came to the end of his pipe, and stalking thoughtfully away, he left Leonard Fairfield trying to extract light from the smoke.

CHAPTER IX.

SHORTLY after this discourse of Riccabocca's, an incident occurred to Leonard that served to carry his mind into new directions. One evening, when his mother was out, he was at work on a new mechanical contrivance, and had the misfortune to break one of the instruments which he employed. Now, it will be remembered that his father had been the Squire's head carpenter: the widow had carefully hoarded the tools of his craft, which had belouged to her poor Mark; and though she occasionally lent them to Leonard, she would not give them up to his service. Amongst these, Leonard knew that he should find the one that he wanted; and being much interested in his contrivance, he could not wait till his mother's return. The tools, with other little relics of the lost, were kept in a large trunk in Mrs. Fairfield's sleeping-room; the trunk was not locked, and Leonard went to it without ceremony or scruple. In rummaging for the instrument, his eye fell upon a bundle of MSS.; and he suddenly recollected that when he was a mere child, and before he much knew the difference between verse and prose, his mother had pointed to these MSS., and said, "One day or other, when you can read nicely, I'll let you look at these, Lenny. My poor Mark wrote such verses—ah, he *was* a schollard!" Leonard, reasonably enough, thought that the time had now arrived when he was worthy the privilege of reading the paternal effusions, and he took forth the MSS. with a keen but melancholy interest. He recognised his father's handwriting, which he had often seen before in account-books and memoranda, and read eagerly some trifling poems, which did not show much genius, nor much mastery of language and rhythm—such poems, in short, as a self-educated man, with poetic taste and feeling, rather than poetic inspiration or artistic culture, might compose with credit, but not for fame. But suddenly, as he turned over these "Occasional Pieces," Leonard came to others in a different handwriting — a woman's handwriting, — small, and fine, and exquisitely formed. He had scarcely read six lines of these last, before his attention was irresistibly chained. They were of a different order of merit from poor Mark's; they bore the unmistakable stamp of genius. Like the poetry of women in general, they were devoted to personal feeling; they were not the mirror of a world, but reflections of a solitary heart. Yet this is the kind of poetry most pleasing to the young. And the verses in question had another attraction for Leonard; they seemed to express some struggle akin to his own, — some complaint against the actual condition of the writer's life, — some sweet, melodious murmurs at fortune. For the rest, they were characterised by a vein of sentiment so elevated, that if written by a man it would have run into exaggeration; written by a woman, the romance was carried off by so many genuine revelations of sincere, deep, pathetic feeling, that it was always natural, though true to a nature for which you would not augur happiness.

Leonard was still absorbed in the perusal of these poems, when Mrs. Fairfield entered the room.

"What have you been about, Lenny? — searching in my box?"

"I came to look for my father's bag of tools, mother, and I found these papers, which you said I might read some day."

"I doesn't wonder you did not hear me when I came in," said the widow, sighing. "I used to sit still for the hour together, when my poor Mark read his poems to me. There was such a pretty one about the 'Peasant's Fireside,' Lenny; have you got hold of that?"

"Yes, dear mother; and I remarked the allusion to you; it brought tears to my eyes. But these verses are not my father's, — whose are they? They seem in a woman's handwriting."

Mrs. Fairfield looked, — changed color, — grew faint, and seated herself.

"Poor, poor Nora!" said she, falteringly. "I did not know as they were there; Mark kep 'em; they got among his ——"

Leonard. — Who was Nora?

Mrs. Fairfield. — Who? — child — who? Nora was — was my — own sister.

Leonard (in great amaze, contrasting his ideal of the writer of these musical lines, in that graceful hand, with his homely, uneducated mother, who could neither read nor write). — Your sister ! — is it possible ? My aunt, then. How comes it you never spoke of her before ? Oh ! you should be so proud of her, mother.

Mrs. Fairfield (clasping her hands). – We were proud of her, all of us — father, mother — all ! She was so beautiful and so good, and not proud she ! though she looked like the first lady in the land. Oh ! Nora, Nora !

Leonard (after a pause). — But she must have been highly educated ?

Mrs. Fairfield. — 'Deed she was !

Leonard. — How was that ?

Mrs. Fairfield (rocking herself to and fro in her chair). — Oh ! my Lady was her godmother — Lady Lansmere I mean, — and took a fancy to her when she was that high ! and had her to stay at the Park, and wait on her Ladyship ; and then she put her to school, and Nora was so clever, that nothing would do but she must go to London as a governess. But don't talk of it, boy ! — don't talk of it !

Leonard. — Why not, mother ? What has become of her ? — where is she ?

Mrs. Fairfield (bursting into a paroxysm of tears). — In her grave — in her cold grave ! Dead, dead !

Leonard was inexpressibly grieved and shocked. It is the attribute of the poet to seem always living, — always a friend. Leonard felt as if some one very dear had been suddenly torn from his heart. He tried to console his

28 *

mother; but her emotion was contagious, and he wept with her.

"And how long has she been dead?" he asked, at last, in mournful accents.

"Many's the long year — many; but," added Mrs. Fairfield, rising, and putting her tremulous hand on Leonard's shoulder, "you'll just never talk to me about her,—I can't bear it, — it breaks my heart; I can bear better to talk of Mark. Come down stairs — come."

"May I not keep these verses, mother? Do let me."

"Well, well, those bits o' paper be all she left behind her. Yes, keep them, but put back Mark's. Are *they* all here? — sure?" And the widow, though she could not read her husband's verses, looked jealously at the MSS. written in his irregular large scrawl, and, smoothing them carefully, replaced them in the trunk, and resettled over them some sprigs of lavender, which Leonard had unwittingly disturbed.

"But," said Leonard, as his eye again rested on the beautiful handwriting of his lost aunt — "but you call her Nora — I see she signs herself L."

"Leonora was her name. I said she was my lady's godchild. We called her Nora for short ——"

"Leonora — and I am Leonard — is that how I came by the name?"

"Yes, yes — do hold your tongue, boy," sobbed poor Mrs. Fairfield; and she could not be soothed nor coaxed into continuing or renewing a subject which was evidently associated with insupportable pain.

CHAPTER X.

It is difficult to exaggerate the effect that this discovery produced on Leonard's train of thought. Some one belonging to his own humble race had, then, preceded him in his struggling flight towards the loftier regions of Intelligence and Desire. It was like the mariner amidst unknown seas, who finds carved upon some desert isle a familiar household name. And this creature of genius and of sorrow — whose existence he had only learned by her song, and whose death created, in the simple heart of her sister, so passionate a grief, after the lapse of so many years — supplied to the romance awaking in his young heart the ideal which it unconsciously sought. He was pleased to hear that she had been beautiful and good. He paused from his books to muse on her, and picture her image to his fancy. That there was some mystery in her fate was evident to him; and while that conviction deepened his interest, the mystery itself, by degrees, took a charm which he was not anxious to dispel. He resigned himself to Mrs. Fairfield's obstinate silence. He was contented to rank the dead amongst those holy and ineffable images which we do not seek to unveil. Youth and Fancy have many secret hoards of idea which they do not desire to impart, even to those most in their confidence.

I doubt the depth of feeling in any man who has not certain recesses in his soul into which none may enter.

Hitherto, as I have said, the talents of Leonard Fairfield had been more turned to things positive than to the ideal; to science and investigation of fact than to poetry, and that airier truth in which poetry has its element. He had read our greater poets, indeed, but without thought of imitating; and rather from the general curiosity to inspect all celebrated monuments of the human mind, than from that especial predilection for verse which is too common in childhood and youth to be any sure sign of a poet. But now these melodies, unknown to all the world beside, rang in his ear, mingled with his thoughts — set, as it were, his whole life to music. He read poetry with a different sentiment — it seemed to him that he had discovered its secret. And so reading, the passion seized him, and "the numbers came."

To many minds, at the commencement of our grave and earnest pilgrimage, I am Vandal enough to think that the indulgence of poetic taste and reverie does great and lasting harm; that it serves to enervate the character, give false ideas of life, impart the semblance of drudgery to the noble toils and duties of the active man. All poetry would not do this — not, for instance, the Classical, in its diviner masters — not the poetry of Homer, of Virgil, of Sophocles — not, perhaps, even that of the indolent Horace. But the poetry which youth usually loves and appreciates the best — the poetry of mere sentiment — does so in minds already over-predisposed to the sentimental, and which require bracing to grow into healthful manhood.

On the other hand, even this latter kind of poetry, which is peculiarly modern, does suit many minds of another mould — minds which our modern life, with its hard positive forms, tends to produce. And as in certain climates plants and herbs, peculiarly adapted as antidotes to those diseases most prevalent in the atmosphere, are profusely sown, as it were, by the benignant providence of nature — so it may be that the softer and more romantic species of poetry, which comes forth in harsh, money-making, unromantic times, is intended as curatives and counter-poisons. The world is so much with us, now-a-days, that we need have something that prates to us, albeit even in too fine an euphuism, of the moon and stars.

Certes, to Leonard Fairfield, at that period of his intellectual life, the softness of our Helicon descended as healing dews. In his turbulent and unsettled ambition, in his vague grapple with the giant forms of political truths, in his bias towards the application of science to immediate practical purposes, this lovely vision of the Muse came in the white robe of the Peacemaker; and with upraised hand, pointing to serene skies, she opened to him fair glimpses of the Beautiful, which is given to Peasant as to Prince — showed to him that on the surface of earth there is something nobler than fortune — that he who can view the world as a poet is always at soul a king; while to practical purpose itself, that larger and more profound invention, which poetry stimulates, supplied the grand design and the subtle view — leading him beyond the mere ingenuity of the mechanic, and habituating him to regard the inert force of the matter at his command with the ambition of the Discoverer. But, above all, the discontent that was within him finding a vent, not in deliberate war upon this actual world, but through the purifying channels of song — in the vent itself it evaporated, it was lost. By accustoming ourselves to survey all things with the spirit that retains and reproduces them only in their lovelier or grander aspects, a vast philosophy of toleration for what we before gazed on with scorn or hate insensibly grows upon us. Leonard looked into his heart after the Enchantress had breathed upon it; and through the mists of the fleeting and tender melancholy which betrayed where she had been, he beheld a new sum of delight and joy dawning over the landscape of human life.

Thus, though she was dead and gone from his actual knowledge, this mysterious kinswoman — "a voice, and nothing more" — had spoken to him, soothed, elevated, cheered, attuned each discord into harmony; and, if now permitted from some serener sphere to behold the life that her soul thus strangely influenced, verily with yet holier joy, the saving and lovely spirit might have glided onward in the Eternal Progress.

We call the large majority of human lives *obscure.* Presumptuous that we are! How know we what lives a single thought retained from the dust of nameless graves may have lighted to renown?

CHAPTER XI.

It was about a year after Leonard's discovery of the family MSS. that Parson Dale borrowed the quietest pad mare in the Squire's stables, and set out on an equestrian excursion. He said that he was bound on business connected with his old parishioners of Lansmere; for, as it has been incidentally implied in a previous chapter, he had been connected with that borough town (and, I may here add, in the capacity of curate) before he had been inducted into the living of Hazeldean.

It was so rarely that the Parson stirred from home, that this journey to a town more than twenty miles off was regarded as a most daring adventure, both at the Hall and at the Parsonage. Mrs. Dale could not sleep the whole previous night with thinking of it; and though she had naturally one of her worst nervous headaches on the eventful morn, she yet suffered no hands less thoughtful than her own to pack up the saddlebags which the Parson had borrowed along with the pad. Nay, so distrustful was she of the possibility of the good man's exerting the slightest common sense in her absence, that she kept him close at her side while she was engaged in that same operation of packing up — showing him the exact spot in which the clean shirt was put, and how nicely the old slippers were packed up in one of his own sermons. She implored him not to mistake the sandwiches for his shaving-soap, and made him observe how carefully she had provided against such confusion, by placing them as far apart from each other as the nature of saddle-bags will admit. The poor Parson — who was really by no means an absent man, but as little likely to shave himself with sandwiches and lunch upon soap as the most common-place mortal may be — listened with conjugal patience, and thought that man never had such a wife before; nor was it without tears in his own eyes that he tore himself from the farewell embrace of his weeping Carry.

I confess, however, that it was with some apprehension that he set his foot in the stirrup, and trusted his person to the mercies of an unfamiliar animal. For, whatever might be Mr. Dale's minor accomplishments as man and parson, horsemanship was not his *forte;* indeed, I doubt if he had taken the reins in his hand more than twice since he had been married.

The Squire's surly old groom, Mat, was in attendance with the pad; and, to the Parson's gentle inquiry whether Mat was quite sure that the pad was quite safe, replied laconically, "Oi, oi, give her her head."

"Give her her head!" repeated Mr. Dale, rather amazed, for he had not the slightest intention of taking away that part of the beast's frame so essential to its vital economy — "Give her her head!"

"Oi, oi; and don't jerk her up like that, or she'll fall a doincing on her hind-legs."

The Parson instantly slackened the reins; and Mrs. Dale — who had tarried behind to control her tears — now running to the door for "more last words," he waved his hand with courageous amenity, and ambled forth into the lane.

Our equestrian was absorbed at first in studying the idiosyncrasies of the pad-mare, and trying thereby to arrive at some notion of her general character: guessing, for instance, why she raised one ear and laid down the other; why she kept bearing so close to the left that she brushed his leg against the hedge; and why, when she arrived at a little side-gate in the fields, which led towards the home-farm, she came to a full stop, and fell to rubbing her nose against the rail — an occupation from which the Parson, finding all civil remonstrances in vain, at length diverted her by a timorous application of the whip.

This crisis on the road fairly passed, the pad seemed to comprehend that she had a journey before her, and giving a petulant whisk of her tail, quickened her amble into a short trot, which soon brought the Parson into the high-road, and nearly opposite the Casino.

Here, sitting on the gate which led to his abode, and shaded by his umbrella, he beheld Dr. Riccabocca.

The Italian lifted his eyes from the book he was reading, and stared hard at the Parson; and he — not venturing to withdraw his whole attention from the pad (who, indeed, set up both her ears at the apparition of Riccabocca, and evinced symptoms of that surprise and superstitious repugnance at unknown objects, which goes by the name of "shying")—looked askance at Riccabocca.

"Don't stir, please," said the Parson, "or I fear you'll alarm this creature; it seems a nervous, timid thing;—soho—gently—gently."

And he fell to patting the mare with great unction.

The pad, thus encouraged, overcame her first natural astonishment at the sight of Riccabocca and the red umbrella; and having before been at the Casino on sundry occasions, and sagaciously preferring places within the range of her experience to bournes neither cognate nor conjecturable, she moved gravely up towards the gate on which the Italian sat; and, after eyeing him a moment—as much as to say, "I wish you would get off,"—came to a dead lock.

"Well," said Riccabocca, "since your horse seems more disposed to be polite to me than yourself, Mr. Dale, I take the opportunity of your present involuntary pause to congratulate you on your elevation in life, and to breathe a friendly prayer that pride may not have a fall!"

"Tut," said the Parson, affecting an easy air, though still contemplating the pad, who appeared to have fallen into a quiet doze, "it is true that I have not ridden much of late years, and the Squire's horses are very high-fed and spirited; but there is no more harm in them than their master when one once knows their ways."

"Chi va piano, va sano,
E chi va sano va lontano,"

said Riccabocca, pointing to the saddle-bags. "You go

slowly, therefore safely; and he who goes safely may go far. You seem prepared for a journey?"

"I am," said the Parson; "and on a matter that concerns you a little."

"Me!" exclaimed Riccabocca—"concerns me!"

"Yes, so far as the chance of depriving you of a servant whom you like and esteem affects you."

"Oh," said Riccabocca, "I understand: you have hinted to me very often that I, or knowledge, or both together, have unfitted Leonard Fairfield for service."

"I did not say that exactly; I said that you have fitted him for something higher than service. But do not repeat this to him. And I cannot yet say more to you, for I am very doubtful as to the success of my mission; and it will not do to unsettle poor Leonard until we are sure that we can improve his condition."

"Of that you can never be sure," quoth the wise man, shaking his head; "and I can't say that I am unselfish enough not to bear you a grudge for seeking to decoy away from me an invaluable servant—faithful, steady, intelligent, and" added Riccabocca, warming as he approached the climacteric adjective "exceedingly cheap! nevertheless—go, and Heaven speed you. I am not an Alexander, to stand between man and the sun."

"You are a noble, great-hearted creature, Signor Riccabocca, in spite of your cold-blooded proverbs and villanous books." The Parson, as he said this, brought down the whip-hand with so indiscreet an enthusiasm on the pad's shoulder, that the poor beast, startled out of her innocent doze, made a bolt forward, which nearly precipitated Riccabocca from his seat on the stile, and then turning round — as the Parson tugged desperately at the rein — caught the bit between her teeth, and set off at a canter. The Parson lost both his stirrups; and when he regained them (as the pad slackened her pace), and had time to breathe and look about him, Riccabocca and the Casino were both out of sight.

"Certainly," quoth Parson Dale, as he resettled himself with great complacency, and a conscious triumph that he was still on the pad's back — "Certainly it is true 'that the noblest conquest ever made by man was that of the horse:' a fine creature it is — a very fine creature — and uncommonly difficult to sit on, especially without stirrups." Firmly in *his* stirrups the Parson planted his feet; and the heart within him was very proud.

CHAPTER XII.

THE borough town of Lansmere was situated in the county adjoining that which contained the village of Hazeldean. Late at noon the Parson crossed the little stream which divided the two shires, and came to an inn, which was placed at an angle where the great main road branched off into two directions — the one leading towards Lansmere, the other going more direct to London. At this inn the pad stopped, and put down both ears with the air of a pad who has made up her mind to bait. And the Parson himself, feeling very warm and somewhat sore, said to the pad benignly, "It is just — thou shalt have corn and water!"

Dismounting, therefore, and finding himself very stiff, as soon as he reached *terra firma,* the Parson consigned the pad to the ostler, and walked into the sanded parlor of the inn, to repose himself on a very hard windsor chair.

He had been alone rather more than half an hour, reading a county newspaper which smelt much of tobacco, and trying to keep off the flies that gathered round him in swarms, as if they had never before seen a Parson, and were anxious to ascertain how the flesh of one tasted, — when a stage-coach stopped at the inn. A traveller got out with his carpet-bag in his hand, and was shown into the sanded parlor.

The Parson rose politely, and made a bow.

The traveller touched his hat, without taking it off — looked at Mr. Dale from top to toe — then walked to the window, and whistled a lively impatient tune, then strode towards the fire-place and rang the bell; then stared again at the Parson; and that gentleman having courteously laid down the newspaper, the traveller seized it, threw himself into a chair, flung one of his legs over the table, tossed the other up on the mantelpiece, and began reading the paper, while he tilted the chair on its hind-legs with so daring a disregard to the ordinary position of chairs and their occupants, that the shuddering Parson expected every moment to see him come down on the back of his skull.

Moved, therefore, to compassion, Mr. Dale said mildly—

"Those chairs are very treacherous, sir. I'm afraid you'll be down."

"Eh!" said the traveller, looking up much astonished—"Eh! down?—oh, you're satirical, sir."

"Satirical, sir? upon my word, no!" exclaimed the Parson, earnestly.

"I think every free-born man has a right to sit as he pleases in his own house," resumed the traveller, with warmth; "and an inn is his own house, I guess, so long as he pays his score. Betty, my dear."

For the chambermaid had now replied to the bell.

"I han't Betty, sir; do you want she?"

"No, Sally—cold brandy-and-water—and a biscuit."

"I han't Sally, either," muttered the chambermaid; but the traveller, turning round, showed so smart a neck-cloth and so comely a face, that she smiled, colored, and went her way.

The traveller now rose, and flung down the paper. He took out a penknife, and began paring his nails. Suddenly desisting from this elegant occupation, his eye caught sight of the Parson's shovel-hat, which lay on a chair in the corner.

"You're a clergyman, I reckon, sir," said the traveller, with a slight sneer.

Again Mr. Dale bowed—bowed in part deprecatingly—in part with dignity. It was a bow that said, "No offence, sir, but I *am* a clergyman, and I'm not ashamed of it."

Going far?" asked the traveller.

PARSON. — Not very.

TRAVELLER. — In a chaise or fly? If so, and we are going the same way — halves.

PARSON. — Halves?

TRAVELLER. — Yes, I'll pay half the damage — pikes inclusive.

PARSON. — You are very good, sir. But [spoken with pride] I am on horseback.

TRAVELLER. — On horseback! Well, I should not have guessed that! You don't look like it. Where did you say you were going?

"I did *not* say where I was going, sir," said the Parson drily, for he was much offended at that vague and ungrammatical remark applicable to his horsemanship, that "he did not look like it."

"Close!" said the traveller laughing; "an old traveller, I reckon."

The Parson made no reply, but he took up his shovel-hat, and, with a bow more majestic than the previous one, walked out to see if his pad had finished her corn.

The animal had indeed finished all the corn afforded to her, which was not much, and in a few minutes more Mr. Dale resumed his journey. He had performed about three miles, when the sound of wheels behind him made him turn his head, and he perceived a chaise driven very fast, while out of the windows thereof dangled strangely a pair of human legs. The pad began to curvet as the post-horses rattled behind, and the Parson had only an indistinct vision of a human face supplanting those human legs. The traveller peered out at him as he whirled by — saw Mr. Dale tossed up and down on the saddle, and cried out, "How's the leather?"

"Leather!" soliloquised the Parson, as the pad recomposed herself. "What does he mean by that? Leather! a very vulgar man. But I got rid of him cleverly."

Mr. Dale arrived without farther adventure at Lansmere. He put up at the principal inn — refreshed himself by a general ablution — and sat down with good appetite to his beef-steak and pint of port.

The Parson was a better judge of the physiognomy of man than that of the horse; and after a satisfactory glance at the civil smirking landlord, who removed the cover and set on the wine, he ventured on an attempt at conversation. "Is my lord at the Park?"

Landlord (still more civilly than before). — No, sir: his lordship and my lady have gone to town to meet Lord L'Estrange."

"Lord L'Estrange! He is in England, then?"

"Why, so I heard," replied the landlord; "but we never see him here now. I remember him a very pretty young man. Every one was fond of him and proud of him. But what pranks he did play when he was a lad! We hoped he would come in for our boro' some of these days, but he has taken to foren parts — more's the pity. I am a reg'lar Blue, sir, as I ought to be. The Blue candidate always does me the honor to come to the Lansmere Arms. 'Tis only the low party puts up with the Boar," added the landlord with a look of ineffable disgust. "I hope you like the wine, sir?"

"Very good, and seems old."

"Bottled these eighteen years, sir. I had in the cask for the great election of Dashmore and Egerton. I have little left of it, and I never give it but to old friends like—for, I think, sir, though you be grown stout, and look more grand, I may say that I've had the pleasure of seeing you before."

"That's true, I dare say, though I fear I was never a very good customer."

"Ah, it *is* Mr. Dale, then! I thought so when you came into the hall. I hope your lady is quite well, and the Squire, too; fine pleasant-spoken gentleman; no fault of his, if Mr. Egerton went wrong. Well, we have never seen him—I mean Mr. Egerton—since that time. I don't wonder he stays away; but my lord's son, who was brought up here, it an't nat'ral like that *he* should turn his back on us!"

Mr. Dale made no reply, and the landlord was about to retire, when the Parson, pouring out another glass of port, said—"There must be great changes in the parish. Is Mr. Morgan, the medical man, still here?"

"No, indeed; he took out his ploma after you left, and became a real doctor; and a pretty practice he had too, when he took, all of a sudden, to some new-fangled way of physicking;—I think they calls it homy—something."

"Homœopathy?"

"That's it — something against all reason: and so he lost his practice here and went up to Lunnun. I've not heard of him since."

"Do the Avenels still reside in their old house?"

"Oh yes!—and are pretty well off, I hear say. John is always poorly; though he still goes now and then to the Odd Fellows, and takes his glass; but his wife comes and fetches him away before he can do himself any harm."

"Mrs. Avenel is the same as ever?"

"She holds her head higher, I think," said the landlord, smiling. "She was always—not exactly proud like, but what I calls gumptious."

"I never heard that word before," said the Parson, laying down his knife and fork. "Bumptious, indeed, though I believe it is not in the dictionary, has crept into familiar parlance, especially amongst young folks at school and college."

"Bumptious is bumptious, and gumptious is gumptious," said the landlord, delighted to puzzle a parson. "Now, the town beadle is bumptious, and Mrs. Avenel is gumptious."

"She is a very respectable woman," said Mr. Dale, somewhat rebukingly.

"In course, sir; all gumptious folks are; they value themselves on their respectability, and looks down on their neighbors."

Parson (still philologically occupied).—Gumptious — gumptious. I think I remember the substantive at school

—not that my master taught it to me. "Gumption,"—it means cleverness.

LANDLORD (doggedly).—There's gumption and gumptious! Gumption is knowing; but when I say that sum un is gumptious, I mean—though that's more vulgar like -sum un who does not think small beer of hisself. You take me, sir?"

"I think I do," said the Parson, half-smiling. "I believe the Avenels have only two of their children alive still—their daughter, who married Mark Fairfield, and a son who went to America?"

"Ah, but he made his fortune there, and has come back."

"Indeed! I'm very glad to hear it. He has settled at Lansmere?"

"No, sir. I hear as he's bought a property a long way off. But he comes to see his parents pretty often—so John tells me—but I can't say that I ever see him. I fancy Dick doesn't like to be seen by folks who remember him playing in the kennel."

"Not unnatural," said the Parson, indulgently; "but he visits his parents; he is a good son at all events, then?"

"I've nothing to say against him. Dick was a wild chap before he took himself off. I never thought he would make his fortune; but the Avenels are a clever set. Do you remember poor Nora—the Rose of Lansmere, as they called her? Ah, no, I think she went up to Lunnun afore your time, sir."

"Humph!" said the Parson drily. "Well, I think you may take away now. It will be dark soon, and I'll just stroll out and look about me."

"There's a nice tart coming, sir."

"Thank you, I've dined."

The Parson put on his hat and sallied forth into the streets. He eyed the houses on either hand with that melancholy and wistful interest with which, in middle life, men revisit scenes familiar to them in youth — surprised to find either so little change or so much, and recalling, by fits and snatches, old associations and past emotions. The long High Street which he threaded now began to change its bustling character, and slide, as it were gradually, into the high-road of a suburb. On the left, the houses gave way to the moss-grown pales of Lansmere Park: to the right, though houses still remained, they were separated from each other by gardens, and took the pleasing appearance of villas — such villas as retired tradesmen or their widows, old maids, and half-pay officers, select for the evening of their days.

Mr. Dale looked at these villas with the deliberate attention of a man awakening his power of memory, and at last stopped before one, almost the last on the road, and which faced the broad patch of sward that lay before the lodge of Lansmere Park. An old pollard oak stood near it, and from the oak there came a low discordant sound; it was the hungry cry of young ravens, awaiting the belated return of the parent bird. Mr. Dale put his hand to his brow, paused a moment, and then, with a hurried step, passed through the little garden, and knocked at the door. A light was burning in the parlor, and Mr. Dale's eye caught through the window a vague outline of three forms. There was an evident bustle within at the sound of the knock. One of the forms rose and disappeared. A very prim, neat, middle-aged maid-servant now appeared at the threshold, and austerely inquired the visitor's business.

"I want to see Mr. or Mrs. Avenel. Say that I have come many miles to see them; and take in this card."

The maid-servant took the card, and half closed the door. At least three minutes elapsed before she reappeared.

"Missis says it's late, but walk in."

The Parson accepted the not very gracious invitation, stepped across the little hall, and entered the little parlor.

Old John Avenel, a mild-looking man, who seemed slightly paralytic, rose slowly from his arm-chair. Mrs. Avenel, in an awfully stiff, clean, Calvinistical cap, and a grey dress, every fold of which bespoke respectability and staid repute — stood erect on the floor, and fixing on the Parson a cold and cautious eye, said —

"You do the like of us great honor, Mr. Dale — take a chair! You call upon business?"

"Of which I apprised Mr. Avenel, by letter."

"My husband is very poorly."

"A poor creature!" said John, feebly, and as if in compassion of himself. "I can't get about as I used to do. But it ben't near election time, be it, sir?"

"No, John," said Mrs. Avenel, placing her husband's arm within her own. "You must lie down a bit, while I talk to the gentleman."

"I'm a real good Blue," said poor John; "but I ain't quite the man I was;" and leaning heavily on his wife he left the room, turning round at the threshold, and saying with great urbanity — "Anything to oblige, sir!"

Mr. Dale was much touched. He had remembered John Avenel the comeliest, the most active, and the most cheerful man in Lansmere; great at glee-club and cricket (though then somewhat stricken in years), greater in vestries; reputed greatest in elections.

"Last scene of all," murmured the Parson; "and oh well, turning from the poet, may we cry with the disbelieving philosopher, 'Poor, poor humanity!'" *

In a few minutes Mrs. Avenel returned. She took a chair at some distance from the Parson's, and, resting one hand on the elbow of the chair, while with the other she stiffly smoothed the stiff gown, she said —

"Now, sir."

That "Now sir," had in its sound something sinister and warlike. This the shrewd Parson recognised with his usual tact. He edged his chair nearer to Mrs. Avenel, and placing his hand on hers —

"Yes, now then, and as friend to friend."

* Mr. Dale probably here alludes to Lord Bolingbroke's ejaculation as he stood by the dying Pope; but his memory does not serve him with the exact words.

CHAPTER XIII.

Mr. Dale had been more than a quarter of an hour conversing with Mrs. Avenel, and had seemingly made little progress in the object of his diplomatic mission, for now, slowly drawing on his gloves, he said —

"I grieve to think, Mrs. Avenel, that you should have so hardened your heart — yes — you must pardon me — it is my vocation to speak stern truths. You cannot say that I have not kept faith with you, but I must now invite you to remember that I specially reserved to myself the right of exercising a discretion to act as I judged best, for the child's interests, on any future occasion; and it was upon this understanding that you gave me the promise, which you would now evade, of providing for him when he came into manhood."

"I say I will provide for him. I say that you may 'prentice him in any distant town, and by-and-by we will stock a shop for him. What would you have more, sir, from folks like us, who have kept shop ourselves? It ain't reasonable what you ask, sir."

"My dear friend," said the Parson, "what I ask of you at present is but to see him — to receive him kindly — to listen to his conversation — to judge for yourselves. We can have but a common object — that your grandson should succeed in life, and do you credit. Now, I doubt very much whether we can effect this by making him a small shopkeeper."

"And has Jane Fairfield, who married a common carpenter, brought him up to despise small shopkeepers?" exclaimed Mrs. Avenel, angrily.

"Heaven forbid! Some of the first men in England have been the sons of small shopkeepers. But is it a crime in them, or in their parents, if their talents have lifted them into such rank or renown as the haughtiest duke might envy? England were not England if a man must rest where his father began."

"Good!" said, or rather grunted, an approving voice, but neither Mrs. Avenel nor the Parson heard it.

"All very fine," said Mrs. Avenel, bluntly. "But to send a boy like that to the university — where's the money to come from?"

"My dear Mrs. Avenel," said the Parson, coaxingly, "the cost need not be great at a small college at Cambridge; and if you will pay half the expense, I will pay the other half. I have no children of my own, and can afford it."

"That's very handsome in you, sir," said Mrs. Avenel, somewhat touched, yet still not graciously. "But the money is not the only point."

"Once at Cambridge," continued Mr. Dale, speaking rapidly, "at Cambridge, where the studies are mathematical — that is, of a nature for which he has shown so great an aptitude — and I have no doubt he will distinguish himself; if he does, he will obtain, on leaving, what is called a fellowship — that is, a collegiate dignity accompanied by an income on which he could maintain himself until he made his way in life. Come, Mrs. Avenel, you are well off; you have no relations nearer to you in want of your aid. Your son, I hear, has been very fortunate."

"Sir," said Mrs. Avenel, interrupting the Parson, "it is not because my son Richard is an honor to us, and is a good son, and has made his fortin, that we are to rob him of what we have to leave, and give it to a boy whom we know nothing about, and who, in spite of what you say, can't bring upon us any credit at all."

"Why? I don't see that."

"Why!" exclaimed Mrs. Avenel, fiercely—"why! you know why. No, I don't want him to rise in life: I don't want folks to be speiring and asking about him. I think it is a very wicked thing to have put fine notions in his head, and I am sure my daughter Fairfield could not have done it herself. And now, to ask me to rob Richard, and bring out a great boy — who's been a gardener or ploughman, or such like — to disgrace a gentleman who keeps his carriage, as my son Richard does—I would have you to know, sir. — No! I won't do it, and there's an end of the matter."

During the last two or three minutes, and just before that approving "good" had responded to the Parson's popular sentiment, a door communicating with an inner room had been gently opened, and stood ajar; but this incident neither party had even noticed. But now the door was thrown boldly open, and the traveller whom the

Parson had met at the inn walked up to Mr. Dale, and said, "No! that's not the end of the matter. You say the boy's a 'cute, clever lad?"

"Richard, have you been listening?" exclaimed Mrs. Avenel.

"Well, I guess, yes — the last few minutes."

"And what have you heard?"

"Why, that this reverend gentleman thinks so highly of my sister Fairfield's boy, that he offers to pay half of his keep at college. Sir, I'm very much obliged to you, and there's my hand, if you'll take it."

The Parson jumped up, overjoyed, and with a triumphant glance towards Mrs. Avenel, shook hands heartily with Mr. Richard.

"Now," said the latter, "just put on your hat, sir, and take a stroll with me, and we'll discuss the thing business-like. Women don't understand business: never talk to women on business."

With these words, Mr. Richard drew out a cigar-case, selected a cigar, which he applied to the candle, and walked into the hall.

Mrs. Avenel caught hold of the Parson. "Sir, you'll be on your guard with Richard. Remember your promise."

"He does not know all, then?"

"He? No! And you see he did not overhear more than what he says. I'm sure you're a gentleman, and won't go against your word."

"My word was conditional; but I will promise you never to break the silence without more reason than I think there is here for it. Indeed, Mr. Richard Avenel seems to save all necessity for that."

"Are you coming, sir?" cried Richard, as he opened the street-door.

CHAPTER XIV.

THE Parson joined Mr. Richard Avenel on the road. It was a fine night, and the moon clear and shining.

"So then," said Mr. Richard, thoughtfully, "poor Jane, who was always the drudge of the family, has contrived to bring up her son well; and the boy is really what you say, eh? — could make a figure at college?"

"I am sure of it," said the Parson, hooking himself on to the arm which Mr. Avenel proffered.

"I should like to see him," said Richard. "Has he any manner? Is he genteel? or a mere country lout?"

"Indeed, he speaks with so much propriety, and has so much modest dignity about him, that there's many a rich gentleman who would be proud of such a son."

"It is odd," observed Richard, "what difference there is in families. There's Jane, now — who can't read nor write, and was just fit to be a workman's wife — had not a thought above her station; and when I think of my poor sister Nora — you would not believe it, sir, but *she* was the most elegant creature in the world — yes, even as a child (she was but a child when I went off to America). And often, as I was getting on in life, often I used to say to myself, 'My little Nora shall be a lady after all.' Poor thing — but she died young."

Richard's voice grew husky.

The Parson kindly pressed the arm on which he leaned, and said, after a pause —

"Nothing refines us like education, sir. I believe your sister Nora had received much instruction, and had the talents to profit by it: it is the same with your nephew."

"I'll see him," said Richard, stamping his foot firmly on the ground, "and if I like him, I'll be as good as a father to him. Look you, Mr. — what's your name, sir?"

"Dale."

"Mr. Dale, look you, I'm a single man. Perhaps I may marry some day; perhaps I shan't. I'm not going to throw myself away. If I can get a lady of quality, why — but that's neither here nor there; meanwhile I should be glad of a nephew whom I need not be ashamed of. You see, sir, I am a new man, the builder of my own fortunes; and though I have picked up a little education — I don't well know how — as I scrambled on, still, now I come back to the old country, I'm well aware that I am not exactly a match for those d—d aristocrats; don't show so well in a drawing-room as I could wish. I could be a Parliament man if I liked, but I might make a goose of myself; so, all things considered, if I can get a sort of junior partner to do the polite work, and show off the goods, I think the house of Avenel and Co. might become a pretty considerable honor to the Britishers. You understand me, sir?"

"Oh very well," answered Mr. Dale, smiling, though rather gravely.

"Now," continued the New Man, "I'm not ashamed to have risen in life by my own merits; and I don't disguise what I've been. And when I'm in my own grand house, I'm fond of saying, 'I landed at New York with £10 in my purse, and here I am!' But it would not do to have the old folks with me. People take you with all your faults if you're rich; but they won't swallow your family into the bargain. So if I don't have at my house my own father and mother, whom I love dearly, and should like to see sitting at table, with my servants behind their chairs, I could still less have sister Jane. I recollect her very well, and she can't have got genteeler as she's grown older. Therefore I beg you'll not set her on coming after me; it would not do by any manner of means. Don't say a word about me to her. But send the boy down here to his grandfather, and I'll see him quietly, you understand."

"Yes, but it will be hard to separate her from her boy."

"Stuff! all boys are separated from their parents when they go into the world. So that's settled. Now, just tell me. I know the old folks always snubbed Jane—that is, mother did. My poor dear father never snubbed any of us. Perhaps mother has not behaved well to Jane. But we must not blame her for that; you see this is how it happened. There were a good many of us, while father and mother kept shop in the High Street, so we were all to be provided for anyhow; and Jane, being very useful and handy at work, got a place when she was a little girl, and had no time for learning. Afterwards my father made a lucky hit, in getting my Lord Lansmere's custom after an election, in which he did a great deal for the Blues (for which he was a famous electioneer, my poor father). My Lady stood godmother to Nora; and then all my brothers, and two of my sisters, died off, and father retired from business; and when he took Jane from service, she was so common-like that mother could not help contrasting her with Nora. You see Jane was their child when they were poor little shop-people, with their heads scarce above water; and Nora was their child when they were well off, and had retired from trade, and lived genteel: so that makes a great difference. And mother did not quite look on her as on her own child. But it was Jane's own fault: for mother would have made it up with her if she had married the son of our neighbor the great linendraper, as she might have done; but she would take Mark Fairfield, a common carpenter. Parents like best those of their children who succeed best in life. Natural. Why, they did not care for me till I came back the man I am. But to return to Jane: I'm afraid they've neglected her. How is she off?"

"She earns her livelihood, and is poor, but contented."

"Ah, just be good enough to give her this," (and Richard took a bank-note of £50 from his pocket-book). "You can say the old folks sent it to her; or that it is a present from Dick, without telling her he has come back from America."

"My dear sir," said the Parson, "I am more and more thankful to have made your acquaintance. This is a very liberal gift of yours; but your best plan will be to send it through your mother. For, though I don't want to betray any confidence you place in me, I should not know what to answer if Mrs. Fairfield began to question me about her brother. I never had but one secret to keep, and I hope I shall never have another. A secret is very like a lie!"

"You had a secret then!" said Richard, as he took back the bank-note. He had learned, perhaps in America, to be a very inquisitive man. He added point-blank, "Pray, what was it?"

"Why, what it would not be if I told you," said the Parson, with a forced laugh — "a secret!"

"Well, I guess we're in a land of liberty. Do as you like. Now, I dare say you think me a very odd fellow to come out of my shell to you in this off-hand way. But I liked the look of you, even when we were at the inn together. And just now I was uncommonly pleased to find that, though you are a Parson, you don't want to keep a man's nose down to a shop-board, if he has anything in him. You're not one of the aristocrats —"

"Indeed," said the Parson, with imprudent warmth, "it is not the character of the aristocracy of this country to keep people down. They make way amongst themselves for any man, whatever his birth, who has the talent and energy to aspire to their level. That's the especial boast of the British constitution, sir!"

"Oh, you think so, do you!" said Mr. Richard, looking sourly at the Parson. "I dare say those are the opinions in which you have brought up the lad. Just keep him yourself, and let the aristocracy provide for him!"

The Parson's generous and patriotic warmth evaporated at once, at this sudden inlet of cold air into the conversation. He perceived that he had made a terrible blunder; and, as it was not his business at that moment to vindicate the British constitution, but to serve Leonard Fairfield, he abandoned the cause of the aristocracy with the most poltroon and scandalous abruptness. Catching at the arm which Mr. Avenel had withdrawn from him, he exclaimed —

"Indeed, sir, you are mistaken; I have never attempted to influence your nephew's political opinions. On the contrary, if, at his age, he can be said to have formed any opinions, I am greatly afraid — that is, I think his opinions are by no means sound — that is, constitutional. I mean, I mean —" And the poor Parson, anxious to select a word that would not offend his listener, stopped short in lamentable confusion of idea.

Mr. Avenel enjoyed his distress for a moment, with a saturnine smile, and then said —

"Well, I calculate he's a Radical. Natural enough, if he has not got a sixpence to lose — all come right by and by. I'm not a Radical — at least not a Destructive — much too clever a man for that, I hope. But I wish to see things very different from what they are. Don't fancy that I want the common people, who've got nothing, to pretend to dictate to their betters, because I hate to see a parcel of fellows, who are called lords and squires, trying to rule the roast. I think, sir, that it is men like me who ought to be at the top of the tree! and that's the long and the short of it. What do you say?"

"I've not the least objection," said the crestfallen Parson basely. But, to do him justice, I must add, that he did not the least know what he was saying!

CHAPTER XV.

UNCONSCIOUS of the change in his fate which the diplomacy of the Parson sought to effect, Leonard Fairfield was enjoying the first virgin sweetness of fame; for the principal town in his neighborhood had followed the then growing fashion of the age, and set up a Mechanics' Institute; and some worthy persons interested in the formation of that provincial Athenæum had offered a prize for the best Essay on the Diffusion of Knowledge, — a very trite subject, on which persons seem to think they can never say too much, and on which there is, nevertheless, a great deal yet to be said. This prize Leonard Fairfield had recently won. His Essay had been publicly complimented by a full meeting of the Institute; it had been printed at the expense of the Society, and had been rewarded by a silver medal —

delineative of Apollo crowning Merit (poor Merit had not a rag to his back; but Merit, left only to the care of Apollo, never is too good a customer to the tailor!) And the "County Gazette" had declared that Britain had produced another prodigy in the person of Dr. Riccabocca's self-educated gardener.

Attention was now directed to Leonard's mechanical contrivances. The Squire, ever eagerly bent on improvements, had brought an engineer to inspect the lad's system of irrigatiou, and the engineer had been greatly struck by the simple means by which a very considerable technical difficulty had been overcome. The neighboring farmers now called Leonard "*Mr.* Fairfield," and invited him, on equal terms, to their houses. Mr. Stirn had met him on the high road, touched his hat, and hoped that "he bore no malice." All this, I say, was the first sweetness of fame; and if Leonard Fairfield comes to be a great man, he will never find such sweets in the after-fruit. It was this success which had determined the Parson on the step which he had just taken, and which he had long before anxiously meditated. For, during the last year or so, he had renewed his old intimacy with the widow and the boy; and he had noticed, with great hope and great fear, the rapid growth of an intellect, which now stood out from the lowly circumstances that surrounded it in bold and unharmonising relief.

It was the evening after his return home that the Parson strolled up to the Casino. He put Leonard Fairfield's Prize Essay in his pocket. For he felt that he could not let the young man go forth into the world without a preparatory lecture, and he intended to scourge poor Merit with the very laurel wreath which it had received from Apollo. But in this he wanted Riccabocca's assistance; or rather he feared that, if he did not get the Philosopher on his side, the Philosopher might undo all the work of the Parson.

END OF THE FIRST VOLUME.

www.ingramcontent.com/pod-product-compliance
Lightning Source LLC
LaVergne TN
LVHW020059110826
845151LV00001B/30

* 9 7 8 1 4 2 5 5 4 5 1 4 7 *